New York City
Specialized High Schools Admissions Test

Sixth Edition

New York City
Specialized High Schools
Admissions Test

Advanced Prep for Advanced Students

Sixth Edition

By Darcy Galane
and the Staff of Kaplan Test Prep and Admissions

This publication is designed to provide accurate and authoritative information in regard to the subject matter covered. It is sold with the understanding that the publisher is not engaged in rendering legal, accounting, or other professional service. If legal advice or other expert assistance is required, the services of a competent professional should be sought.

Published by Kaplan Publishing, a division of Kaplan, Inc.
395 Hudson Street
New York, NY 10014

Printed in the United States of America

May 2011
10 9 8 7 6 5 4 3 2

ISBN-13: 978-1-60978-108-8

Kaplan Publishing books are available at special quantity discounts to use for sales promotions, employee premiums, or educational purposes. For more information or to purchase books, please call the Simon & Schuster special sales department at 866-506-1949.

Table of Contents

Section 5: SHSAT Practice Tests and Explanations

Resource Section

About the Author

Darcy L. Galane is Project Manager for Graduate Product Research and Development at Kaplan; while writing this book she served as the Associate Director of Pre-College Curriculum. She received a BA from the University of California–Los Angeles and began teaching SAT and LSAT classes for Kaplan while earning her JD at the University of Connecticut School of Law. Having taught and written curriculum for most of Kaplan's courses, Darcy has helped thousands of students to raise their scores on standardized tests.

Available Online

FOR ANY TEST CHANGES OR LATE-BREAKING DEVELOPMENTS

kaptest.com/publishing

The material in this book is up-to-date at the time of publication. However, the NYC Department of Education may have instituted changes in the test or test registration process after this book was published. Be sure to read carefully the materials you receive when you register for the test.

If there are any important late-breaking developments—or any changes or corrections to the Kaplan test preparation materials in this book—we will post that information online at **kaptest.com/publishing**. Check to see if any information has been posted there for readers of this book.

FEEDBACK AND COMMENTS

kaplansurveys.com/books

What did you think of this book? We'd welcome your comments and suggestions. Fill out our online survey form at **kaplansurveys.com/books**. Your feedback is extremely helpful as we continue to develop high-quality resources to meet your needs.

How to Use This Book: The Classic Plan

Ideally, you should take a couple of months to work through this book, though it's certainly possible to read it in far less time. Here's how you should go about prepping with it:

1. Read through each chapter completely, learning from the example problems and trying the practice problems. In the SHSAT Study Aids section, you'll find SHSAT "Math in a Nutshell," which summarizes the most important math concepts you can expect to see on the Specialized Science High Schools Admission Test.

2. Read the section entitled "Ready, Set, Go!" to set the stage for your preparation and testing success.

3. Take Practice Test 1 under strictly timed conditions to get a sense of your strengths and weaknesses.

4. Before trying your luck at the other Practice Test, repeat the process of reviewing your areas of weakness.

5. Give yourself a day of rest right before the real exam.

If you have time, do just two or three chapters a week and let the material sink in slowly. Take some time off from your SHSAT preparation when you need to. Nobody can take this stuff day in and day out for weeks at a time without a break.

How to Use This Book:
The Emergency Plan

Maybe you have only two or three weeks—or even less time than that. Don't freak! This book has been designed to work for students in your situation too. If you go through a chapter or two every day, you can finish this book in a couple of weeks. If you have limited time to prepare for the SHSAT (less than six weeks), we suggest you do the following:

1. Take a slow, deep breath. Read the Ready, Set, Go! section to maximize your study and testing time.
2. Read Section 1: The Basics.
3. Complete as many Practice Set problems (located at the end of each chapter) as you can.
4. Take both of the Practice Tests under timed conditions.
5. Review your results, with special attention to the questions you missed.
6. Give yourself the day before the test off.

Scattered throughout the text you'll find special points that we feel deserve emphasis and amplification. Pay special attention to these hints, which spotlight some very important test prep information. Sidebars also highlight key concepts and strategies, fun facts, and real-world stories.

SHSAT Emergency FAQs

Q.   It's two days before the SHSAT and I'm clueless. What should I do?

A.   First of all, don't panic. If you have only a day or two to prepare for the test, then you don't have time to prepare thoroughly. But that doesn't mean you should just give up. There's still a lot you can do to improve your potential score. First and foremost, you should become familiar with the test. Read Section 1: The Basics. And if you don't do anything else, take one of the full-length practice tests at the back of this book under reasonably testlike conditions. When you finish the practice test, check your answers and look at the explanations for the questions you didn't get right.

Q. Math is my weak spot. What can I do to get better at math in a big hurry?

A. Read through 100 Essential Math Concepts in the appendix of the book. Read Introducing SHSAT Math in Section 3. Review the rest of Section 3, focusing on the content areas that give you the most trouble. Then do as many of the problems in the Math Practice Sets at the end of each chapter as you can. If you don't have time to do the problems, just read the sidebars in the math chapters. They contain really helpful facts and tips.

Q. I'm great at Math, but Verbal scares me. How can I improve my Verbal score right away?

A. Turn to Section 2 and read through Introducing SHSAT Verbal. Then do as many of the Practice Set problems in the Verbal chapters as you have time for. If you don't have time to do the problems, just read the sidebars in those chapters. These strategies can help boost your score.

Q. My parents are upset with me for waiting till the last minute to study, and now I can't concentrate. Help!

A. Take a deep breath! Anxiety and stress are the enemies of all test takers—no matter how much time they have to prepare. Turn to Section 4 and read through the Stress Management chapter. Do the suggested exercises. And don't forget to think positively!

Q: The SHSAT is tomorrow. Should I stay up all night studying geometry formulas?

A: The best thing to do right now is to try to stay calm. Read the Countdown to the Test chapter in Section 4 to find out the best way to survive, and thrive, on test day. And get a good night's sleep.

Q: I don't feel confident. Should I just guess?

A: There is no wrong-answer penalty, so you should definitely fill in an answer for every question. However, this does not mean that you should always guess randomly. Whenever you can eliminate wrong answers, you increase your chances of guessing correctly. Therefore, you should guess strategically whenever possible.

Q: What's the most important thing I can do to get ready for the SHSAT quickly?

A. In addition to basic Math and Verbal skills, the SHSAT mainly tests your ability to take the SHSAT. Therefore, the most important thing you can do is to familiarize yourself with the directions, the question types, the answer grid, and the overall structure of the test. Make sure you know how to get to your testing location and so forth. Read every question carefully—many mistakes are the result of simply not reading thoroughly.

Q. So it's a good idea to panic, right? RIGHT?

A. No! No matter how prepared you are for the SHSAT, stress will hurt your performance, and it's really no fun. Stay confident and don't cram. Just breathe, stay calm, and do your best.

A Special Note for Parents

The nine specialized high schools in New York City are Fiorello H. LaGuardia High School of Music and Art and Performing Arts; Bronx High School of Science; Brooklyn Latin School; Brooklyn Technical High School; High School for Math, Science and Engineering at City College; High School for American Studies at Lehman College; Queens High School for the Sciences at York College; Staten Island Technical High School; and Stuyvesant High School. The Specialized High Schools Admission Test (SHSAT), administered once a year, is required for admission to all of these schools except for Fiorello H. LaGuardia High School of Music & Art and Performing Arts. If a student is applying only to LaGuardia, then admission is based on an audition and a review of academic records. However, if a student is applying to LaGuardia and any of the other schools, he or she must take the SHSAT.

Approximately 20,000 applicants apply for about 2,000 spots at just three of the specialized New York City schools each year (Stuyvesant, Brooklyn Tech, and Bronx Science).

You have the opportunity to play an important role in your child's preparation for the Specialized High Schools Admissions Test. The SHSAT is difficult and the stakes are high, so your child may be feeling quite a lot of stress. You are the best judge of how much supervision and structure he or she needs in order to prepare. Similarly, since you know how your child handles stress, you are the best person to reassure and motivate your child during his or her preparation.

Much of the information that follows can be found elsewhere in this book. However, the information most salient for parents has been summarized here so that you don't have to search for it.

GETTING STARTED

If you do not have it already, you should get a copy of the *Specialized High Schools Student Handbook*. This is published by the Department of Education and is available on the website at **schools.nyc.gov** (look for the link in the "Choices & Enrollment" section) and should also be available in your son or daughter's guidance office. Get this handbook early and spend some time reading through it. Additionally, it's worth your while to do a little research into the individual schools. Take some time to learn the features and strengths of each.

Bronx High School of Science
75 West 205th Street
Bronx, NY 10468
(718) 817-7700
www.bxscience.edu

Brooklyn Latin School
325 Bushwick Avenue
Brooklyn, NY 11206
(718) 366-0154
www.brooklynlatin.org

Brooklyn Technical High School
29 Fort Greene Place
Brooklyn, NY 11217
(718) 804-6400
www.bths.edu

Fiorello H. LaGuardia High School of Music & Art and Performing Arts
100 Amsterdam Avenue
New York, NY 10023
(212) 496-0700
www.laguardiahs.org

High School for Math, Science and Engineering at The City College
240 Convent Avenue
New York, NY 10031
(212) 281-6490
www.hsmse.org

High School of American Studies at Lehman College
2925 Goulden Avenue
Bronx, NY 10468
(718) 329-2144
www.hsas-lehman.org

Queens High School for the Sciences at York College
94-50 159th Street
Jamaica, NY 11451
(718) 657-3181
www.qhss.org

Staten Island Technical High School
485 Clawson Street
Staten Island, NY 10306
(718) 667-5725
www.siths.org

Stuyvesant High School
345 Chambers Street
New York, NY 10282
(212) 312-4800
www.stuy.edu

THE SHSAT

Format

The test is broken into two sections, Verbal and Math. The Verbal Section contains 5 Scrambled Paragraphs, 10 Logical Reasoning questions, and 5 Reading Passages accompanied by 30 questions. The Math Section contains 50 questions covering arithmetic, algebra, and geometry. All questions except for Scrambled Paragraphs are multiple choice. Scrambled Paragraphs require test takers to arrange five sentences to form a coherent paragraph.

Timing

Test takers have 150 minutes (2 1/2 hours) for the entire test. The recommended time for each section is 75 minutes. However, test takers can break up the time however they choose.

Scoring

Although the Verbal Section contains five fewer questions than the Math Section, both sections contribute equally to the final score. (Scrambled Paragraphs are weighted a little more heavily than the other question types). The test taker's raw score out of 100 is converted to a scaled score on an 800-point scale.

Admission

Admission is determined exclusively by test takers' scores on this 800-point scale. Essentially, roughly the top 5,500 scorers are admitted to the eight specialized high schools requiring the SHSAT. It is impossible to know what the "cutoff" scores will be for each school, since this depends on the number of test takers and their overall performance.

THINGS TO KEEP IN MIND

The test is the sole criterion for admission.

Other test scores, grades, and connections do not help. If your child does not have straight As, he or she can still gain admission to one of the specialized high schools. If your child does have straight As, he or she may not get in. It may seem unfair—and it certainly puts a lot of pressure on the test takers—but it's the most objective method the Board of Education could devise to open the admissions process to all applicants.

Only students prepared to attend one of the specialized science high schools should take the SHSAT.

Your child should *not* take the SHSAT just to see how he or she would do. Only students who are serious about attending one of the specialized high schools should take the test. Any student who is admitted to one of these schools is expected to attend. Make sure that your child is serious about this commitment before taking the test.

Applying to more than one science high school increases your child's chances of admission.

The application asks the applicant to rank his or her choices of schools. If your child is interested in all of the schools, he or she should indicate an order of preference. Obviously, applying to six schools increases an applicant's odds of being admitted into one. However, this does not mean that all applicants should apply to all of the schools. Consider issues such as location and school size when making this decision. Think very seriously about how long a commute is acceptable.

HOW TO HELP YOUR SON OR DAUGHTER PREPARE FOR THE TEST

Help your child identify his or her priorities.

There are two reasons to do this. First, it's a good to idea to verify that your child actually wants to attend one of the specialized high schools and is prepared to make the accompanying commitment. Second, if your child identifies what she or he wants from this process, his or her motivation is likely to be clearer. Consequently, she or he may feel more control over the application and test-taking process.

Help your child design and maintain a study schedule.

This is a self-study book. Self-study requires a lot of self-discipline—not a quality for which eighth graders are generally known. Creating a schedule will increase your child's chance of working through and deriving the benefit from the entire book. You know your child and consequently know how much supervision she or he needs to stick to the schedule. A little supervision and prodding can help keep a lot of students on track. Of course, too much oversight can become oppressive for all parties.

Let your child know that you understand that this process is stressful.

The bottom line is that this is a difficult, high-stakes test. Preparing to take it can be extraordinarily stressful. While the high stakes can provide motivation, they can also induce fear—which can be paralyzing. Encourage your child to read Section 4: Ready, Set, Go! Make sure that your child realizes that it will be disappointing, but not the end of the world, if he or she does not gain admission to one of the specialized high schools.

The Basics

1

SHSAT Mastery

Highlights

- Get the Answers to Common Questions about the Specialized High Schools Admissions Test

- Find Out How to Take Advantage of the Test's Structure

- Learn How to Approach the Questions Strategically

You're reading this book because you're serious about attending high school at Brooklyn Latin, Stuyvesant, Bronx Science, Brooklyn Tech, City College, Lehman College, Staten Island Tech, or York College. You probably already know that if you want to go to one of these specialized high schools, you have to take the Specialized High Schools Admissions Test (SHSAT). If you want to get a high score on the test, there are some steps you can take to maximize your score. Essentially, you need to

- understand the structure of the test;

- hone your math and verbal skills;

- develop strategies and test-taking techniques; and

- practice what you've learned.

The Specialized High Schools Admissions Test (SHSAT) is a standardized test. It's certainly not easy, but it is a fairly predictable test. This means that you can prepare for the content and question types that you'll see on test day.

Before delving into the specific content and strategies you will need to perform well on the SHSAT, you should know some basic information about the test. Here are answers to some common questions about the test.

COMMON QUESTIONS ABOUT THE SHSAT

Why Should I Take the SHSAT Exam?

If you want to attend high school at Brooklyn Latin, Stuyvesant, Bronx Science, Brooklyn Tech, City College, Lehman College, Staten Island Tech, or York College, you must take the SHSAT. It is the sole criterion for admission. This means that your grades, extracurricular activities, etc. play no role in the admissions process. **Do not take the test if you are not serious about attending one of the schools!** If you score high enough to be accepted at a school, you will be expected to attend.

Who Administers the Test?

What Does SHSAT Stand For?

The full name of the test is the Specialized High Schools Admissions Test. SHSAT is just a wee bit easier to say.

The New York City Department of Education administers the test. The Department of Education is composed of teachers and administrators who decide what students at New York City high schools need to learn.

Why Is the Test the Sole Criterion for Admission?

Having one test be the only factor that determines whether you are accepted at the school of your choice is rough. However, more than 20,000 students apply for admission, and the Department of Education needs a way to pare down that number to roughly 5,500. A multiple-choice test given to all applicants is a very efficient way to make the cut because it subjects all applicants to the exact same standard and is very easy to grade. You might not be thrilled about this process, but it is not going to change before October. Therefore, regardless of your personal feelings about standardized tests in general or this test in particular, you need to take some time to prepare for the SHSAT.

Forget Your Connections

The test—and only the test— will determine whether you're admitted to one of the specialized high schools. It won't matter if your uncle's bowling partner's half-sister's son once played golf with the president and thinks he can wrangle you a letter of recommendation.

Is There *Any* Other Way to Get into the Specialized High Schools?

A limited number of students may be eligible to participate in a Discovery program, which is designed to give disadvantaged students who have demonstrated high potential a chance to enroll in a specialized high school program. For more information about this program, see the *Specialized High Schools Student Handbook*.

How Is the Test Scored?

The test contains 95 questions. Ninety of them are worth 1 "raw" point and five are worth 2 "raw" points, giving you a "raw score" on a 100-point scale. Your raw score is multiplied by a formula known only to the Department of Education to arrive at a scaled score out of 800.

What Is a "Good Score"?

That's a good question. Alas, there's really no answer to it. Admission works like this: The Department of Education identifies the number of places available at each school. If there are 500 spaces available at Stuyvesant, the Board of Education accepts the top 500 scorers who identified Stuyvesant as their first choice. Therefore, there is no magic number for admission.

What Should I Bring to the Test?

You need your admissions ticket, two or more No. 2 pencils, an eraser, and a watch that does not contain a calculator. You may not bring a calculator to the test.

TAKING ADVANTAGE OF THE SHSAT'S STRUCTURE

While it's possible that next year's SHSAT will be a little different from last year's, you can be confident that the test will look pretty much the same. Therefore, you can take advantage of the test's predictability and use what you know about the structure to raise your score.

You Do Not Need to Answer the Questions in Order

Usually when taking a test, you automatically answer the questions in the order that they're written. However, there are a lot of questions on the SHSAT, and you may be able to make it easier on yourself by doing the stuff you find easier first. For example, if you're good at Logical Reasoning questions, build your confidence and grab some quick points by doing them first. Or if you have a tough time with coordinate geometry, skip the Coordinate Geometry questions and go back to them when you have time.

You Can Go Back to the Verbal Section Once You've Finished the Math Section

Most standardized tests don't let you move between sections. On the SHSAT, however, you can go back to the Verbal Section after you've finished the Math Section.

There Is No Penalty for Wrong Answers

Don't leave anything blank on the SHSAT. A correct answer is a correct answer. It makes no difference to your score if you get the question correct by solving the question or by guessing. Of course, you should solve the questions you know, but there's no harm in guessing when you don't know how to answer a question or are running out of time. Remember, you have a 0 percent chance of getting a question correct if you leave it blank. Your chances of getting it correct if you guess are at least 20 percent. Go with the odds.

Don't Leave It Blank

Don't leave any questions blank! There's no penalty for wrong answers, so a guess can only help and will never hurt.

The SHSAT Answer Grid Has No Heart

Don't lose valuable points on the test by misgridding! The answer choices are labeled A–E and F–K to help you keep track of answers.

Always circle questions you skip.

Whenever you choose not to answer a question, circle it in your test book. This can help you in two ways. The first is that it will be easier to find the questions you skipped if they're circled. The second is that you are less likely to misgrid when you skip questions if you clearly mark the ones you skip. Anything that will help you approach the test efficiently is worth doing. Circling questions that you skip is relatively effortless and can save you time and get you points.

Always circle the answer you choose.

A great way to avoid careless gridding errors is to circle your answers in the test book. If you circle your answers, you can quickly check your circled answers against your gridded answers to make sure that you did not misgrid. Additionally, if you have time to recheck your answers, it's easier to do this if the answers are circled.

Grid Smart

> Instead of gridding each answer as you finish the question, circle the answer in your testbook and grid the answers after every five questions.

Grid your answers in blocks of five.

Don't grid in each answer after you answer each question. Instead, grid your answers after every five questions. As you're entering the answers into the grid, silently say, "1, A," "2, G," etc. This will help you to avoid any omissions. Since questions alternate between A–E choices and F–K choices, you should be able to catch a mistake if you have skipped a question or entered answers onto the wrong line.

APPROACHING SHSAT QUESTIONS STRATEGICALLY

As important as it is to know the setup of the SHSAT, it is equally important to have a system for attacking the questions. You wouldn't venture onto the subway for the first time without looking at a map, and you shouldn't approach the SHSAT without a plan. Remember, the more knowledge you have about the test and the questions, the better you'll be able to take control of the test. The following is the best way to approach SHSAT questions systematically.

Think Before You Answer

> Try to predict the answer—or at least think about it before you look at the answer choices. If nothing else, you may realize what the answer won't be. This will help you to avoid the tempting "traps" set by the test maker.

Think about the Questions Before You Look at the Answers

It's hard to emphasize strenuously enough precisely how important this strategy is. Basically, IT'S REALLY, REALLY IMPORTANT! One of the most damaging mistakes that students make when taking the SHSAT is that they jump immediately from the question to the answers without stopping to think first. This is particularly true in the Reading section but is a problem with most question types. Here's what will happen if you read the questions and then go directly to the answer choices: You will be confronted with very tempting, but very wrong, answer choices. If you take the time to think before looking at the choices, you will be much less likely to fall for the traps.

Use Backdoor Strategies and Guess

You'll learn more about backdoor strategies later, but the gist of them is that sometimes there are shortcuts to solving problems and guessing strategically. No one sees your work, so you do not have to solve problems the way you would in school. Any method that gets you the correct answer is the "right" way on the SHSAT. Additionally, since there is no penalty for wrong answers, don't leave any answers blank!

Go for the Points

You don't gain any points for leaving questions blank, and you don't lose any points for getting them wrong. You're better off guessing than leaving questions blank.

Pace Yourself

The SHSAT gives you a lot of questions in a relatively short period of time. To get through the test, you need to be in control of your pace. Remember, although you should enter an answer for every question, you don't have to answer *every* question correctly to score well. There are a few strategies you can employ to take control of your pace.

Take Control

Taking control of your pace will help you take control of your testing experience.

- Don't spend too much time on any one question. You can always circle a question and come back to it later.

- Give yourself a rough time limit for each question—move on if you run out of time.

- Be flexible—you can answer questions out of order.

- Don't spend more than 3–4 minutes on any one Reading Passage—keep reading and move on. Remember, your points come from answering the questions.

- Practice under timed conditions.

Locate Quick Points If You're Running Out of Time

Some questions can be answered more quickly than others. Some are simply amenable to shortcuts. For example, a Reading question that contains a line number or asks for the meaning of an *italicized* word may be easier to answer quickly than one that does not give you a clue. Other questions will be easier because of your particular strengths. If you're comfortable with geometry and are running out of time, look for the geometry questions.

Know Thyself

You know your strengths and weaknesses better than anyone else. Use this knowledge to work efficiently.

2

Inside the SHSAT

Highlights

- Understand the Structure of the Test

- Learn How the Test is Scored and Timed

- Get Practical Advice on Pacing Yourself During the Test

- Get Information on the Schools That the SHSAT Can Get You Into

The SHSAT is a standardized test, which means that it is pretty predictable. Although the Department of Education is free to change the test (and occasionally does), the test is unlikely to change dramatically. Therefore, you can take control and build your confidence by knowing what to expect. When you sit down to take the test, you should know what the test will look like, how it will be scored, and how long you'll have to complete it.

STRUCTURE OF THE TEST

There are two sections on the test: Verbal and Math. The Verbal Section has three question types: Scrambled Paragraphs, Logical Reasoning, and Reading. Though the Math Section has only one question type, students can expect to see arithmetic, algebra, geometry, and other math topics on the test.

Verbal Section

On the Verbal Section, you'll see the following types of questions:

• 5 Scrambled Paragraphs
Scrambled Paragraphs questions require you to arrange six sentences into a logical paragraph. These questions test your ability to identify a logical flow and sequence of ideas. The main skill they test is your ability to identify transitional words and phrases.

• 10 Logical Reasoning Questions
As the name suggests, Logical Reasoning questions present you with a situation or a set of facts and require you to reason logically based on the information you are given. The specific tasks include figuring out codes, identifying correct assumptions, determining the relative positions of people or things, or drawing valid conclusions.

• 30 Reading Questions
The Reading questions don't exactly test your ability to read. They test your ability to comprehend what you've read. You'll get five Reading passages on a variety of subjects, each of which will be followed by six questions. One question for each passage will test your understanding of the main idea. Other questions will ask you to identify details from the passage or to make inferences based on what you read.

Know the Test's Structure

You'll see 45 Verbal and 50 Math questions on the test. The Verbal and Math Sections are equally weighted.

The Verbal Section will appear first on the test, and you will have approximately 75 minutes to complete the section.

Math

In the Math Section, you'll find the following:

• 50 Questions Covering a Variety of Math Topics
Most Math questions will be arithmetic, algebra, and geometry questions. However, you may also see problems dealing with simple probability and statistics. Additionally, you're likely to see questions that seem somewhat unfamiliar. The Department of Education believes that your ability to deal with novel situations is a good indicator of mathematical ability. However, most of the subject matter will be familiar. The ninth-grade test will contain basic trigonometry, which is not covered in this book. Refer to your school textbook or to Kaplan's *Math Power* for trig review.

The Math Section will follow the Verbal Section. You will have approximately 75 minutes to complete the section.

SCORING

Scoring for the SHSAT is a little strange. It's not that the scoring is difficult to understand; it's just that individual scores matter only to the extent that they are above or below a cutoff line.

Here's how the scoring works. First, you get a "raw score" based on the number of questions you answer correctly. You get two points for every correct Scrambled Paragraph and one point for every other correct answer you mark on your answer grid. Since there are 5 Scrambled Paragraphs and 90 other questions on the test, the highest possible "raw score" is 100.

> ### Know the Score
>
> You'll get a "raw" score and a scaled score for each section. The highest possible "raw" score is 100 for each section. The highest possible composite scaled score is 800. This is the score that will determine admissions.

Next, your raw score is multiplied by a formula known only to the Department of Education to arrive at a scaled score. You receive a scaled score for each section and a composite score for the entire test. The highest possible composite score is 800.

Admission to all specialized high schools except LaGuardia is based solely on your composite score. The way this works is that all of the students are ranked from high score to low score and then assigned to the school of their first preference until all the available seats are filled. For example, if Stuyvesant had exactly 500 spaces available and the top 500 scorers all picked Stuyvesant as their first choice, all 500 scorers would be admitted. If the 501st scorer listed Stuyvesant as her first choice and Bronx Science as her second choice, she would be assigned to Bronx Science. In other words, if 500 students were admitted to Stuyvesant and the 500th highest score was 560, then 560 would be the "cutoff" score for Stuyvesant. Therefore, scores are relative; it matters only whether they are above the cutoff, but there is no way of accurately knowing what the cutoff score will be. All you know is that it will likely be a little higher than last year's cutoff because the test becomes increasingly competitive every year.

SHSAT TIMING

When the test begins and you open to the first page, here's what you'll see:

PART 1—VERBAL

Time—75 Minutes

45 Questions

The most important thing to remember about SHSAT timing suggestions is that they are just that—**suggestions!**

Here's the way it works. You'll have 150 minutes to complete the entire test. It is recommended that you spend approximately half the time (75 minutes or 1 hour and 15 minutes) on each section. However, if you finish the Verbal Section early, you can move on to the Math Section without waiting for the 75 minutes to end. Similarly, if you finish the Math Section with time to spare, you can go back over both the Math and Verbal Sections of the test.

What this means is that you have both the freedom to structure your time and the responsibility to use your time wisely. While you can spend more than 75 minutes working on the first section, it may not be wise to do so. However, the flexibility you have in skipping around and going back to one section after finishing the other gives you ample opportunity to play to your strengths.

PACING

You are responsible for setting your own pace on the test. This is a big responsibility that you should take very seriously. Here are some rough guidelines to follow.

Verbal	**Scrambled Paragraphs:**	2–3 minutes each
	Logical Reasoning:	$1\frac{1}{2}$ minutes each
	Reading:	2–3 minutes per passage
		1–$1\frac{1}{2}$ minutes per question
Math	$1\frac{1}{2}$ minutes per question	

Remember that these guidelines are rough. You will spend more time on some questions and less time on others. However, you must be aware of time if you want to maximize your score. If you're casual about it, you could get yourself into big trouble.

THE SCHOOLS

In addition to preparing for the test, you should be doing some research about the schools. Remember, if you get accepted into a school, you will be expected to attend. Therefore, you want to make an informed decision here. The best way to get information about the schools is to contact them or check out their websites. Here's the contact information for each school:

Bronx High School of Science	75 West 205th Street Bronx, NY 10468 (718) 817-7700 *www.bxscience.edu*
Brooklyn Latin School	325 Bushwick Avenue Brooklyn, NY 11206 (718) 366-0154 *www.brooklynlatin.org*
Brooklyn Technical High School	29 Fort Greene Place Brooklyn, NY 11217 (718) 804-6400 *www.bths.edu*

Fiorello H. LaGuardia High School of Music & Art and Performing Arts	100 Amsterdam Avenue New York, NY 10023 (212) 496-0700 *www.laguardiahs.org*
High School for Math, Science and Engineering at The City College	240 Convent Avenue New York, NY 10031 (212) 281-6490 *www.hsmse.org*
High School of American Studies at Lehman College	2925 Goulden Avenue Bronx, NY 10468 (718) 329-2144 *www.hsas-lehman.org*
Queens High School for the Sciences at York College	94-50 159th Street Jamaica, NY 11451 (718) 657-3181 *www.qhss.org*
Staten Island Technical High School	485 Clawson Street Staten Island, NY 10306 (718) 667-5725 *www.siths.org*
Stuyvesant High School	345 Chambers Street New York, NY 10282 (212) 312-4800 *www.stuy.edu*

Do some research. Talk to your parents, teachers, and guidance counselor. Some factors that you may want to consider are these:

- Location
- Age and condition of facilities
- Class size
- School size
- Areas of concentration
- Advanced Placement courses
- Research programs
- Availability of hands-on tech courses
- College courses offered
- Extracurricular activities

Additionally, here are a few trivia facts about some of the specialized high schools that you may or may not know:

- Brooklyn Tech is one of the ten largest high schools in the country, according to *U.S. News and World Report.*

- Stuyvesant was recognized by the President's Commission on Excellence as one of the best schools in the country.

- Five Nobel Prize winners attended Bronx Science: Leon Cooper, 1972; Sheldon Glashow, 1979; Steven Weinberg, 1979; Melvin Schwartz, 1988; Russell A. Hulse, 1993.

- Brooklyn Latin, which opened in 2006, features a curriculum that is focused on the humanities.

TEST DATE

The test is administered during a weekend in late October for eighth graders and during a weekend in late October or early November for ninth graders.

Log on to **schools.nyc.gov** for updated information.

SHSAT
Verbal

3

Introducing SHSAT Verbal

Highlights

- Discover the Good News and the Bad News about the Verbal Section of the Test

- Get an Overview of the Verbal Section

- Familiarize Yourself with the Question Types You'll Encounter

- Find Out How to Approach SHSAT Verbal

THE GOOD NEWS AND THE BAD NEWS

First, the Good News...

Let's start with the good news about the Verbal Section of the SHSAT: **There is no content to study or memorize for the Verbal Section of the SHSAT.** The SHSAT does not test vocabulary, so you don't have to spend time memorizing lists of words or word roots. The SHSAT does not test grammar or punctuation, so you don't have to bone up on gerunds or dangling participles.

This is good news. You'll have plenty of math content to study between now and test day, so it's a pretty good deal that you don't have to study any verbal content. Success on this section of the test is dependent on your ability to read and to think. There's a pretty good chance that you know how to do both of these things.

No Vocabulary or Grammar

There is no Verbal content on the SHSAT. Put away your dictionary and English textbook. The Verbal Section does not test vocabulary or grammar.

Now for the Bad News...

The bad news is that the SHSAT does not test Verbal content. Okay, so this is a little contradictory. If the fact that that the test maker does not test Verbal content is good news, you may wonder why this same piece of information constitutes bad news. The short answer is that while Verbal content may be tedious, it's also fairly easy to study. Preparing for the Verbal Section of the SHSAT is a little trickier than simply memorizing a list of vocabulary words or grammar rules.

To prepare for the Verbal Section of the SHSAT, you must become familiar with the test and practice strategies for each question type. This includes getting used to unfamiliar question types and reading a lot of dry reading passages.

VERBAL OVERVIEW

The Verbal Section is the first section on the test. It contains 45 questions but accounts for one-half of your total points on the SHSAT. The suggested time for the section is 75 minutes, or 1 hour and 15 minutes.

The breakdown of the Verbal Section is as follows:

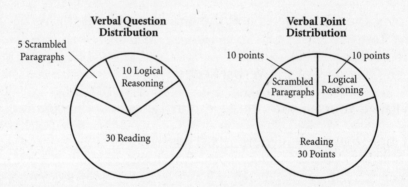

As you can see from the graphs, there are five fewer Scrambled Paragraphs than Logical Reasoning questions, but the two subsections account for the same total value on the test. This is because each Scrambled Paragraph has the same value as two of any other question type. However, what should be abundantly clear is that the bulk of your points on the SHSAT will come from the Reading section.

This does not mean, by the way, that you should not prepare for Scrambled Paragraphs or Logical Reasoning. Rather, it's just good to know where the bulk of the points will come from. Also, if you're running out of time before the test and cannot devote as much time as you would like to prepare, dedicate more time to Reading than to the other Verbal question types.

THE QUESTION TYPES

Scrambled Paragraphs

The Directions: When you begin the Verbal Section, you will see the following:

> ### SCRAMBLED PARAGRAPHS
> ### Paragraphs 1–5
>
> Below are six sentences that form a paragraph. The first sentence is the first sentence of the paragraph. The remaining five sentences are listed in random order. Choose the order for the five sentences that will create the **best** paragraph, one that is both well organized and grammatically correct. Each correctly ordered paragraph will be worth **two** points. No credit will be given for responses that are only partially correct.

Basically, Scrambled Paragraphs test your ability to organize sentences into a logical progression of ideas. The main thing about them is that each paragraph is either all right or all wrong. In other words, you have to put all five sentences in the correct order in order to get credit. If you get any part of it wrong, the whole thing is wrong. This means you have to be very careful to avoid wasting time and points.

You may find Scrambled Paragraphs a little strange at first. Stick with them. They get easier with practice. An important thing to remember is that what's being tested is your ability to arrange the sentences in the way that the test maker believes is correct. As you practice Scrambled Paragraphs, pay close attention to the explanations and make sure you know why correct answers are correct.

Logical Reasoning

The Directions: When you reach the Logical Reasoning questions, the following is what you'll see:

> ### LOGICAL REASONING
> ### Questions 11–20
>
> Read the information given and choose the **best** answer to each question. Base your answer **only on the information given**.

These directions are pretty straightforward. The key is the bolded words: You need to pay attention to only the information you've been given. You'll learn more about this later, but it's incredibly easy to make mistakes on Logical Reasoning questions by making unwarranted assumptions.

You'll notice that Logical Reasoning questions are kind of like games or puzzles. They're designed to test your skills at making deduction and understanding arguments. If you find them a little intimidating at first, relax. If you practice the Kaplan strategies, they'll get easier. If you find them kind of fun, go with it. Many test takers find that Logical Reasoning questions liven up the Verbal Section.

Reading

The Directions: The beginning of the Reading section will look like this:

READING
Questions 21–50

Read each passage below and answer the questions following it. Base your answers **only on what you have read in the passage**. You may reread a passage if you need to. Mark the **best** answer for each question.

As with Logical Reasoning questions, it is crucial that you restrict your answers to Reading questions to what you have read in the passage. Bringing in outside information is a great way to get yourself in trouble. These questions test your understanding of what you've read in the passages.

Everything You Need Is on the Page

Stick to the passage. Don't bring outside knowledge into Reading questions. You don't need it.

Although the Department of Education calls this section "Reading," Kaplan calls this section "Reading Comprehension" because the questions don't test your ability to read as much as they test your ability to understand what you've read. You'll get five passages, each followed by six questions, covering a range of topics. Remember, the fact that you may be applying to a "science" high school does not mean that you want to show off on the science passages. These questions do not test any outside knowledge of science.

HOW TO APPROACH SHSAT VERBAL

To do well on the SHSAT Verbal Section, you need to be systematic in your approach. In other words, you need to know how you are going to deal with each question type and the section as a whole before you open the test booklet. You need to know your strengths and weaknesses. For example, if you find Logical Reasoning questions easy, you can jump directly to them and get some quick points. Or you can leave them in the middle to break up the section. It's up to you. You have to be aware of timing. Five Reading passages are a lot. You have to be aware of your time and plan it well. If you spend an hour making certain that all your Scrambled Paragraphs are correct, you're going to be in trouble later.

Use What You Know

Once again, this means that you need to focus on strategy rather than content. In case you missed the point the 12,000 times it's been mentioned so far in this chapter—the Verbal

Section of the SHSAT does not test any specific content. Therefore, the best way to prepare for the test is to become thoroughly familiar with the question types and the strategies that will help you answer them correctly.

What you may not have thought about is that the Verbal Section tests skills that you already use both in school and in day-to-day life. You've written paragraphs before; you know how to organize sentences. You've make deductions based on information you've been given. You've read prose and answered questions. You also use these skills outside of the classroom.

Say you take a seat on the subway and realize that people sitting near you are having what seems to be an interesting conversation. Do you choose not to eavesdrop because you haven't heard the entire thing and assume that you will not be able to follow it? Probably not. Odds are, you use your inference skills—the ability to draw valid conclusions from limited information—to figure out what they're talking about and enjoy the espionage. When you tell your friends about it later, do you relay it word for word? You probably distinguish the important points from the unimportant details and use your paraphasing skills—the ability to condense complex ideas into a few words—to give them the highlights.

> **What Matters**
>
> Your performance on the Verbal Section of the SHSAT is based on your ability to do the following:
>
> - Put sentences in order.
> - Make deductions based on a few pieces of information.
> - Read a passage and answer a bunch of question about it.

Know What to Expect

Remember that this is a standardized test. Doing your best on test day comes from knowing what to expect and realizing that you have the skills to handle it. Although the Department of Education can change the test, odds are that it won't do anything too radical. The combination of practice and confidence should get you pretty far.

4

Scrambled Paragraphs

Highlights

- Familiarize Yourself with the Format

- Practice Kaplan's 3-Step Method for Scrambled Paragraphs

- Figure Out How to Work with Structural Clues

- Learn How to Identify Classic Paragraph Structures

Scrambled Paragraphs seem strange at first—there's no getting around that. They're probably pretty different from anything you've seen on any other test or in any class. However, the fact that they're different does not mean that they have to be difficult. Scrambled Paragraphs are designed to test your understanding of paragraph structure. You've seen—and written—plenty of paragraphs in your day, so understanding paragraph structure is not a radical concept. What's tricky is getting used to the rather strange format.

Unfamiliar, but Not Impossible

Don't be afraid of new things. The fact that Scrambled Paragraphs are a little strange does not make them inherently difficult. You just have to get used to them.

THE FORMAT

This is what the questions look like. You'll see six sentences—one Topic Sentence and five other sentences listed in no particular order. The five sentences will be lettered Q, R, S, T, and U. Each sentence will have a line short line next to it.

Paragraph 1

Porpoises and sharks appear to be similar in that they are streamlined, are good swimmers, and live in the sea.

___2___ **Q.** For example, the shark has gills, cold blood, and scales, whereas the porpoise has lungs, warm blood, and hair.

___1___ **R.** Important differences are apparent, however, to marine biologists who study these species.

___4___ **S.** The porpoise, on the other hand, is fundamentally more like man than like the shark—and it therefore belongs to the order of mammals.

___5___ **T.** Armed with the knowledge that the porpoise is a mammal, the biologist can then confidently predict that porpoises have a four-chambered heart and bones of a particular type.

___3___ **U.** From this contrast in features, the zoologist knows that the shark has the physiology of a fish.

Use the lines next to each sentence to keep track of your work. For example, if sentence Q were the sentence following the Topic Sentence (it's not, by the way), then you would jot down a "1" on the line next to Q. This would help you keep the sentences straight when you transfer your answers to the answer grid.

The Scrambled Paragraph section of the answer grid will look like this:

Paragraph 1

The first sentence is	Q	R	S	T	U
The second sentence is	Q	R	S	T	U
The third sentence is	Q	R	S	T	U
The fourth sentence is	Q	R	S	T	U
The fifth sentence is	Q	R	S	T	U

Again, if Q were the first sentence folowing the Topic Sentence (which it still is not), you would bubble in Q where it says, "The first sentence is."

KAPLAN'S 3-STEP METHOD FOR SCRAMBLED PARAGRAPHS

The key to taking control of the test is knowing how you're going to approach each problem before you ever see it. Because the test is standardized, you can do this. You can learn and practice a method to help you get through each problem quickly and efficiently.

The Kaplan Method for unscrambling Scrambled Paragraphs has three simple steps:

1. Read through each sentence, circling any important Structural Clues.

2. Use Structural Clues to connect the sentences in such a way that they logically follow the Topic Sentence.

3. Read through your paragraph to make sure it makes sense.

Have a Plan

It's about the methodology. If you decide ahead of time how you will approach every question type on the test, you'll work faster and more accurately on test day.

Step 1: Read Through Each Sentence, Circling Any Important Structural Clues

Structural Clues are words that provide information about the relationship between sentences. They're words or phrases that help you predict where the paragraph is going or follow where it has been.

Paragraph 1

Porpoises and sharks appear to be similar in that they are streamlined, are good swimmers, and live in the sea.

_____ Q. **For example**, the shark has gills, cold blood, and scales, whereas the porpoise has lungs, warm blood, and hair.

_____ R. Important differences are apparent, **however**, to marine biologists who study these species.

_____ S. The porpoise, **on the other hand**, is fundamentally more like man than like the shark—and it therefore belongs to the order of mammals.

_____ T. **Armed with the knowledge that the porpoise is a mammal**, the biologist can then confidently predict that porpoises have a four-chambered heart and bones of a particular type.

_____ U. **From this contrast in features**, the zoologist knows that the shark has the physiology of a fish.

Contextual Clues— Right on the Page

Scrambled Paragraphs test active reading. Success is about your ability to figure out what an author is going to say next or what the author must have already said.

Each of the sentences contains clues that provide information about its relationship to other sentences. Look at sentence Q. It begins with the words "For example." This tells you that sentence Q must refer back to something specific in a previous sentence.

Step 2: Use Structural Clues to Connect the Sentences in Such a Way That They Logically Follow the Topic Sentence

The key to connecting the sentences is to keep in mind that endings connect with beginnings. Every sentence has to connect smoothly to the next, without any ambiguity or loose ends. Structural clues are the tools that enable you to make these connections.

Your topic sentence says:

Porpoises and sharks appear to be similar in that they are streamlined, are good swimmers, and live in the sea.

The phrase **"appear to be"** should make you suspicious that despite the fact that porpoises and sharks appear similar, the author is going to tell you how they are not similar. Therefore, it's a good idea to *actively look* for a sentence that talks about differences. As soon as you do this, voilá, Sentence R leaps out at you:

R. **Important differences are apparent, however, to marine biologists who study these species.**

This sentence starts by talking about the **important differences** that you predicted would be discussed. Furthermore, the sentence uses the big Structural Clue "**however.**" "However" tells you that there is some type of *contrast* (i.e., that even though things seem one way, in reality they are another).

Now that you've seen how the second sentence connects with the first, you have to think about how the second sentence will connect with the third. Sentence R mentioned differences between porpoises and sharks generally. What do you think the next sentence will address? Here's a hint: Paragraphs tend to move from the general to the specific.

At this point, Sentence Q should be screaming for you to look at it:

Q. **For example, the shark has gills, cold blood, and scales, whereas the porpoise has lungs, warm blood, and hair.**

This sentence begins with the words "**For example.**" This is a pretty big clue that the rest of the sentence is going to present a specific example of something. And this sentence delivers exactly what it promises. It discusses specific differences between porpoises and sharks.

Be a Detective

Use your deductive reasoning skills. Scrambled paragraphs tend to move from the general to the specific.

Sentence U picks up where Sentence Q ends: "From this contrast in features..." refers specifically to the physiological differences mentioned in Sentence Q.

You now have two sentences left. Take a look at them to see which should come first. Which of the two better connects to the fourth sentence, and which sentence best wraps up the paragraph? In other words, which sentence doesn't leave anything hanging at the end?

S.   The porpoise, on the other hand, is fundamentally more like man than like the shark—and it therefore belongs to the order of mammals.

T.   Armed with the knowledge that the porpoise is a mammal, the biologist can then confidently predict that porpoises have a four-chambered heart and bones of a particular type.

Think about where the paragraph has gone so far. The Topic sentence noted similarities between porpoises and sharks. Sentence R noted that they were different despite their similarities. Sentence Q identified some differences. Sentence U drew a conclusion about sharks based on these differences. **Sentence S** begins by distinguishing porpoises from something mentioned previously—"The porpoise, **on the other hand**...." (You know that the porpoise is being distinguished from the shark.) **Sentence T** then picks up on the reference to the porpoises as mammals and finishes the idea (i.e., it mentions how scientists can use this data).

Step 3: Read Through Your Paragraph to Make Sure It Makes Sense

Paragraph 1

Porpoises and sharks appear to be similar in that they are streamlined, are good swimmers, and live in the sea.

R.   Important differences are apparent, however, to marine biologists who study these species.

Q.   For example, the shark has gills, cold blood, and scales, whereas the porpoise has lungs, warm blood, and hair.

U.   From this contrast in features, the zoologist knows that the shark has the physiology of a fish.

S.   The porpoise, on the other hand, is fundamentally more like man than like the shark—and it therefore belongs to the order of mammals.

T.   Armed with the knowledge that the porpoise is a mammal, the biologist can then confidently predict that porpoises have a four-chambered heart and bones of a particular type.

When you put these sentences together in order, they make logical sense. There are no awkward transitions or phrases that seem out of sequence.

WORKING WITH STRUCTURAL CLUES

Structural Clues are words that authors use to indicate the function of each sentence in relation to other sentences and the author's argument as a whole. They indicate the logical progression of the argument. Fundamental rules of sentence construction and grammar also dictate an argument's progression or "architecture." Therefore, understanding these rules can also help you identify sentence order. Identifying both these words and grammatical constructions is the key to arranging the sentences.

Sentence Pairs

As a general rule, it's a good idea to work with sentences in pairs. It is often easier to look for the relationship between two sentences than it is to deal with the paragraph as a whole. For example, if a sentence contains a pronoun, look for the sentence that contains the antecedent.

Nouns and Pronouns

Nouns and Pronouns

Paying attention to pronouns and nouns can help you unscramble the sentences.

Paying attention to pronouns and nouns can help you unscramble sentences 2–5. Basically, any time you see an ambiguous pronoun (a pronoun whose antecedent is not found in the same sentence), you know that the previous sentence must define the pronoun. For example, if you come across the sentence, "Rather than finish college, she dropped out to pursue her dream of building the world's largest popsicle stick sculpture," you know that the sentence preceding this one has to tell you who "she" is.

A Rule Without Exception

Scrambled paragraphs will never contain a pronoun without an antecedent.

Similarly, if a person is referred to by a last name or nickname (i.e., by something other than a full name), there will be a previous sentence in which the person is mentioned by his or her full name. So if you came across the sentence "The popularity of Michener's *Kent State* was renewed as the anniversary of the Kent State shootings neared," you would have a previous sentence identifying "Michener" by his full name, James Michener.

> EXERCISE

Use ambiguous nouns and pronouns to determine the order of the following sentence pairs.

Q. The diminutive Shetland pony has been a protected species for many years.

R. Though largely protected by isolation from other species, the pony is vulnerable because of small numbers.

Q. Some of these standing stones were decorated with carvings depicting harvest rituals.

R. Dotted across the Scottish countryside, the Pictish stones serve as a reminder of a lost race.

Q. Recent research suggests that they will last well into the twenty-first century.

R. Earth's fossil fuels may not be as scarce as scientists once thought.

Answers can be found at the end of this chapter.

More Structural Clues

Example

Example clues indicate that the author is providing specific evidence to back up an argument or opinion: *example, for example, for instance, one illustration of this,* etc.

Sequence

Sequence clues indicate the chronological order of a series of events or the order in which an author wants to discuss a series of issues: *first...second, until recently...today, in the 1920s... by the 1940s,* etc.

Continuity

Continuity clues indicate that the author is following up a statement with an additional, consistent statement: *similarly, consequently, therefore, hence,* etc.

Contrast

Contrast clues indicate that the author is presenting an idea that is inconsistent with the preceding idea: *however, on the other hand, but, nevertheless,* etc.

Classic Paragraph Structures

The more you practice Scrambled Paragraphs, the more you'll recognize paragraph structures that appear repeatedly. For example, Scrambled Paragraphs usually start off pretty general and get progressively more specific and detailed. Often, the author will introduce some sort of contrast and counterexample at the end. (Look for clues such as "however" or "nevertheless.") As a general rule, with practice you'll find that the basic structure of Scrambled Paragraphs becomes more and more familiar.

Scrambled Paragraph Practice Set

Paragraph 1

It is ironic that, despite the many successes of scientific medicine, many afflictions stubbornly resist all attempts to combat them.

Q. Those affected by this deadly virus and other modern plagues cannot be blamed for suspecting that scientific medicine is somehow missing something important.

R. If body and mind are indeed linked, future doctors may be able to manipulate the mind in order to have a healing effect on currently intransigent physical problems.

S. This connection would appear to be an obvious factor for examination, since the brain has long been established as the command center of the body.

_3_ T. ① Perhaps the gap in understanding stems from the fact that doctors have overlooked a potent connection between body and mind.

① U. Until recently, for example, science has been largely powerless in the face of HIV, which seems designed by nature to withstand the weapons of immunologists.

Paragraph 2

Modern compendia of the stories of Greek classical mythology have relied on the Latin poet Ovid as their chief source.

_5_ Q. The original Greek mythologists would no doubt have been dismayed to learn that such liberties had been taken with their work.

_1_ R. Latin, the mother of major European languages and the medium of the Catholic Church, pushed Greek into a minor occupation of scholars.

_3_ S. Unfortunately, however, the myths were not factual truth to Ovid as they had been to the early Greek poets; he viewed them as sheer nonsense.

_2_ T. Hence, not surprisingly, some of the most famous stories come down to us only in Ovid's pages.

_4_ U. As a consequence, he felt free to transform what once had been vehicles of deep religious truth into idle tales that were witty but often sentimental.

Paragraph 3

Early in the eighteenth century, the astronomer Edmund Halley wondered to himself why it was that the night sky is dark.

_1_ Q. Such an apparently naive question is far from useless.

_4_ R. A star's brightness stays the same over any distance, so each of those stars would be visible to us, and the heavens would be filled with light.

_5_ S. The fact that they are not indicates that there is something fundamentally wrong with the popular conception of the universe.

_3_ T. In an infinite universe, after all, there would have to be a star lying in every possible line of sight in the sky.

_2_ U. Halley's question is in fact interesting to consider because if the universe were truly infinite, as most suppose, the entire sky would be ablaze at night.

Paragraph 4

The philosophers in eighteenth-century France had a direct and strong influence upon the revolutionary movement of 1789.

_____ **Q.** This may seem surprising, given that most French people experienced poverty and starvation.

_____ **R.** This miserable situation would appear to have been enough by itself to inflame the masses.

_____ **S.** However, until they were provided with the idea of revolution, the people expressed their dissatisfaction only in occasional riots.

_____ **T.** In fact, it is safe to say that there would have been no revolution at all without their writings and lectures.

_____ **U.** They provided a dramatic example of the cliché "The pen is mightier than the sword."

Paragraph 5

The study of indoor environmental pollution is a controversial new area of scientific research.

_____ **Q.** For example, inhabitants of houses with statistically "average" levels of radon are exposed to approximately 300 percent more radiation than the average American receives from X-ray medical procedures in a lifetime.

_____ **R.** Consequently, it is a serious concern that hundreds of thousands of homes exceed "average" pollution levels.

_____ **S.** One area of debate is that the use of the terms "high," "low," and "average" in reports of the concentrations of indoor pollutants can be misleading.

_____ **T.** Clearly, more attention needs to be paid to issues such as the labeling of indoor pollutant concentrations.

_____ **U.** Such labels do not necessarily imply any correlation with "acceptable" or "unacceptable" health risks.

Paragraph 6

Many people find it puzzling that groups of people sometimes engage in behavior that seems to be clearly dangerous or, at least, ill-conceived.

__4__ Q. For that reason, when the leader exhibits a preference for a specific solution to the crisis, the other members may choose to ignore any other alternatives.

__5__ R. The resulting lack of balanced judgment—groupthink—may well cause the group to reach a decision that in retrospect is obviously wrong.

__3__ S. Individual members of the group prize the high morale derived from its cohesion and fear rejection if they break ranks.

__1__ T. Irving Janis developed the "groupthink" hypothesis in 1972 in an attempt to explain how fatal errors can occur in a group's decision making.

__2__ U. According to this hypothesis, groupthink can arise when a highly cohesive group with a strong-willed leader faces a crisis.

Paragraph 7

In spite of a recent revival of interest in nineteenth-century women writers, Lydia Maria Child remains an obscure name.

__2__ Q. Child's writing was, by contrast, politically passionate; she devoted her literary energies to vindicating the rights of women, Indians, and African American slaves.

__1__ R. The most likely explanation for this oversight is that she cannot be classified with her female contemporaries, who mainly produced stylized domestic fiction.

__5__ S. Our gain, though, would not compensate for the fact that her voice was not sufficiently heard when it would have been most relevant.

__3__ T. So powerful was her voice, in fact, that the abolitionist William Lloyd Garrison hailed her as "first woman in the Republic."

__4__ U. His endorsement leaves no room for doubt that the modern reader should be made aware of her work.

Paragraph 8

The famous economist Adam Smith was notorious for his absent-mindedness and tendency to enter strange fits of distraction.

4 Q. When the spell was broken, he stopped and took up the conversation where he had left off, not realizing he had done anything out of the ordinary.

1 R. On one occasion, Smith was walking in Edinburgh with a friend when a guard presented his pike in salute.

3 S. He returned the honor with his cane and then astonished his friend by following exactly in the guard's footsteps, duplicating with his cane every motion of the pike.

2 T. Smith, who had been thus honored on countless occasions, was suddenly hypnotized by the saluting soldier.

5 U. Encountering the organized reliability of *The Wealth of Nations*, it is difficult to imagine the spellbound principal of this anecdote as the father of modern economics.

Paragraph 9

When we read newspaper quotations, we assume them to represent exactly what the speaker said.

3 Q. People speak with bizarre syntax, hesitations, repetitions, and contradictions, making it necessary for the journalist to translate speech into prose.

2 R. Journalists must contend, however, with the fact that exact quotations of human speech would be virtually unreadable.

1 S. Indeed, the idea of a reporter inventing rather than reporting speech is repugnant because so much of our knowledge comes from what we read in the press.

5 T. When the speaker does not recognize the quote as his or her own, however, the journalist has taken too much license.

4 U. These translations may not be exact quotes, but they are valid as long as they remain faithful to the subject's thought and characteristic way of expression.

Paragraph 10

The thistle is a type of prickly plant that grows throughout North America.

___T___ **Q.**   His cry awoke the Scots, who fell upon their attackers and saved their nation from conquest.

___S___ **R.**   In Scotland, however, the thistle has been the cherished national flower for centuries.

___R___ **S.**   According to legend, as marauding Norsemen crept toward a camp full of sleeping Scottish soldiers, one invader stepped on a thistle and let out a yelp.

___Q___ **T.**   On that continent, most thistles are considered wildflowers not worthy of much attention.

___U___ **U.**   Ironically, the thistle's self-protective feature protected not only the flower, but the nation.

EXPLANATIONS TO EXERCISES

Nouns and Pronouns Exercise

1. **QR**   In Q, the noun "Shetland pony" is spelled out. In R, it's contracted to "pony," so R must follow Q. Logically, Q indicates that the Shetland pony is protected, and R explains why.

2. **RQ**   In R, "Pictish stones" is the subject, whereas in Q it's referred to as "these standing stones." Q must therefore follow R. Logically, R makes a general statement about Pictish stones, while Q narrows the scope of the discussion to focus on the carvings on them.

3. **RQ**   In Q, "they" is ambiguous—it must refer to "earth's fossil fuels" from sentence R. Q must therefore follow R. Logically, R introduces the topic of fossil fuels, and Q provides more detail on how long they will last.

Practice Set Explanations

1. **UQTSR.** U is the most logical first sentence—it provides an *example* of an affliction or illness resisting doctors' attempts to combat it. Q must follow, as "this deadly virus" must refer to HIV in sentence U. T's "gap in understanding" refers to the concept of "missing something important" in Q. "This connection" in S refers to the mind/body reference in T. R concludes by suggesting how mind/body medicine might improve the medicine of the future.

2. **RTSUQ.** R provides an explanation for why a Latin poet would be the source for Greek myths. T must come next, as "only in Ovid's pages" must refer to "relied on the Latin poet Ovid." S introduces a contrasting idea—the idea that Ovid thought the stories were nonsense. U spells out the "consequence" of this belief—that he changed all the stories. Finally, Q concludes by speculating on what the Greeks would have thought of Ovid's destruction of their stories.

3. **QUTRS.** Q must come first because this "naive question" can refer to only the question posed in the Topic Sentence. U must follow Q because it provides a reason why the "question" in Q is "in fact interesting." T must follow, as "in an infinite universe" expands on the issue mentioned in U. R's "each of those stars" connects back to "a star lying in every possible line of sight" in T. Finally, "the fact that they are not" in S refers to "the heavens would be filled with light" in R.

4. **UTQRS.** "They" in U refers to the philosophers in the Topic Sentence. T must come next, as "without their writing and lectures" must follow "the philosophers in eighteenth-century France." Q spells out one "surprising" aspect of this fact: that you'd think that the people would have rebelled without needing the writings of philosophers. R's "miserable situation" refers to "poverty and starvation" in Q. Finally, "they" in S must refer to "the masses" in R.

5. **SUQRT.** S logically follows the Topic Sentence, as "one area of debate" expands on *why* the study of indoor pollution is "controversial." Only sentence U can come next, as "such labels" must refer to "high, low" and so forth in S. Q follows logically because it explains why such labels might not correlate with "acceptable" health risks. Finally, R draws a conclusion from the statement in Q—that people in above-average pollution households deserve wider concern. T raises a future policy consideration.

6. **TUSQR.** T provides the beginning of an explanation for the phenomenon described in the Topic Sentence. U logically follows by explaining when "groupthink" typically occurs. The last three sentences are more challenging. Why does groupthink occur? Sentence S tells us why—group members prize the solidarity of the group above all other considerations. What would happen as a result? Q tells us—whatever the leader says, the group will tend to agree. Finally, R spells out the consequence—wrong decisions are often made.

7. **RQTUS.** R logically follows the Topic Sentence because it begins the explanation of why Child was ignored. Q expands on the contrast between Child and other nineteenth-century women writers mentioned in R. Finally, TUS conclude the paragraph, as "his endorsement" in U must refer to "William Lloyd Garrison" in T, and S must follow U because "our gain" refers to the "modern reader" in U.

8. **RTSQU.** R logically follows the Topic Sentence by providing a specific example of the phenomenon mentioned in the Topic Sentence. TSQ follow in chronological sequence, and U wraps it up with a mention of how paradoxical this anecdote seems.

9.   **SRQUT.** S logically follows the Topic Sentence because it explains *why* we assume that newspaper quotes must be direct quotations. R introduces the contrasting point in the paragraph—that journalists often find it impossible to directly translate real speech. Q explains why, and U draws a conclusion from R and Q—that approximations of a speaker's actual words are OK, as long as they're true to the spirit of the speaker's ideas. T follows up with an example of when the journalist has gone too far.

10.   **TRSQU.** T follows from the Topic Sentence because "that continent" in T relates to "North America" in the Topic Sentence. R logically follows T because "however" sets up a contrast between the way the thistle plant is viewed in North America and in Scotland. SQU relate in a chronological sequence a historical myth or legend that explains why the thistle is so important to the Scots.

5

Logical Reasoning

Logical Reasoning

Highlights

- Learn to Work with Logical Clues

- Practice with Kaplan's 4-Step Method for Logical Reasoning

- Familiarize Yourself with All the Logical Reasoning Question Types

MIGHT VERSUS MUST

Here's the scoop about Logical Reasoning questions on the SHSAT. These ten questions do not require any prior training in formal logic or philosophy or anything like that. Rather, they are designed to test your ability to sort through evidence, make logical deductions, and separate what might be true from what must be true. That's it.

This **might** versus **must** idea is the key to Logical Reasoning. What **must** be true is a logical deduction. What **might** be true is guesswork. Not surprisingly, the test rewards logical deductions, not guesswork.

Logical Reasoning Strategy

Sort through evidence. Make reasonable deductions. Separate what **might** be true from what **must** be true.

Take a look at the following example.

EXAMPLE

1. Jill sees that Blythe has only peanut butter in her cupboard. Jill concludes that Blythe must be unemployed.

   Given no other information, which of the following statements must be true in order for Jill's conclusion to be valid?

   A. Blythe has been unemployed in the past.

   B. Blythe's cupboard is usually quite full.

   C. Blythe's cupboard would contain just peanut butter only if she were unemployed.

   D. Blythe usually consumes a lot of food that would be stored in a cupboard.

   E. Jill believes that Blythe should find a new job.

Which of these answers must be true? Which of these answers might—or might not—be true?

Jill's conclusion is that Blythe must be unemployed. She believes this because Blythe has only peanut butter in her cupboard. The correct answer must make a connection between Jill's employment status and the contents of her cupboard. (A) makes a certain amount of sense. If Blythe has been unemployed in the past, she could be again—but where's the connection to the peanut butter? (B) and (D) both suggest that it is unusual for Blythe's cupboard to be empty. However, neither explains why this means she is unemployed. (E) might be true, but so what?

Only (C) makes a connection between Blythe's peanut butter and her employment status. If the only reason that Blythe's cupboard would be bare—except for peanut butter—is because she is unemployed, then the fact that her cupboard contained only peanut butter means that she **must** be unemployed. Again, (A), (B), (D), and (E) *could* be true—but they do not *have* to be for the conclusion to be valid.

LOGICAL CLUES

The easiest way to distinguish what must be true from what might be true is to pay attention to Logical Clues. For example . . .

"**If** you score above your first-choice school's cutoff score on the SHSAT exam, then you will be admitted to your first-choice school."

If and **then** tell you something about cause and effect. This statement tells you that if your score is high enough, it **must** be true that you will be admitted to your first-choice school. In other words, if you were not admitted to your first-choice school, it **could not** be true that you scored above the cutoff.

The following are some Logical Clues that frequently appear in Logical Reasoning questions.

Logical Clue	Example	Deductions
Sequence	There are four cats in the household: Cici, Foster, Monty, and Whitney. Whitney is **larger than** Cici. Foster is **larger than** Whitney. Monty is the **largest** cat in the house.	Relative size of the cats: Monty > Foster > Whitney > Cici
Necessary Conditions	Four diners sit around a round table: Julia, Amy, David, and Ben. Amy **never** sits next to Ben. Julia **will only** sit to Amy's right.	Amy and Ben sit opposite each other. Julia is to Amy's right. The order of seating (counterclockwise) is Amy, Julia, Ben, David.
If/Then	If Adam is a prize-winning playwright, **then** he must be talented.	All prize-winning playwrights are talented.
All/Some/None	**All** dinosaurs were reptiles. **Some** dinosaurs were bipeds. **No** bats are reptiles.	Some reptiles were (are) bipeds. Some dinosaurs were not bipeds. No bats are dinosaurs.

Logical Clues Exercise

Identify the Logical Clues in the following statements and write down your deductions.

1. All of Joanna's colleagues are highly motivated. None of Joanna's colleagues went to business school.

   Deduction: _____ All/None. None of Joanna's collegues like business._____

2. Chontelle's Ferrari is more expensive than her Jaguar. Her Jeep is more durable and less expensive than her Jaguar.

   Deduction: _____ sequence. Her ferrari is more expensive than her Jeep._____

Explanations can be found at the end of the chapter.

KAPLAN'S 4-STEP METHOD FOR LOGICAL REASONING QUESTIONS

The key to success on the SHSAT is approaching every question type systematically. If you know exactly how you're going to approach every Logical Reasoning question—regardless of content—you'll save yourself a lot of time that you can put to good use on the test.

Don't Just Jump into the Answer Choices

You've got to work through the problem step-by-step.

1. Read through the entire problem.

2. Identify exactly what the question is asking.

3. Reread the problem sentence by sentence, making logical deductions.

4. Draw any diagrams, pictures, or charts that are helpful.

Step 1: Read Through the Entire Problem

EXAMPLE

2. The smartest girl in the junior class can read seven books in one week. Christine can read only four books in one week.

    Based on only the information above, which of the following must be true?

    F. Christine is not a member of the junior class.

    G. Christine is not the smartest girl in the junior class.

    H. The ability to read books is related to intelligence.

    J. Other members of the junior class can read more than seven books in one week.

    K. The smartest girl in the junior class can read more than any other girl in the class.

The first time through, just read the question. Don't try to figure out the answer yet.

Step 2: Identify Exactly What the Question Is Asking

The question gives you information about the smartest girl in the class and information about Christine and asks you what **must** be true based on this information. Since you are limited to the information given, you are being asked what you can *definitively* deduce from the information given.

Step 3: Reread the Problem Sentence by Sentence, Making Logical Deductions

The smartest girl in the junior class can read seven books in one week. This tells you how many books the smartest girl in the class can read in a week. That's it. You do not know who the smartest girl in the class is. You do not know whether she is the fastest reader in the class. You do not know that there is a connection between her reading speed and her intelligence.

Christine can read only four books in a week. This tells you how many books Christine can read in a week. You do not know whether she is a member of the junior class or how smart she is.

Deductions: Christine is not the smartest girl in the junior class because if she were, she could read seven books in one week and we know that Christine can read only four.

Unwarranted Assumptions: Christine is a member of the junior class.
Christine is not as smart as the smartest girl in the junior class.
The smartest girl in the junior class is the fastest reader in the class.
Reading speed is connected to intelligence.

Step 4: Draw Any Diagrams, Charts, or Pictures That Are Helpful

No diagrams, charts, or pictures are necessary here. Since you've made your deductions, you are ready to answer the question.

If you scan the answer choices looking for the deduction you made, you'll see that it's sitting there waiting for you. You deduced that Christine is not the smartest girl in the junior class. Answer choice (G) states that Christine is not the smartest girl in the junior class, so answer (G) is correct. You should note that choices (F), (H), (J), and (K) are all unwarranted assumptions. They **might** be true, but they do not **have** to be true.

In sum, you should apply the same four steps to every Logical Reasoning problem on the SHSAT. As you've seen, sometimes you will not need to do anything for Step 4. You do not always have to draw a diagram. However, if it will help, **always** draw a diagram.

LOGICAL REASONING QUESTION TYPES

The Logical Reasoning questions that you'll see on the test can take a number of different forms. The two most common question types are Verbal Deduction questions and Sequence questions.

Verbal Deduction Questions

Verbal Deduction questions give you between two and four carefully worded statements describing a hypothetical situation. Based on the given information, you're asked what must be true. This is a very common question type. Questions 1 and 2 that we just discussed are Verbal Deduction questions. The key to this type of question is to work only with the information you've been given. Remember, it's very easy to make unwarranted assumptions.

Sequence Questions

Sequence questions test your ability to figure out the order of a set of known variables. The key to sequence questions is to keep track of what isn't known as well as what you know for sure. Do not expect to get complete information about variables, and do not be surprised if the answer is (E) or (K) (i.e., "Cannot be determined from the information given").

EXAMPLE

Five runners cross the finish line of a race one after the other.

1) Nancy finishes ahead of Michael but behind Sue.

2) Michael finishes behind Paul but ahead of Rachel.

3) Paul finishes behind Sue.

3. Who crosses the finish line fourth?
A. Nancy
B. Michael
C. Rachel
D. Paul
E. Cannot be determined from the information given.

Once you've read the question and identified that you must determine who the fourth of five runners is, you can beginning making deductions. Always sketch your deductions on Sequence questions.

First, you can look at each statement individually.

1) **S——N——M**

2) **P——M——R**

3) **S——P**

First to Last

———————————————→

Next, combine the statements.

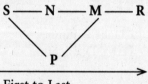

First to Last

Now you can see that Michael has to be fourth. Even though we don't know whether Paul crosses the finish line before or after Nancy, we know that either way, Michael is crossing after Sue, Nancy, and Paul. The answer would therefore be (B).

What if you got a second question here that looked like this?

4. Who crosses the finish line second?

F. Sue

G. Nancy

H. Paul

J. Michael

K. Cannot be determined from the information given.

If you look back at your sketch, you should see that the answer here is (K), cannot be determined from the information given. Here, you do not know whether Nancy or Paul is second. You know that both place between Susan and Michael, but you do not know where they place in relation to each other.

PRACTICE SET

Before moving on to other question types, take some time to work on the following Verbal Deduction and Sequence practice questions. Make sure to practice the Kaplan 4-Step Method. In particular, make certain that you read the question carefully and know exactly what the question is asking. Before selecting an answer, ask yourself, "Does this have to be true?" Answers and explanations can be found at the end of this chapter.

1. A jury reaches a verdict when all of its members have come to a unanimous agreement. In one recent well-publicized trial, the judge thought that the jury had reached a verdict. Eventually, it was learned that one juror had never been able to agree with the others. The proceeding was ultimately declared a mistrial by the judge.

   Based only on the information above, which of the following statements is a valid conclusion?

   A. The jury never actually reached a verdict.

   B. The jury had reached a verdict but been disrupted by a single juror.

   C. There have been other trials in which the jury failed to reach a verdict.

   D. Only trials in which the jury fails to reach a verdict are declared mistrials.

   E. The judge's role is not as important as that of the individual jurors.

   Ⓐ Ⓑ Ⓒ Ⓓ Ⓔ

2. In the 1920s, people diagnosed with disease X were not expected to live beyond six months to a year. Now many people diagnosed with disease X are able to survive for five years and even longer if they receive early treatment.

   According to the above information, which of the following **must** be true?

F. Modern medicine is now capable of curing disease X.

G. Most people no longer die from disease X.

H. Disease X is more easily cured than other serious diseases.

J. Progress has been made in the treatment of disease X.

K. The worst outbreak of disease X was in the 1920s.

Ⓕ Ⓖ Ⓗ Ⓙ Ⓚ

3. The maximum time a member is allowed to run on a treadmill at City Fitness is 30 minutes. Bernard has been running on a treadmill for at least 45 minutes.

   Based only on the information above, which of the following statements is a valid conclusion?

   A. The time limit has been established in order to give every member a chance to run.

   B. If Bernard is not violating City Fitness rules, then he is not running at City Fitness.

   C. If Bernard is running at City Fitness, he will have his membership revoked.

   D. Bernard will be getting off the treadmill as soon as possible.

   E. Bernard is not running on a treadmill at City Fitness.

   Ⓐ Ⓑ Ⓒ Ⓓ Ⓔ

4. In a foreign language class for students who know nothing of the language being taught, those who have already studied another foreign language do much better at first than those who have had no previous foreign language training. After about three months, both groups perform at the same level.

Which of the following conclusions is best supported by the information above?

F. Students with previous foreign language training studied more at the beginning of the course.

G. Many foreign languages are very similar to one another.

H. Students who like learning foreign languages learn better than those who do not.

J. The ability to learn a new language is initially increased by previous experience in learning a new language.

K. Advanced knowledge of one subject can interfere with an attempt to learn a new subject.

Ⓕ Ⓖ Ⓗ Ⓙ Ⓚ

5. Athletes who accept money to endorse brand X cola are expected to appear in at least three commercials for the cola per year. Basketball star Patrick Ewing appeared in only one commercial for brand X cola last year.

Based only on the information above, which of the following statements is a valid conclusion?

A. Ewing did not accept money to endorse brand X cola.

B. If Ewing were playing better, he would be appearing in more commercials.

C. If all athletes appeared in only one commercial for brand X cola, no one would buy it.

D. If Ewing accepted money to endorse brand X cola, he has not done what is expected of him.

E. Ewing must do public appearances for brand X cola to make up for missed commercials.

Ⓐ Ⓑ Ⓒ Ⓓ Ⓔ

6. There are two paintings on the wall.

1) One painting is a portrait; the other is of a landscape.

2) The portrait has a brown frame.

3) One painting was signed by its painter.

4) One painting has a gray frame and hangs at eye level.

5) The painting that does not hang at eye level was signed by its painter.

Based only on the information above, which of the following **must** be true?

F. The landscape painting was signed by its painter.

G. The landscape painting has a brown frame.

H. The portrait hangs at eye level.

J. The portrait was signed by its painter.

K. The landscape painting does not have a gray frame.

Ⓕ Ⓖ Ⓗ Ⓙ Ⓚ

7. A woman has exactly four daughters: Carla, Deirdre, Edith, and Flora. Carla is older than Edith, but younger than Deirdre. If Flora is Carla's only twin, then we know that

A. Deirdre is the youngest of the daughters.

B. Edith is the youngest of the daughters.

C. Edith is older than both Carla and Flora.

D. Edith is older than both Carla and Deirdre.

E. Carla and Deirdre are both younger than Flora.

Ⓐ Ⓑ Ⓒ Ⓓ Ⓔ

Questions 8 and 9 refer to the following information.

The five Benton children each arrive home from school at a different time.

(A) Alicia arrives home before Jim but after Rene.

(B) Rene arrives home before Robert but after Martha.

(C) Robert arrives before Jim. M < R < A < 3R < 7

8. Which child is the last to arrive home from school?

F. Alicia

G. Robert

H. Jim

J. Rene

K. Cannot be determined from the information given.

9. Which child is the second one to arrive home from school?

A. Martha

B. Rene

C. Alicia

D. Jim

E. Cannot be determined from the information given.

10. Max, Juan, Larry, Ellen, Olivia, and Pete are seated around a circular table with exactly six chairs. Max is not sitting next to Olivia, although Ellen is. There is at least one person sitting between Larry and Pete. If Max sits next to Ellen, and if Larry sits next to Olivia, how many people are seated between Max and Larry?

F. 0

G. 1

H. 2

J. 3

K. Cannot be determined from the information given.

11. Marion is out running errands and needs to stop by the post office, the supermarket, the library, the drug store, and the bank. She must stop at the bank before she goes to the supermarket. She will make either the post office or the library her third stop and either the post office or the library her final stop. If the drug store is her first stop, which of the following must be true?

A. The post office is her third stop.

B. The supermarket is her fourth stop.

C. She stops at the library after she stops at the post office.

D. She stops at the supermarket before she stops at the library.

E. She stops at the bank after she stops at the post office.

12. Duane has received job offers from four different engineering firms, and he must decide which offer he will accept.

1) Firm A is offering a higher salary than Firm B and more fringe benefits than Firm D.

2) Firm C is offering a lower salary and fewer fringe benefits than Firm A.

3) Firm B is offering a lower salary than Firm D and more fringe benefits than Firm A.

Based only on the information above, which of the following must be true?

F. Firm B offers the most fringe benefits.

G. Firm B offers a higher salary than Firm C.

H. Firm D offers more fringe benefits than Firm B.

J. Firm C offers the fewest fringe benefits.

K. Firm D offers a lower salary than Firm A.

Oddball Questions

The rest of the Logical Reasoning question types are less common than Verbal Deductions and Sequence Questions. In fact, you may not see all of the following question types on the SHSAT. However, since it's impossible to know precisely which question types you will see, it's important to prepare for any question type that you know you might see.

Math-Type Questions

Math-type questions test your ability to make mathematical deductions from verbal statements. These questions tend to ask for very specific information so it is crucial that you identify precisely what the question is asking. Look out for logical clue words such as "all but," "none," "only," or "at least." Additionally, a big mistake that many people make is that they try to figure out the answer all at once. You're much better off if you work through the problem one stage at a time.

Strategy

Focus on exactly what the question is asking. Look for logical clues. Piece your answer together a step at a time.

EXAMPLE

Dr. Roosevelt is scheduled to see a number of patients during the first week of June. Although his first patient is scheduled for a root canal, at least two are not. All but three of his patients are coming for yearly checkups. What is the **fewest** number of patients that Dr. Roosevelt can be scheduled to see during the first week of June?

A. 3

B. 4

C. 5

D. 6

E. Cannot be determined from the information given.

Instead of trying to get directly to the answer, take the question apart and deal with it in pieces.

The first sentence, "Dr. Roosevelt is scheduled to see a number of patients during the first week of June," just sets the stage. It does not contain any logical clues.

The next sentence, "Although his first patient is scheduled for a root canal, **at least two** are not," contains logical clues that should catch your eye. You have enough information to deduce that Dr. Roosevelt has to see at least three patients—the root canal and at least two more.

$$RC + 2 = 3$$

Don't stop here assuming that you're done. The third sentence tells you, "**All but three** of his patients are coming for yearly checkups." You can make another deduction here. If **all but three** are coming for yearly checkups, then a **minimum of one** patient must be coming for a checkup and **exactly three** are coming for other purposes.

$$YC + 3 = 4$$

Or

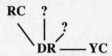

The answer, therefore, is (**B**). 4. Dr. Roosevelt must see a minimum of four patients to meet the specified conditions, but does not have to see more than four patients to meet the specified conditions.

Translation Questions

Translation questions test your ability to break code patterns. You'll be given code words or letters that correspond to real words. Your job is to deduce a word from the evidence you're given. Make sure that you take these questions slowly and deal with them a step at a time. Do not try to do these in your head. Use your test booklet to make notes and cross things out.

> **Use What You Know First**
>
> Start by translating words you know for sure.

EXAMPLE

Questions 6 and 7 refer to the following information.

In the code below, (1) each letter represents the same word in all three sentences, (2) each word is represented by only one letter, and (3) in any given sentence, the position of a letter is never the same as that of the word it represents.

Always read Translation questions carefully. The information given in Statements 1 and 2 is usually identical to the information given in this example problem, telling you that each letter always represents the same word and that each word is represented by a single letter. However, the information in Statement 3 may vary in different Translation questions. Sometimes it may say that "the position of a letter is never the same as that of the word it represents." On the other hand, Statement 3 might tell you that "the letters may or may not be presented in the same order as the words." Therefore, pay careful attention to Statement 3 in Translation questions.

Here, you're told that: (1) the same letter will always represent the same word each time it appears.
(2) each word is represented by only one letter.
(3) the position of the letter is never the same as the word it represents in a given sentence. For example, "my" cannot be represented by R, Q, or S since it is in the same position as R, Q, and S.

R	X	Y	S	N	means
"My	dog	has	four	toys."	

Q	R	N	X	Y	means
"My	cat	has	four	toys."	

S	R	Y	Z	N	means
"My	dog	has	four	legs."	

Next, it's time to work with the code. If you work with the code two lines at a time, you should be able to narrow down your options. Look at the first two lines. Notice how only one word is different between these two lines. Since four of the five words in these two lines are the same, four of the five letters in the two lines are also the same. Therefore, the letter in the first line that doesn't appear in the second represents "dog" and the letter in the second that doesn't appear in the first represents "cat."

R, X, Y, and N appear in both lines. This means that S represents "dog" and Q represents "cat." Make note of this.

> S = dog
> Q = cat

Now do the same thing for the first and third lines. The only difference between these two sentences is "toys" and "legs." Both lines contain the letters R, S, Y, and N. This means that X must represent "toys" and Z must represent "legs."

> S = dog
> Q = cat
> X = toys
> Z = legs

EXAMPLE

6. Which letter represents "toys"?

    F. Q

    G. Y

    H. X

    J. S

    K. N

You now have enough information to answer question #6—"toys" is represented by X so the answer is (H).

EXAMPLE

7. Which word is represented by R?

    A. My

    B. Dog

    C. Has

    D. Either "my" or "dog" but cannot determine which one.

    E. Either "my" or "has" but cannot determine which one.

Since your initial work did not tell you which word was represented by R, you need to do a little more work. First identify what you know so far.

My	=
Dog	= S
Has	=
Four	=
Toys	= X
Cat	= Q
Legs	= Z

R can represent only "my," "has," or "four." However, according to statement 3, no letter can be in the same position in any of the sentences as the word it represents. R is in the same position as "my" in the first sentence, so R cannot represent "my." Before going any further, take a look at your answer choices. Once you know that R cannot represent "my," you can eliminate choices (A), (D), and (E). Additionally, you can eliminate (B), dog, because you already know that dog is represented by S. Therefore the answer is (C), has.

You should notice a key point here. On this particular question, looking at the answer choices and using elimination provide a quicker path to the right answer than poring over the code to determine on your own which word must be represented by R. You'll read more about pacing and elimination later, but you should always be on the lookout for ways to save yourself time and avoid unnecessary work.

All/Some/None Questions

All/Some/None questions test your understanding of sets. You'll be given two to four "all," "some," or "none" statements on a given topic and asked to make deductions. Again, the key to this question type will be to distinguish what **must** be true from what **might** be true. To get yourself on the right track with these questions, work with "all" statements first and use Venn diagrams (those diagrams with overlapping circles) to visualize your work.

EXAMPLE

8. All archeologists are scientists. Some of the lab assistants at the dig site are archeologists. None of the technicians at the dig site are lab assistants.

If the above statements are true, which of the following **must** also be true?

F. Some of the technicians at the dig site are not scientists.

G. None of the technicians at the dig are archeologists.

H. All of the lab assistants at the dig site are scientists.

J. All archeologists are lab assistants at the dig site.

K. Some scientists are lab assistants at the dig site.

Find a Common Thread

Look for connections between statements that describe the same sets. Begin with "all" statements. Draw Venn diagrams to visualize your work.

First deal with the "all" statement.

Archeologists who are scientists

**All archeologists are scientists.
This can be represented by:**

Next, add what you know about the lab assistants.

Archeologists who are scientists

**Some lab assistants are archeologists,
so there is an overlap.**

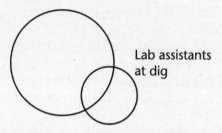

Lab assistants
at dig

The sentence about the technicians is the tricky part.

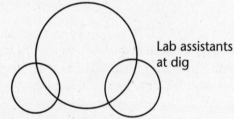

Archeologists who are scientists

Lab assistants
at dig

Technicians at dig

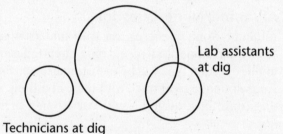

Archeologists who are scientists

Lab assistants
at dig

Technicians at dig

No technicians are lab assistants, but the some or all technicians may or may not be archeologists/scientists. You've been told nothing about the relationship between technicians and archeologists/scientists, so there may or may not be overlap. **Do not assume anything about this relationship!**

If you note that you know nothing about the relationship between technicians and archeologists, you can eliminate answers (F) and (G), since both deal with this relationship. (H) is too extreme. You know that at least one lab assistant must be an archeologist. This does not mean that **all** lab assistants are scientists. (J) is also too extreme. There is no reason to deduce that **all** archeologists (at the dig or otherwise) are lab assistants. This leaves you with (K), which is correct. Some scientists **must** be lab assistants since there is an overlap between the two groups.

If/Then Questions

If/then questions test your understanding of cause-and-effect scenarios. You are given a statement that tells you, "**If X happens, then Y occurs.**" There is *only one deduction* that you can make from an if/then statement—**the contrapositive**.

You may never have heard of a contrapositive before. This doesn't matter. All you have to know about the contrapositive is that it is formed by reversing and negating the if/then statement. Here's how it works. Say you have the following statement:

If I live in New York, **then** I am a New Yorker.

This makes a certain amount of sense, doesn't it? If I live in New York, then I have to be a New Yorker.

To find the contrapositive, you reverse the **if** and **then** clauses and make both negative. It should look like this.

>**If** I am not a New Yorker, **then** I do not live in New York.

This follows from the first statement. If living in New York makes me a New Yorker, then if I am not a New Yorker, I cannot live in New York.

Try a couple of these on your own.

Contrapositive Exercise

1. If Louis eats another cheeseburger, then he will get sick.

   Contrapositive: _____

2. If aliens take over Earth, I will not have to do my homework.

   Contrapositive: _____

(See end of section for answers.)

Now try a question in testlike format.

EXAMPLE

9. If Carlos follows the safety precautions, then his experiment will go according to plan.

    According to the statement above, which of the following **must** be true?

    A. If Carlos's experiment goes according to plan, then he followed the safety precautions.

    B. If Carlos does not follow the safety precautions, his experiment is potentially dangerous.

    C. If Carlos's experiment does not go according to plan, then he did not follow the safety precautions.

    D. Carlos's experiment will only go according to plan if he follows the safety precautions.

    E. If Carlos does not follow the safety precautions, then his experiment will not go according to plan.

On if/then questions, identify the contrapositive of the statement and then locate it among the answer choices. The answer choices will contain a number of tempting wrong-answer traps.

Here, you are told that if Carlos follows the safety precautions, his experiment will go according to plan. The contrapositive of this statement is that if Carlos's experiment did not go according to plan, then he did not follow the safety precautions. You should see that this is choice (C).

Choices (A) and (B) **might** be true. They do seem logical. However, we don't know that they **must** be true. The fact that his experiment will go according to plan if he follows the safety precautions does not mean that it could not go according to plan if he didn't follow them. That's too big a leap to make. The issue of danger is beyond the scope of the argument. You might assume that the experiment is potentially dangerous, but you do not **know** this. (D) is too extreme—just because following the safety precautions will lead to a successful experiment does not mean that this is the **only** thing that will work. This is the same reasoning that eliminates (E)—you simply do not know what will happen if Carlos fails to follow safety precautions. You only know what happens if he follows them.

PRACTICE SET

When you do the following practice problems, make sure to think about what you learned in this chapter. Do not jump immediately to the answers and do not go with your gut. Ask yourself whether your answers **must** be true. That's what Logical Reasoning questions are about.

13. Kim and Phil have three sons, all of whom are planning to attend a four-year college. The eldest son, Michael, will enter college this year. He is two grades ahead of Jamie, the middle son. John, the youngest, is three grades behind Jamie.

    Given that each son will complete college in four years and on time, how many years will Kim and Phil have at least one son in college?

    A. five
    B. six
    C. eight
    D. nine
    E. ten

    Ⓐ Ⓑ Ⓒ Ⓓ Ⓔ

14. A group of tourists is being led through a famous cathedral by a guide. One family of four is Japanese, but at least three other tourists in the group are not. All but five of the group are Americans. What is the least number of tourists that can be in this group?

    F. 6
    G. 7
    H. 9
    J. 10
    K. Cannot be determined from the information given.

    Ⓕ Ⓖ Ⓗ Ⓙ Ⓚ

15. Some friends order a pizza that has eight slices. Half are plain, and half are pepperoni. All of the pepperoni slices are eaten by a total of at least three people. The plain slices are eaten by only two of the friends.

    What is the **greatest** number of slices that could have been eaten by a single person?

    A. two
    B. three
    C. four
    D. five
    E. Cannot be determined from the information given.

    Ⓐ Ⓑ Ⓒ Ⓓ Ⓔ

Question 16 relates to the following information:

In the code below, (1) each letter represents the same word in each of the four sentences; (2) each word is represented by one letter only; and (3) in any given sentence, letters may or may not appear in the same order as the words they represent.

H   C   G   M   D   means
Appu watches basketball on TV.

G   E   B   C   F   means
Jay watches movies on cable.

I   L   G   C   H   means
Kyra watches gymnastics on TV.

C   K   F   H   G   means
Carolyn watches movies on TV.

16. Which letter represents "cable"?

    F. G
    G. B
    H. E
    J. F
    K. Cannot be determined from the information given.

    Ⓕ Ⓖ Ⓗ Ⓙ Ⓚ

17. In a foreign language, "nyeer cog joch" means "big yellow taxi," "shaw joch" means "big house," and "nyeer deniro" means "taxi driver."

    Which word means "yellow"?

    A. nyeer

    B. deniro

    C. shaw

    D. cog

    E. joch

18. In the code below, each letter represents one syllable. The letters are not necessarily listed in the correct order.

    BGZ   = "leverage"

    OMD   = "extracting"

    TF   = "lighten"

    CDT   = "engraving"

    GHP   = "levitate"

    Which letters are needed to write the code for "gravitate"?

    F. PCH

    G. FOD

    H. CDG

    J. DPH

    K. GPC

19. All scuba divers are experienced swimmers.

    Some experienced swimmers swim every day.

    No businessman swims every day.

    If the above statements are true, which of the following must also be true?

    A. No businessman is an experienced swimmer.

    B. Some scuba divers are not businessmen.

    C. All of those who swim every day are scuba divers.

    D. Some scuba divers swim every day.

    E. Some experienced swimmers are scuba divers.

20. All actors are Democrats.

    Some writers are actors.

    No doctor is a writer.

    If the above statements are true, which of the following **must** also be true?

    F. Some doctors are not Democrats.

    G. No doctor is an actor.

    H. All writers are Democrats.

    J. All actors are writers.

    K. Some Democrats are writers.

    Ⓕ Ⓖ Ⓗ Ⓙ Ⓚ

21. Whenever Dieter sings, Jarik gets a headache and Kari groans. If Kari is not groaning, which of the following statements **must** be true?

    A. Dieter is singing and Jarik has a headache.

    B. Jarik has a headache but Dieter is not necessarily singing.

    C. Dieter is singing but Jarik does not necessarily have a headache.

    D. Dieter has been singing and Jarik is beginning to get a headache.

    E. Dieter is not singing.

22. Since the bill to institute reform in business practices passed in the Senate, it must have been supported by a majority of the senators.

    Which of the following most clearly leads to the above conclusion?

    F. All of the senators supported the bill to institute reform in business practices.

    G. There were several bills that the senators voted on, but only the bill to reform business practices passed.

    H. Only bills that are supported by the majority of the senators can pass in the Senate.

    J. Reform in business practices is considered by senators to be more important than other types of reform.

    K. The bill to institute reform in business practices was the first of its kind to pass in the Senate.

    Ⓕ Ⓖ Ⓗ Ⓙ Ⓚ

23. The partners of the law firm all eat at the Doylestown country club every Friday night. Johann eats at the Doylestown country club every Friday night. Therefore, Johann may be a partner of the law firm.

    Which of the following uses reasoning that is most similar to that in the paragraph above?

    A. Every baseball umpire has played the game in his youth. Vito is a baseball umpire. Therefore, Vito has probably played the game in his youth.

    B. People who have lied always look guilty. Matthew looks guilty. Therefore, it is possible that Matthew has lied.

    C. The surgeons in a hospital all operate in the morning and play golf in the afternoon. Ben is a surgeon who operates in the morning. Therefore, he probably plays golf in the afternoon.

    D. All of the reporters working for the *Times* want to win a Pulitzer prize. Melissa wants to win a Pulitzer prize. Therefore, she is a *Times* reporter.

    E. Stefan practices the piano for hours every day. Practicing for hours every day increases one's skill. Therefore, Stefan may well master the piano.

Explanations to Exercises

Logical Clues Exercise

1. Clues: All, none

   Deduction: Some people who did not go to business school are highly motivated.

   Do you know:

   - If people who went to business school are highly motivated? (No)

   - What makes Joanna's colleagues highly motivated? (No)

2. Clues: More expensive, more durable, less expensive.

   Deduction: Pricewise, Chontelle's Ferrari > Jaguar > Jeep. Durability: Jeep > Jaguar.

   Do you know:

   - If the Ferrari is more durable than the Jeep or the Jaguar? (No—remember not to bring in outside knowledge!)

Contrapositive Exercise

1. **If** Louis did not get sick, **then** he did not eat another cheeseburger.

2. **If** I have to do my homework, **then** aliens did not take over the Earth.

PRACTICE SET EXPLANATIONS

1. **A** If one juror had never been able to agree with the others, then the members of the jury never came to a unanimous agreement; they never reached a verdict (A). (B) is wrong because it contradicts this idea. (C), (D), and (E) may all be true statements, but we have no know way of knowing for sure from the information in the question stem.

2. **J** This Verbal Deduction question revolves around an improvement in medicine. We're told that people diagnosed with disease X lived only six months to a year in the 1920s—whereas nowadays with treatment they can live five years or longer. (J) is the valid conclusion. The other choices involve too much inference; nothing is said about curing the disease (F) or how many people survive the disease (G). Likewise, there is no information about how disease X compares to other serious diseases (H) or whether the 1920s saw the worst outbreak of disease X (K).

3. **B** The trick here is to recognize that the second sentence does **not** say where Bernard's treadmill is; it may or may not be at City Fitness. Only if the treadmill is at City Fitness is he violating the rules; in other words, if he is not violating the rules, he is not running at City Fitness (B). (E), the closest wrong answer, is out because Bernard could be running at City Fitness and just flouting the rules.

4. **J** Choice (J)'s conclusion is based solidly on (and is really not much more than a restatement of) the information we have, that students who have already studied one foreign language initially learn a second language faster than do students with no prior foreign-language learning experience. Choices (F), (G), and (H) base their conclusions on unwarranted assumptions as well as the information in the question stem, so they are wrong. Choice (K) contradicts the information in the question stem.

5. **D** Let's go through the answer choices. (A) may be true—Ewing could have done one commercial for free—but it doesn't **have** to be true; we need the choice that **has** to be true. (B) is not a conclusion based strictly on information in the question stem; neither is (C) or (E). Choice (D) is the choice that has to be true: If athletes who accept money are expected to appear in three commercials and Ewing accepted money but appeared in only one commercial, then he has not done what is expected of him.

6. **J** Set up two different columns to keep track of each painting's features.

	portrait	landscape
Statement 2	brown frame	
Statement 3	??	??
Statement 4		gray frame, hangs at eye level
Statement 5	signed	

Statement 4 (gray frame, hangs at eye level) must refer to the landscape painting, since statement 2 says the portrait has a brown frame. Statement 5 must refer to the portrait, then, since the landscape painting hangs at eye level. From this we conclude that the portrait was signed by its painter (J).

7. **B** It nearly always helps to draw a diagram when you're answering a sequence problem. Carla, we're told, is older than Edith but younger than Deirdre:

Deirdre

Carla

Edith

If the fourth daughter Flora is Carla's only twin, then we know that Flora and Carla are the same age:

Deirdre

Carla and Flora

Edith

Based on this information, the only conclusion that is true is that Edith must be the youngest daughter (B).

8. **H** Let's diagram each statement.

Arrival home

	earlier		later Δ
Statement A:	Re	A	J
Statement B:	M	Re	Ro
Statement C	Ro	J	

We can put Statements A and B together to get M Re A J. Robert isn't included here because we know Robert came home before Jim and after Rene, but we have no way of knowing whether Robert came home before or after Alicia. In any case, Jim is clearly the laggard of the group, so (H) is the correct answer.

9. **B** Referring to the diagrams above, we can clearly see that Rene (B) had to be the second one home.

10. **H** This is a circular sequence problem. The first clue tells us two things: that Ellen is sitting next to Olivia, and that Max is **not** sitting next to Olivia. You can sketch a diagram and fill them in. Somewhere on the table we've got Ellen and Olivia sitting next to each other. We're told that Max sits next to Ellen. So that gives us "Max, then Ellen, then Olivia." We're then told that Larry sits next to Olivia. This leaves only Pete and Juan for the remaining two seats, so our diagram looks like this:

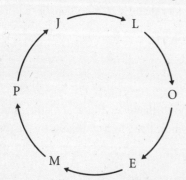

Thus, to answer the question, two people must sit between Max and Larry, making (H) correct.

11. **B** Here's an initial diagram for this question:

Stop   1   2   3   4   5

From the last two sentences:

	D		PO		PO
			L		L

We know from the last two sentences that Marion is going to stop at the drug store first and make the third and the fifth stops her post office/library stops. Whether she goes to the post office or the library first is not a question we can answer. However, we also know that she has to go to the bank before she goes to the supermarket. Since there are only two spots left, she must go to the bank second and the supermarket fourth:

D	B	PO	S	PO
		L		L

(B) is therefore correct. Choices (A), (C), and (D) are wrong because none of them absolutely has to be true (since the positions of the post office and library are interchangeable). Choice (E) is wrong no matter what; from the diagram, we can see that Marion has to stop at the bank before she stops at the post office.

12. **F** This question requires you to set up two diagrams:

	Salary		Benefits	
	higher	lower	more	fewer
Statement 1:	A	B	A	D
Statement 2:	A	C	A	C
Statement 3:	D	B	B	A

It's pretty hard to combine the salary information into anything more substantial. A is higher than B and C, but we don't know the order of B and C; B is less than A and D, but we don't know the order of A and D. This rules out choices (G) and (K). With benefits, however, we can learn a bit more from the diagram. If B is more than A, which is more than both C and D, then B must offer the most benefits (F). This also rules out (H). Choice (J) is wrong because there is no way to know whether C has fewer benefits than D or vice versa.

13. **D** It will take Michael four years to complete college. Since Jamie is two years behind Michael, he will have finished two years of college when Michael graduates. Thus it will take Jamie two more years to finish (4 + 2 = 6 years total so far for Michael and Jamie). At the end of this six years, when Jamie graduates, John will have completed only one year of college since he is three years behind Jamie. It will take John three years to graduate, so the grand total comes to 6 + 3 = 9 years for all three brothers to finish college.

14. **G** The second sentence here implies that there are at least seven tourists: four in the Japanese family and three others. Now, the third sentence specifies that all but five of the group are Americans. Does this mean we need to add more tourists to the total of seven from the second sentence? No, because if two of the "three others" from the second sentence are Americans and one is, say, Spanish, then it would be true that 1) four tourists are Japanese, 2) three others are not, and 3) all but five of the group are American. The least number of tourists we need, then, is seven.

15. **D** The greatest number of pepperoni slices any one person could eat is two: There have to be at least three people eating the pepperoni slices, so you have one person eating two slices and two people eating one apiece. The greatest number of plain slices any one person could eat is three: There are two people eating them, and one person gets three while the other person gets one. Now, if the person who gets the two pepperoni slices also gets three plain (nothing in the question stem forbids this), then that person is eating a total of five slices (D).

16. **K** Let's see how close we can get to figuring out the letter for "cable." "Watches" and "on" appear in all four sentences, as do the letters C and G, so "watches" and "on" are C and G, or vice versa. That leaves us with E, B, and F for "Jay," "movies," and "cable" in the second sentence. We also find F in the code for the last sentence, which happens to be the only other sentence that has "movies" in it.

The second and fourth sentences have no other word besides "movies" in common (and "watches" and "on," whose code letters we already know) so the letter F must stand for "movies." Now we're down to two letters, E and B, for the last two words in the second sentence, "Jay" and "cable," that we don't know. The problem is that neither word and neither letter shows up in any other sentence, so there's no way to know which letter stands for which word. (K) is therefore the correct choice.

17. **D** Start by figuring out which words are shared by two phrases. "Big yellow taxi" and "big house" have only the word "big" in common, so "joch" must mean "big." Similarly, "taxi" is the only word that appears in "big yellow taxi" and "taxi driver," so "nyeer" must mean "taxi." Two words in "nyeer cog joch" have been translated, so the remaining word "cog" must mean "yellow."

18. **F** The syllables you need to find are "grav," "i," and "tate." Let's go after "grav" first. "Grav" only appears in "engraving" so we have to figure out by a process of elimination which letter (of C, D, and T) represents "grav." When we compare "enlighten" and "engraving," they have only "en" and the letter T in common. T must represent "en." When we compare "extracting" and "engraving," they have only "ing" and D in common, so D must represent "ing." If T is "en" and D is "ing," then C must be "grav." We cannot figure out which letter represents "i" and which represents "tate," but we can determine which two letters represent "itate," which is enough to get the answer. "Levitate" and "leverage" have "lev" and G in common. If G represents "lev," then HP (or PH) must represent "itate." "Gravitate," then, is a combination of C, H, and P (F).

19. **E** If all scuba divers are experienced swimmers, then it must also be true that at least some experienced swimmers are scuba divers (E). Just because some experienced swimmers swim every day and no businessman does, this does not mean that no businessman is an experienced swimmer (A). (B) is not necessarily true: All scuba divers could be businessmen without contradicting any statement here. (C) takes a wild inferential leap from very shaky ground. (D) is wrong because it is possible that there are no scuba divers among the experienced crowd that swims every day, even though all scuba divers are experienced swimmers.

20. **K** Another tricky all/some/none question. The first statement tells us that all actors are Democrats. The next statement says that some writers are actors. Therefore, we can conclude that some writers (the ones who are actors) must be Democrats—or as choice (K) puts it, some Democrats are writers. (F) and (G) make unwarranted conclusions about doctors. The third statement tells us that no doctors are writers—but this doesn't tell us whether or not doctors can be actors or Democrats. (H) is wrong because we know only that some writers are Democrats—we don't know that all writers are Democrats. (J) is a similar leap—we can't infer that all actors must be writers.

21. **E** We're told that if Dieter sings, then Jarik gets a headache and Kari groans. Then we're told that Kari is not groaning. Using the contrapositive, we get the following logic: If Jarik **doesn't** have a headache and/or if Kari **isn't** groaning, then Dieter **must not** be singing. So if Kari is not groaning, then there is no way that Dieter is singing—choice (E). (A), (B), and (C) are wrong because we know that Dieter cannot be singing if Kari is not groaning. (D) is wrong because we're not given information about what happens after Dieter stops singing.

22. **H** If you learn that a bill has passed in the Senate and you immediately conclude that it must have been supported by a majority of the senators, then you are assuming that bills can only pass if they are supported by a majority of the senators. (H) paraphrases this. There is no reason to assume that every senator approved the bill (F), that there was more than one bill (G), or that this bill was the most important (J) or the first of its kind (K) in order to reach the conclusion of the question stem.

23. **B** We need an answer choice here that shows correct reasoning because the paragraph in the question stem exhibits reasoning that is correct. It would have been wrong to conclude that Johann is definitely a partner of the law firm just because he eats at the country club every time the partners do, but you can at least conclude that he may be a partner (nothing rules out this possibility). Choice (B) uses similar reasoning. We cannot definitely say that Matthew lied just because he looks guilty like all liars do (he may easily look guilty because of something else he did), but we can say that he may have lied. (A) is wrong because it uses incorrect reasoning; Vito must have (not probably has) played baseball in his youth. (C)'s reasoning is incorrect because we don't know whether Ben works in a hospital, and if he did, he would definitely, not probably, play golf in the afternoon. (D) also uses false reasoning: Melissa could easily be a reporter for some other newspaper and still want to win a Pulitzer. Finally, (E) is very soft reasoning that does not resemble the logic in the question stem at all.

6

Reading Comprehension

- Practice wth Kaplan's 4-Step Method for Reading Comprehension

- Learn Useful SHSAT Reading Strategies

- Familiarize Yourself with All the Question Types

OVERVIEW

The Reading section is a huge part of the SHSAT. In fact, it's 60 percent of the Verbal Section. You'll be presented with 5 passages (350–450 words each) and 30 questions (6 per passage). The section is called Reading, but if you think about it, you know that the Department of Education knows you can read. What's being tested is your ability to comprehend what you've read. Specifically, you're being tested on your ability to answer five multiple-choice questions about a given passage.

The scope of these questions is actually pretty narrow. One question will require you to identify the main point of the passage. Expect this question to be very straightforward. The remaining five questions will either ask you to identify specific details of the passage or to read between the lines a little.

On the one hand, it's a good thing that you're inherently prepared for this section because you already know how to read. On the other hand, your previous reading experience has the potential to get you into a little bit of trouble on this section of the test. Reading habits that may serve you well in school can get in the way on the test. There are three big reading traps that you need to avoid on the SHSAT.

Basic Format

Reading Comprehension consists of five passages and six questions per passage.

Common Reading Traps

There are no points in the passage, so don't linger over it. You earn points by answering questions.

1. Reading too slowly.

2. Continually rereading things you do not understand.

3. Spending more time on the passages than on the questions.

All of these traps revolve around timing. Usually, it's good to read slowly and deliberately. Usually, it's good to stick with something that you are reading until you understand it. Which brings us to our next point . . .

SHSAT Reading Is Different from Everyday Reading!

So this isn't exactly subtle. It's an important point. You already know how to read, but the way that you normally read may not help you maximize your points on the SHSAT. The other major point is . . .

The Points Come from the Questions, Not the Passages!

This needs to be your mantra as you prepare for this section. This test is about points. If you understand all the nuances of a given passage but don't get the points from the questions, you have not spent your time well. Yes, you may know details about tenth-century Swahili trading patterns or traveling performers in India. You may even be a better person for knowing this information. None of this, however, will help you get into one of New York City's specialized high schools—and that is the point here.

Therefore, as you work through this section, there are two things that you need to do:

1. Pay attention to your habits. Note how you are approaching the passages and whether you are getting bogged down in the details.

2. Remember that the point of the Reading Section is to get points by answering questions correctly. Save your character-building exercises for more interesting reading material.

The Kaplan 4-Step Method for Reading Comprehension

You've probably realized by now that Kaplan has a 4-Step Method for all of the question types on the SHSAT. The point of this is that it is in your best interest to approach the test as a whole and the individual sections systematically. If you approach every passage the same way, you will work your way through the Reading Section efficiently.

The Kaplan 4-Step Method

1. Read the passage.

2. Decode the question.

3. Research the detail.

4. Predict the answer and check the answer choices.

Like the methods for the other question types, the Kaplan 4-Step Method for Reading questions requires you to do most of your work before you actually get around to answering the questions. It's very tempting to read the questions and immediately jump to the answer choices. Don't do this. The work you do up front not only saves you time in the long run, but it increases your chances of avoiding the tempting wrong answers.

Step 1: Read the Passage

The first thing you're going to do is to read the passage. This should not come as a big surprise. It's important to realize that while you do not want to memorize or dissect the passage, you do need to read it. If you try to answer the questions without reading it, you're likely to waste time and make mistakes. Although you'll learn more about how to read the passages later, keep in mind that the main things you're looking for when you read the passage are the Big Idea and the Paragraph topics. Additionally, you're going to note where the passage seems to be going.

For example, if you saw the following passage (which, admittedly, is a little shorter than the average SHSAT passage), these are some of the things you might want to note…

The first detective stories, written by Edgar Allan Poe and Arthur Conan Doyle, emerged in the mid-nineteenth century, at a time when there was an
Line enormous public interest in scientific progress. The
(5) newspapers of the day continually publicized the latest scientific discoveries, and scientists were acclaimed as the heroes of the age. Poe and Conan Doyle shared this fascination with the step-by-step, logical approach used by scientists in their experiments, and instilled
(10) their detective heroes with outstanding powers of scientific reasoning.
　　The character of Sherlock Holmes, for example, illustrates Conan Doyle's admiration for the scientific mind. In each case that Holmes investigates, he is
(15) able to use the most insubstantial evidence to track down his opponent. Using only his restless eye and ingenious reasoning powers, Holmes pieces together the identity of the villain from such unremarkable details as the type of cigar ashes left at the crime
(20) scene, or the kind of ink used in a handwritten letter. In fact, Holmes's painstaking attention to detail often reminds the reader of Charles Darwin's *On the Origin of the Species*, published some twenty years earlier.

Comparison between Holmes and Darwin

This passage is basically about detective stories … and science.

Poe and Conan ~~Doyle~~ seem to be important.

Holmes is an example of a detective hero with a brilliant scientific mind.

Ways that Holmes uses a scientific approach.

Again, you'll spend more time a little later learning how to read the passage. The point here is that the first thing you'll do is read through the entire passage, noting the topic of each paragraph and the overall purpose of the passage.

Translating for Yourself

Make the question make sense to you.

Step 2: Decode the Question

Six questions will follow the passage. The first thing you'll need to do with each question is to decode it. In other words, you need to figure out exactly what is being asked before you can answer the question. Basically, you need to make the question make sense to you.

1. Which of the following is implied by the statement that Holmes was able to identify the villain based on "unremarkable details"?

   A. Holmes's enemies left no traces at the crime scene.

   B. The character of Holmes was based on Charles Darwin.

   C. Few real detectives would have been capable of solving Holmes's cases.

   D. Holmes was particularly brilliant in powers of detection.

   E. Criminal investigation often involves tedious, time-consuming tasks.

In other words, *why* does the author mention "unremarkable details"?

Step 3: Research the Detail

Do the Research

Do not try to answer questions just from your memory—glance at the passage again.

This does not mean that you should start rereading the passage from the beginning to find the reference to "unremarkable details." Focus your research. Where does the author mention Holmes? You should have noted when you read the passage that the author discusses Holmes in the second paragraph. So scan the second paragraph for the reference to "unremarkable details." (Hint: You can find the reference in lines 17–20.)

Another mistake to avoid is answering questions based on your memory. Go back and do the research. Generally, if you can answer questions based on your memory, you have spent too much time on the passage.

Step 4: Predict the Answer and Check the Answer Choices

When you find the detail in the passage, think about the purpose that it serves. Why does the author mention the "unremarkable details"? If you read the lines surrounding the phrase, you should see that the author is talking about how amazing it is that Holmes can solve mysteries based on such little evidence. Therefore, the reason the author mentions "unremarkable details" is to show how impressive Holmes is. Now scan your answer choices.

   A. Holmes's enemies left no traces at the crime scene.

   B. The character of Holmes was based on Charles Darwin.

   C. Few real detectives would have been capable of solving Holmes's cases.

   D. Holmes was particularly brilliant in powers of detection.

   E. Criminal investigation often involves tedious, time-consuming tasks.

Answer choice (D) should leap out at you.

Now that you've seen how to apply the Kaplan method, it's time to back up a little and look more specifically at how to deal with the passages.

THE PASSAGE

As you learned earlier, reading for the SHSAT is not exactly like the reading that you do in school or at home. As a general rule, you read to learn or you read for pleasure. It's a pretty safe bet that you're not reading SHSAT Reading passages for the fun of it. If you happen to enjoy it, that's a fabulous perk, but most people find these passages pretty dry. You should also be clear about the fact that you are not reading these passages to learn anything. You are reading these passages so that you can answer six questions about each one. That's it. Reading to answer a few questions is not the same thing as reading to learn.

The main difference between reading to learn and reading to answer questions is that the former is about knowledge and the latter is only about points. Anything that doesn't get you points is a waste of time for the purposes of the test. The SHSAT Reading section is not a place to learn anything new. Therefore, your goal is to read in such a way that you maximize your chances of getting points on the questions. The questions will ask you about the main idea, a few details, and a few inferences. You need to get enough out of the passage to deal with these questions.

> **Don't Attempt to Memorize the Info**
>
> You are not reading the passages to learn. You're reading to answer questions. There's a difference.

Seven SHSAT Reading Strategies

1. **Mark it up.**
    You can write in the test booklet, so use this to your advantage. Do not take a lot of notes, but do not leave the passage and surrounding space blank! If you do not jot down notes and circle and underline anything, you are putting yourself at a disadvantage. These passages are boring and difficult to remember. Make it easy to find the stuff you'll need to answer the questions.

2. **Focus on the first third of the passage.**
    You may find the passages boring. That's just a fact of the test. However, while you cannot count on being entertained, you can count on being presented with a well-organized passage. This means that the author is overwhelmingly likely to spell out most the important stuff in the beginning of the passage. Odds are that you'll be able to answer the main idea question based on the first third of the passage.

3. **Look for the big idea.**
    All you really need to pick up is the gist of the passage (i.e., the main idea and the paragraph topics). Remember that you can research the details as you need them as long as you have an idea of where to look.

4. Use the paragraph topics.

The first two sentences of each paragraph should tell you what it's about. The rest of the paragraph is likely to be more detail heavy. Just as you should pay more attention to the beginning of the passage, you should also pay more attention to the beginning of each paragraph.

5. Don't sweat the details.

Don't waste time reading and rereading parts you don't understand. As long as you have a general idea of *where* the details are, you don't really have to know *what* the details are. Remember, if you don't get a question about a detail, you don't have to know it. This is another place where marking up the passage comes in handy. You can always circle or underline details that seem as though they may be important. Furthermore, as long as you have made a note of the paragraph topic, you should be able to go back and find the details. Details will always be consistent with the paragraph topics.

6. Make it simple.

Sometimes you'll come across difficult language and technical jargon in the passages. As much as possible, try not to get bogged down by language you find confusing. The underlying topics are generally pretty straightforward. It can be very helpful to put confusing-sounding language into your own words. You don't have to understand every word in order to summarize or paraphrase. All you need is a very general understanding.

7. Keep moving.

Aim to spend no more than two to three minutes reading each passage. Remember, just reading the passage doesn't get you points.

Critical Reading Skills

So far, you've learned a method by which to approach all Reading passages and questions. Additionally, you've been introduced to seven strategies that should help you work through the passages efficiently. Now, it's time to look a little more closely at the skills you'll need to employ in this section of the test—summarizing, researching, and inferencing. (OK, *inferencing* is not exactly a real word, but you get the gist.) Practicing these skills will make you a more effective SHSAT reader.

Summarizing

For the purposes of the SHSAT, summarizing means capturing in a single phrase what the entire passage is about. You can expect to get a question following each passage that deals with the passage as a whole. Wrong answers will include choices that deal with only one paragraph or some other subset of the passage. You need to recognize the choice that encompasses the passage as a whole. If you've thought about the Big Picture ahead of time, you're more likely to home in on the correct answer.

The four brightest moons of Jupiter were the first objects in the solar system discovered with the use of the telescope. Their proven existence played a central
Line role in Galileo's famous argument in support of the
(5) Copernican model of the solar system, in which the planets are described as revolving around the Sun.

For several hundred years after their discovery by Galileo in 1610, scientific understanding of these moons increased fairly slowly. Observers on
(10) earth succeeded in measuring their approximate diameters, their relative densities, and eventually some of their light-reflecting characteristics. However, the spectacular close-up photographs sent back by the 1979 Voyager missions forever changed our
(15) impressions of these bodies.

2. Which of the following best tells what this passage is about?

F. Galileo's invention of the telescope

G. the discovery of the Galilean moons

H. scientific knowledge about Jupiter's four brightest moons

J. the Copernican model of the solar system

K. the early history of astronomy

Which choice sums up the entire passage?

There is only one answer choice here that sums up the contents of both paragraphs. (G) is just a detail. (F) cannot be correct because Galileo's telescope is not even mentioned. (J) is only mentioned in the first paragraph and is a distortion of the author's point. (K) is too broad in scope.

Only (H) summarizes the entire passage. The passage deals with scientific knowledge about Jupiter's four brightest moons. The four moons are the first thing mentioned in the first paragraph, and the rest of the first paragraph discusses the role they played for Galileo. The second paragraph discusses how the moons were perceived by scientists throughout history. In sum, both paragraphs are concerned with scientific knowledge about these moons.

Researching

Researching is essentially about knowing where to look for the details. Generally, if you take brief margin notes on paragraph topics, you should be in pretty good shape to figure out where to find the details. Once you know where to look, just scan the passage for key phrases found in the question.

A human body can survive without water for several days and without food for as many as several weeks. If breathing stops for as little as three to six
Line minutes, however, death is likely. All animals require
(5) a constant supply of oxygen to the body tissues, and especially to the heart or brain. In the human body, the respiratory system performs this function by delivering air containing oxygen to the blood.

But respiration in large animals possessing lungs
(10) involves more than just breathing. It is a complex process that delivers oxygen to internal tissues while eliminating waste carbon dioxide produced by cells. More specifically, respiration involves two processes known as bulk flow and diffusion. Oxygen and carbon
(15) dioxide are moved in bulk through the respiratory and circulatory systems; gaseous diffusion occurs at different points across thin tissue membranes.

Breathing = critical bodily function

Respiration—large animals = complex process

Take a look at the passage and paragraph notes. You should see that the margin notes are very brief and general. They note only the gist of the paragraphs. If you saw the following questions, would you know where to go find the answers?

3. Which bodily function, according to the passage, is least essential to the survival of the average human being?

The first paragraph deals with bodily functions. Lines 2–3 note that food is most expendable.

  A. eating
  B. drinking
  C. breathing
  D. blood circulation
  E. the oxygen supply

4. Which part of an animal's body is responsible for producing waste carbon dioxide?

The second paragraph deals with the complex details of respiration. Carbon dioxide is mentioned in lines 12 and 14–15.

  F. the internal tissues
  G. the circulatory systems
  H. the tissue membranes
  J. the bloodstream
  K. the cells

Both questions here can be answered simply by finding the appropriate part of the passage and reading carefully to get the details straight. The answer to question 3 is in the first sentence. A person can survive "without food for as many as several weeks" (lines 2–3). In contrast, a person can live without water for only "several days" (line 2) and requires "a constant supply of oxygen" (line 5). Because a person can go longest without eating, you know that eating is the least essential of the functions mentioned. (A) is the correct answer. Notice that the correct answer is clearly based on what is stated in the passage.

For question 4, you have to find the right spot to reread in the passage. Carbon dioxide is mentioned twice in the second paragraph. The first reference is the one that lets you answer this question. Line 12 states that carbon dioxide is "produced by cells." (K) is the correct answer.

Inference

Inference means you're looking for something that is strongly implied, but not stated explicitly. In other words, "inferencing" means "reading between the lines." What did the author almost say, but not say exactly?

Inferences will not stray too far from the language of the text. Wrong answers on inference questions will often fall beyond the subject matter of the passage.

Children have an amazing talent for learning vocabulary. Between the ages of one and seventeen, the average person learns the meaning of about 80,000 words—about 14 per day. Dictionaries and traditional
(5) classroom vocabulary lessons only account for part of this spectacular knowledge growth. More influential are individuals' reading habits and their interaction with people whose vocabularies are larger than their own. Reading shows students how words are used in
(10) sentences. Conversation offers several extra benefits that make vocabulary learning engaging—it supplies visual information, offers frequent repetition of new words, and gives students the chance to ask questions.

5. When is a child most receptive to learning the meaning of new words?

A. when the child reaches high school age

B. when the child is talking to other students

C. when the child is assigned vocabulary exercises

D. when the child is regularly told that he or she needs to improve

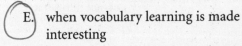 E. when vocabulary learning is made interesting

This short passage discusses how children learn vocabulary. The question asks when children are most receptive to learning new words. There is no sentence in the passage that states, "Children are most receptive to learning new words . . . ." In lines 6–8, however, the author mentions that reading and conversation are particularly helpful. Lines 10–13 note how conversation is engaging. This is consistent with (E)—children learn when vocabulary learning is made interesting.

There is nothing in the passage to suggest that children learn more at high school age (A). (B) might have been tempting, but it is too specific. There's no reason to believe that talking to students is more helpful than talking to anyone else. (C) contradicts the passage, and (D) is never mentioned at all.

Practice Exercise

Now it's time to put some of this together. Take about three minutes to read the following passage. Then take about four minutes to answer the questions that follow. Answers are at the end of the chapter.

The poems of the earliest Greeks, like those of other ancient societies, consisted of magical charms, mysterious predictions, prayers, and traditional
Line songs of work and war. These poems were intended
(5) to be sung or recited, not written down, since they were created before the Greeks began to use writing for literary purposes. All that remains of them are fragments mentioned by later Greek writers. Homer, for example, quoted an ancient work-song for
(10) harvesters, and Simonides adapted the ancient poetry of ritual lamentation, songs of mourning for the dead, in his writing.

The different forms of early Greek poetry all had something in common: They described the way of life
(15) of a whole people. Poetry expressed ideas and feelings that were shared by everyone in a community— their folktales, their memories of historical events, their religious speculation. The poems were wholly impersonal, with little emphasis on individual
(20) achievement. It never occurred to the earliest Greek poets to tell us their names or to try to create anything completely new.

In the "age of heroes," however, the content and purpose of Greek poetry changed. By this later period,
(25) Greek communities had become separated into classes of rulers and ruled. People living in the same community therefore had different, even opposed, interests; they shared fewer ideas and emotions. The particular outlook of the warlike upper class gave poetry a new content,
(30) one that focused on the lives of individuals. Poets were assigned a new task: to celebrate the accomplishments of outstanding characters, whether they were real or imaginary, rather than the activity and history of the community.

(35) In the heroic age, poets became singers of tales who performed long poems about the fates of warriors and kings. One need only study Homer's *Iliad* and *Odyssey,* which are recorded examples of the epic poetry that was sung in the heroic age, to understand
(40) the influence that the upper class had on the poet's performance. Thus, the poetry of the heroic age can no longer be called a folk poetry. Nor was the poetry of the heroic age nameless, and in this period it lost much of its religious character.

1. Which of the following best tells what this passage is about?

   A. how the role of early Greek poetry changed

   B. how Greek communities became separated into classes

   C. the superiority of early Greek poetry

   D. the origin of the *Iliad* and the *Odyssey*

   E. why little is known about early Greek poets   Ⓐ Ⓑ Ⓒ Ⓓ Ⓔ

2. The earliest Greek poems were probably written in order to

   F. bring fame to kings.

   G. bring fame to poets.

   H. express commonly held beliefs.

   J. celebrate the lives of warriors.

   K. tell leaders how they should behave.   Ⓕ Ⓖ Ⓗ Ⓙ Ⓚ

3. The term "folk poetry" (line 42) refers to poetry whose contents depict mainly

   A. the adventures of warriors.

   B. the viewpoint of a ruling class.

   C. the problems of a new lower class.

   D. the concerns of a whole culture.

   E. the fates of heroes.   Ⓐ Ⓑ Ⓒ Ⓓ Ⓔ

4. Which of the following did poetry of the heroic age primarily celebrate?

   F. community life

   G. individuals

   H. religious beliefs

   J. the value of work

   K. common people   Ⓕ Ⓖ Ⓗ Ⓙ Ⓚ

5. The passage suggests that, compared to communities in an earlier period, Greek communities during the heroic period were probably

   A. less prosperous.

   B. less unified.

   C. better organized.

   D. more peaceful.

   E. more artistic.   Ⓐ Ⓑ Ⓒ Ⓓ Ⓔ

6. Which of the following situations is most like the one involving poets in the heroic age as it is presented in the passage?

    F. A school of artists abandons portrait painting in favor of abstract art.

    G. A sports team begins to rely increasingly on the efforts of a star player.

    H. A species of wolf is hunted to the verge of extinction.

    J. A group of reporters publicizes the influence of celebrities on historical events.

    K. A novelist captures the daily lives of a rural community.

THE QUESTIONS

As you already know, Reading points come from answering the questions, not simply reading the passages. This doesn't mean that it is not important to approach the passage strategically—it is. However, if you do not answer the questions correctly, the passage hasn't done you much good.

There are three basic question types in the Reading Section: Main Idea, Detail, and Inference questions.

Main Idea Questions

A Main Idea question asks you to summarize the topic of the passage.

1. Which of the following best tells what this passage is about?

    A. the history of American landscape painting

    B. why an art movement caught the public imagination

    C. how European painters influenced the Hudson River School

    D. why writers began to romanticize the American wilderness

    E. the origins of nationalism in the United States

Detail Questions

A Detail question asks you to research information that is directly stated in the passage.

2. Which of the following is **not** mentioned as one of the reasons for the success of the Hudson River School?

    F. American nationalism increased after the War of 1812.

    G. Americans were nostalgic about the frontier.

    H. Writers began to focus on the wilderness.

    J. The United States wanted to compete with Europe.

    K. City dwellers became concerned about environmental pollution.

Inference Questions

An Inference question, like a Detail question, asks you to find relevant information in the passage. But once you've located the details, you've got to go one step further: to figure out the underlying point of a particular phrase or example.

> **Summarizing Sentences**
>
> A key strategy for Main Idea questions is to look for a choice that summarizes the entire passage—not just a detail that's mentioned once, not just a single paragraph, but the whole passage.

> **Don't Stray from the Text**
>
> Detail questions are straightforward—all you have to do is locate the relevant information in the passage. The key strategy is to research the details by relating facts, figures, and names in the question to a specific paragraph.

> **Always Find the Point— the "So What?" of the Passage**
>
> Use your inference skills to figure out what the author's point is—the answer will not be stated, but it will be strongly implied.

3. Which of the following best describes what is suggested by the statement that the Hudson River School paintings "fitted the bill perfectly" (lines 26–27)?

   A. The paintings depicted famous battle scenes.

   B. The paintings were very successful commercially.

   C. The paintings reflected a new pride in the United States.

   D. The paintings were favorably received in Europe.

   E. The paintings were accurate in their portrayal of nature.

Now that you've been introduced to the question types, it's a good idea to get some practice with them. Take three to four minutes to read the following passage. As usual, mark it up. Read it with the goal of answering questions afterwards.

The first truly American art movement was formed by a group of landscape painters that emerged in the early nineteenth century called the
Line Hudson River School. The first works in this style
(5) were created by Thomas Cole, Thomas Doughty, and Asher Durand, a trio of painters who worked during the 1820s in the Hudson River Valley and surrounding locations. Heavily influenced by European Romanticism, these painters set out to
(10) convey the remoteness and splendor of the American wilderness. The strongly nationalistic tone of their paintings caught the spirit of the times, and within a generation the movement had mushroomed to include landscape painters from all over the United States.
(15) Canvases celebrating such typically American scenes as Niagara Falls, Boston Harbor, and the expansion of the railroad into rural Pennsylvania were greeted with enormous popular acclaim.

One factor contributing to the success of the
(20) Hudson River School was the rapid growth of American nationalism in the early nineteenth century. The War of 1812 had given the United States a new sense of pride in its identity, and as the nation continued to grow, there was a desire to compete with
(25) Europe on both economic and cultural grounds. The vast panoramas of the Hudson River School fitted the bill perfectly by providing a new movement in art that was unmistakably American in origin. The Hudson River School also arrived at a time when writers in
(30) the United States were turning their attention to the wilderness as a unique aspect of their nationality. The Hudson River School profited from this nostalgia because they effectively represented the continent the way it used to be. The view that the American
(35) character was formed by the frontier experience was widely held, and many writers were concerned about the future of a country that was becoming increasingly urbanized.

In keeping with this nationalistic spirit, even the
(40) painting style of the Hudson River School exhibited a strong sense of American identity. Although many of the artists studied in Europe, their paintings show a desire to be free of European artistic rules. Regarding the natural landscape as a direct manifestation of
(45) God, the Hudson River School painters attempted to record what they saw as accurately as possible. Unlike European painters who brought to their canvases the styles and techniques of centuries, they sought neither to embellish nor to idealize their scenes,
(50) portraying nature with the care and attention to detail of naturalists.

We hope you caught that this passage was about why the Hudson River School became so successful. You should have also noted that the second paragraph addresses how American nationalism contributed to the success of the Hudson River School and the third paragraph discusses how nationalist sentiment was evident in the Hudson River School painting style.

Main Idea Question

1. Which of the following best tells what this passage is about?

    A. the history of American landscape painting

    B. why an art movement caught the public imagination

    C. how European painters influenced the Hudson River School

    D. why writers began to romanticize the American wilderness

    E. the origins of nationalism in the United States

Do you see which one of these answers describes the entire passage without being too broad or too narrow?

(A) is too broad, as is (E). The passage is not about all American landscape painting, it's about the Hudson River School. Nationalism in the United States is much larger than the role of nationalism in a particular art movement. (C) and (D) are too narrow. European painters did influence the Hudson River School painters, but that wasn't the point of the whole passage. Similarly, writers are mentioned in paragraph 2, but the passage is about an art movement. Only (B) captures the the essence of the passage—it's about an art movement that caught the public imagination.

Detail Question

2. Which of the following is **not** mentioned as one of the reasons for the success of the Hudson River School?

    F. American nationalism increased after the War of 1812.

    G. Americans were nostalgic about the frontier.

    H. Writers began to focus on the wilderness.

    J. The United States wanted to compete with Europe.

    K. City dwellers became concerned about environmental pollution.

Four of the five answer choices are mentioned explicitly in the passage. (F) is mentioned in lines 19–21. (G) appears in line 32. (H) shows up in lines 28–31. (J) is mentioned in lines 22–25. Only (K) does not appear in the passage.

Inference Questions

3. Which of the following best describes what is suggested by the statement that the Hudson River School paintings "fitted the bill perfectly" (lines 26–27)?

   A. The paintings depicted famous battle scenes.

   B. The paintings were very successful commercially.

   C. The paintings reflected a new pride in the United States.

   D. The paintings were favorably received in Europe.

   E. The paintings were accurate in their portrayal of nature.

First, read the lines surrounding the quote to put the quote in context. Paragraph 2 is talking about American pride—that's why Hudson River School paintings "fitted the bill." Hudson River School paintings were about America. (C) summarizes the point nicely. Note how this question revolves around the interplay between main idea and details. This detail strengthens the topic of the paragraph—the growing sense of nationalism in America. (A) superficially relates to the War of 1812, but it does not answer the question. (B) and (D) aren't mentioned in the passage. (E) is a misused detail. While paragraph 3 does state that Hudson River School painters attempted to depict nature accurately, this fact doesn't answer the question in the question stem.

A Word about Science Passages

You can expect to see at least one passage in the Reading section that deals with a science or technical topic. There is one thing to keep in mind here—you are *not* being tested on any outside science knowledge. Do not answer the questions based on anything other than the information contained in the passage.

A Reminder about Timing

Plan to spend approximately three minutes reading the passage and roughly a minute to a minute and a half on each question. When you first start practicing, you'll probably find yourself spending more time on the passages. That's okay. However, you need to pay attention to your timing and cut the time down to around three minutes. If you do not, it will hurt you on test day.

PRACTICE SET

Now it's time to practice some Reading passages and questions. Make sure you mark up the passage and note the Big Idea and the Paragraph topics. Research the details and predict your answers. Most important, remember that it's about the questions.

The painter Georgia O'Keeffe was born in Wisconsin in 1887 and grew up on her family's farm. At seventeen she decided she wanted to be an artist
Line and left the farm for schools in Chicago and New York,
(5) but she never lost her bond with the land. Like most painters, O'Keeffe painted the things that were most important to her, and nearly all her works are simplified portrayals of nature.

O'Keeffe became famous when her paintings
(10) were discovered and exhibited in New York by the photographer Alfred Stieglitz, whom she married in 1924. During a visit to New Mexico in 1929, O'Keeffe was so moved by the bleak landscape and broad skies of the western desert that she began to paint its images.
(15) Cows' skulls and other bleached bones found in the desert figured prominently in her paintings. When her husband died in 1946, she moved to New Mexico permanently and used the horizon lines of the desert, colorful flowers, rocks, barren hills, and the sky as
(20) subjects for her paintings. Although O'Keeffe painted her best-known works in the 1920s, '30s, and '40s, she continued to produce tributes to the western desert until her death in 1986.

O'Keeffe is widely considered to have been
(25) a pioneering American modernist painter. While most early modern American artists were strongly influenced by European art, O'Keeffe's position was more independent. She established her own vision and preferred to view her painting as a private endeavor.
(30) Almost from the beginning, her work was more identifiably American than that of her contemporaries in its simplified and idealized treatment of color, light, space, and natural forms. Her paintings are generally considered "semi-abstract" because even though they
(35) depict recognizable images and objects, the paintings don't present those images in a very detailed or realistic way.

Rather, the colors and shapes in her paintings are often so reduced and simplified that they begin to
(40) take on a life of their own, independent of the real-life objects from which they are taken.

1. Which of the following best tells what this passage is about?

   A. O'Keeffe was the best painter of her generation.

   B. O'Keeffe was a distinctive modern American painter.

   C. O'Keeffe liked to paint only what was familiar to her.

   D. O'Keeffe never developed fully as an abstract artist.

   E. O'Keeffe used colors and shapes that are too reduced and simple.

2. Which of the following is **not** mentioned as an influence on O'Keeffe's paintings?

   F. her rural upbringing

   G. her life in the west

   H. the work of Mexican artists

   J. the appearance of the natural landscape

   K. animal and plant forms

3. The passage suggests that Stieglitz contributed to O'Keeffe's career by

   A. bringing her work to a wider audience.

   B. supporting her financially for many years.

   C. inspiring her to paint natural forms.

   D. suggesting that she study the work of European artists.

   E. requesting that she accompany him to New Mexico.

4. Which of the following is most similar to O'Keeffe's relationship with nature?

   F. a photographer's relationship with a model

   G. a writer's relationship with a publisher

   H. a student's relationship with a part-time job

   J. a sculptor's relationship with an art dealer

   K. a carpenter's relationship with a hammer

5. Why have O'Keeffe's paintings been described as "semi-abstract" (line 34)?

   A. They involve a carefully realistic use of color and light.

   B. They depict common, everyday things.

   C. They show familiar scenes from nature.

   D. They depict recognizable things in an unfamiliar manner.

   E. They refer directly to real-life activities.

6. Why was O'Keeffe considered an artistic pioneer?

   F. Her work became influential in Europe.

   G. She painted the American Southwest.

   H. Her paintings had a definite American style.

   J. She painted things that were familiar to her.

   K. Her work was very abstract.

EXPLANATIONS TO EXERCISES

Greek Poetry Passage

Big Idea: What the poems of the ancient Greeks were like.

Paragraph 2:   Ancient Greek poetry was an expression of the community, not individuals.

Paragraph 3:   How later ancient Greek poetry (in the "age of heroes") became more individu- alistic. (Note contrast keyword "however" signaling this change in line 23.)

Paragraph 4:   More changes in later Greek poetry.

1   **A**   Main idea. Only (A) captures paragraphs 1–4. (B) is beyond the scope of this passage. (C) expresses an extreme view that the author never takes. (D) men- tions the *Iliad* and the *Odyssey*, which are discussed only in paragraph 4. (E) again does not address the purpose of the entire passage.

2.   **H**   Paragraph Topic. Refer to the topic of paragraph 2. (F), (G), (J), and (K) are never mentioned in this paragraph.

3.   **D**   Inference. You need to use your inference skills to answer this question. The reference to line 42 leads you to the fourth paragraph. Here "folk poetry" refers to the age before the "heroic age" when poetry was about the entire community, and not just the warriors and kings. (A), (B), and (E) do not refer to the "folk" at all and are therefore incorrect. (C) mentions class con- flict—something not discussed in this paragraph.

4.   **G**   Paragraph Topic. The answer is clearly stated in paragraph 4. "In the heroic age, poets became singers of tales who performed long poems about the fates of warriors and kings" (i.e., individuals).

5.   **B**   Paragraph Topic. Refer to the topic of paragraph 3, which focuses on the diversification of the Greeks during the heroic period. Lines 25–26 state that the "communities had become separated into classes of rulers and ruled." The following sentence (lines 27–28) expands on this idea by saying that commu- nity members "had different, even opposed, interests."

6.   **G**   Inference. Here you are asked to apply the ideas of the passage to a hypotheti- cal situation. Paragraphs 3 and 4 discuss the portrayal of individual heroes in later Greek poetry such as Homer's *Iliad*. Journalism focusing on celebrities is analogous.

O'Keeffe Passage

1. **B**   A Main Idea question. Looking at these choices in order, (A) is wrong because it's simply never stated that O'Keeffe was the best painter of her generation. (B) is accurate and may be the best choice, so keep it in mind. (C) is a bit tricky. It's true that O'Keeffe liked to paint things that were familiar to her—primarily certain nature images—but this is just one point about O'Keeffe covered in the passage. The broader, more important idea—the reason the passage was written—is that O'Keeffe was an important modern American painter. (D) is simply never suggested by the passage. (E) focuses too much on a detail, and it also distorts the "message" of the passage. The author never says that O'Keeffe's colors and shapes are "too" reduced and simple; O'Keeffe is never criticized. That leaves (B), which is both accurate and general enough without being so general that the meaning of the passage is lost. That's the kind of answer you always want to look for in Main Idea questions.

2. **H**   A Detail question. You're looking for the factor that did not influence O'Keeffe. The third paragraph describes O'Keeffe's work as distinctly American in style, independent of European influences. Mexican influences are never even mentioned, so (H) is correct here. The four wrong choices are all true. As for (F), the passage's first few sentences make clear that her rural childhood had a lasting influence. (G), (J), and (K) are supported in the second half of the second paragraph: her work was greatly affected by her life in the West, particularly by its natural landscape with bleached animal bones, hills, and colorful flowers.

3. **A**   An Inference question. The first sentence of paragraph 2 states that O'Keeffe "became famous" when Stieglitz "discovered and exhibited" her work in New York City. You can infer, then, that Stieglitz helped O'Keeffe by bringing her work to a wider audience, choice (A). Whatever financial arrangement, if any, existed between Stieglitz and O'Keeffe (B) is not mentioned in the passage. Paragraph 1 strongly implies that O'Keeffe was inspired to paint natural forms (C) long before she met Stieglitz. (D) contradicts paragraph 3, which states that O'Keeffe was not strongly influenced by European artists. As for (E), the circumstances leading to O'Keeffe's visit to New Mexico are not described.

4. **F**   An Inference question. First ask yourself what O'Keeffe's relationship to nature was. O'Keeffe painted from nature—it was the subject of her work. Of the choices offered, which is most similar to the relationship between a painter and her subject? Choice (F) is best, because a model is the subject of a photographer's work. (G) is wrong because a publisher is not the subject of a writer's work; a publisher simply prints and distributes a writer's work. Similarly, (H) is out because a part-time job is not a student's subject. It is not what a student bases her work on. Same with (J): An art dealer buys and sells a sculptor's work, but the art dealer is not the subject of the sculptor's work. Finally, a hammer is simply a carpenter's tool; it doesn't provide a carpenter with a subject or model, so (K) is out.

5. **D** A Detail question. O'Keeffe's "semi-abstract" style is discussed in the passage's last two sentences. Don't worry if the term "semi-abstract" sounds confusing to you because, as always, everything you need to know will be stated or clearly suggested. The next-to-last sentence states that O'Keeffe's paintings are thought of as semi-abstract because they depict recognizable images in a way that is not very detailed or realistic. (D) simply restates this. (A) and (E) are wrong because they refer to "realistic" or "real-life" qualities, descriptions that contradict the passage's explanation of "semi-abstract." While (B) and (C) both describe O'Keeffe's work accurately, they are not reasons for her work being called "semi-abstract." They describe subjects of her paintings, but not the semi-abstract style in which they were painted.

6. **H** A Detail question. The first sentence of the third paragraph states that O'Keeffe is considered a pioneering modern American painter. The following two sentences say why—because her style was independent and identifiably American, not strongly influenced by European art. (H) restates the idea. (F) is never suggested. (G) and (J) are true of O'Keeffe's work, but they are not the reasons she was considered an artistic pioneer. (K) is not true of O'Keeffe's work, which is considered semi-abstract, not very abstract. Furthermore, (K) does not address the question of why O'Keeffe is considered an artistic pioneer.

SHSAT Math

Introducing SHSAT Math

- Find Out What to Expect on SHSAT Math

- Get Useful Strategies to Approach SHSAT Math

- Practice with Backdoor Methods for Getting the Right Answer

MATH OVERVIEW

There's a lot of math out there. Someday you may need or may choose to immerse yourself in the intricacies of number theory or multivariable calculus. However, for the purposes of the SHSAT, you need to know a relatively small subset of all of the math out there. The most commonly tested math concepts fall within the areas of arithmetic, algebra, and geometry. It is also not uncommon to see simple probability and statistics. As you read earlier, you will see some math with which you are unfamiliar because the Department of Education deliberately tests unfamiliar math. The ninth-grade test will cover basic trigonometry, which is not covered in this book. Check out Kaplan's *Math Power* for a basic trig review.

How SHSAT Math Is Set Up

All 50 of the Math questions are multiple-choice. The obvious point here is that the all the answers are right there in front of you. That does not mean that the problems are easy, but it does mean that you can employ strategies to rule out wrong answers and to guess strategically.

Know What to Expect

GENERAL INSTRUCTIONS

Solve each problem. Select the best answer from the choices given. Mark the letter of your answer on the answer sheet. You can do your figuring in the test booklet or on paper provided by the proctor. **DO NOT FIGURE ON YOUR ANSWER SHEET.**

IMPORTANT NOTES:

(1) Formulas and definitions of mathematical terms and symbols are **not** provided.

(2) Diagrams other than graphs are **not** necessarily drawn to scale. Do not assume any relationship in a diagram unless it is specifically stated or can be figured out from the information given.

(3) Assume that a diagram is in one plane unless the problem specifically states that it is not.

(4) Graphs are drawn to scale. Unless stated otherwise, you can assume relationships according to appearance. For example, lines that appear to be parallel can be assumed to be parallel; likewise for concurrent lines, straight lines, collinear points, right angles, etc.

(5) Reduce all fractions to lowest terms.

The directions are pretty straightforward on the Math Section. Essentially, they tell you to answer the questions and mark the answers on your answer sheet. However, the directions do include a few notes that can help with your preparation and save you time on test day. Here are a few things you should know:

Don't Waste Time Reading Directions!

Know what to expect on test day. The directions are not going to change, so learn them now and save yourself time later.

• **Math formulas and definitions are NOT provided.**

What this means: The Department of Education is not going to provide the shortcuts, so memorize those math formulas. Of course, you don't have to know very many, but make certain you know the basics.

• **Diagrams other than graphs are NOT drawn to scale unless otherwise noted.**

What this means: You cannot take much for granted about diagrams unless you are specifically told that they are drawn to scale. For example, lines that look parallel may, in fact, not be parallel. Figures that look like squares may not be square. Lines that look like the diameter of a circle may not be the diameter. You get the picture.

• **Diagrams are in one plane, unless otherwise stated.**

What this means: One thing that you can assume is that diagrams are in one plane. In other words, assume that figures are flat unless you are told otherwise.

- **Graphs are drawn to scale, unless otherwise stated.**

What this means: You can eyeball graphs and take what you see for granted. For example, if lines look parallel, you can assume that they are.

- **Fractions should be reduced to their lowest terms.**

What this means: If you solve a problem that has a fraction for its answer and you do not reduce the fraction to its lowest terms, you will not find your answer among the answer choices.

HOW TO APPROACH SHSAT MATH

You've done math before. You've most likely been exposed to the majority of the math concepts you'll see on the SHSAT. This begs the question as to why you would need to approach SHSAT math differently than you would approach any other math.

The answer to this question is that it's not that you necessarily have to do the math *differently*, it's just that you have to do it very deliberately. What this means is that you'll be under a lot of time pressure when you take the test, so you'll want to use your time well. You may not want to answer every SHSAT math problem the way that you would approach the same problem in math class.

> **The SHSAT Is Not Math Class**
>
> No one is going to check your work. Choose the *fastest* method to solve the problem, even if your math teacher would not approve.

Ultimately, the best way to take control of your testing experience is to approach every SHSAT math problem the same way. This doesn't mean that you will solve every problem the same way. Rather, it means that you'll use the same process to decide how to solve—or whether to solve—each problem.

Read Through the Question

Okay, this may seem a little too obvious. Of course you're going to read the question. How else can you solve the problem? In reality, this is not quite as obvious as it seems. The point here is that you need to read the entire question carefully before you start solving the problem. When you do not read the question carefully, it's incredibly easy to make careless mistakes. Consider the following problem:

EXAMPLE

51. For what positive value of x does

$\frac{6}{5} = \frac{x^2}{30}$?

A. 5

B. 6

C. 10

D. 12

E. 25

It's crucial that you pay close attention to precisely what the question is asking. Question 51 contains a classic trap that's very easy to fall into if you don't read the question carefully. Did you notice how easy it would be to solve for x^2 instead of x? Yes, this would be careless, but it's easy to be careless when you're working quickly. By the way, the answer is (B), 6.

There are other reasons to read the whole question before you start solving the problem. One is that you may save yourself some work. If you start to answer too quickly, you may assume that a problem is more difficult than it actually is. Similarly, you might assume that the problem is less difficult than it actually is and skip a necessary step or two.

Another reason to read carefully before answering is that you probably shouldn't solve every problem on your first pass. A big part of taking control of your SHSAT experience is deciding which problems to answer and which to save for later.

Decide Whether to Do the Problem or Skip It for Now

Every time you approach a new math problem, you have the option of whether or not to answer the question. Therefore, you have to make a decision each time about how to best use your time. You have three options.

1. If you can solve the problem relatively quickly and efficiently, do it! This is the best option.

2. If you think you can solve it but it will take you a long time, circle the number in your test booklet and go back to it later.

3. If you have no idea what to do, skip the problem and circle it. Save your time for the problems you can do.

Remember that when you go back to the problems you skip, you want to fill in an answer even if it's a random guess. You'll see more about this later, but do not underestimate your ability to eliminate wrong answers even when you do not know how to solve a problem. Every time you eliminate a wrong answer, you increase your chances of guessing correctly.

EXAMPLE

52. Tamika, Becky, and Kym were investors in a new restaurant. Tamika and Becky each invested one-half as much as Kym invested. If the total investment made by these three was $5,200, how much did Kym invest?

F. $900
G. $1,300
H. $1,800
J. $2,100
K. $2,600

Different test takers are going to have different reactions to question 52. Some test takers may quickly see the algebra—or the backdoor method for solving this problem—and do the math. Others may see a word problem and run screaming from the room. This approach is not recommended. However, if despite practice, you know that you habitually have difficulty with algebra word problems, you may choose to save this problem for later or make an educated guess.

Here's the algebra, by the way. Kym, Tamika, and Becky contributed a total of $5,200. You can represent this algebraically as $K + T + B = \$5,200$. Since Tamika and Becky each contributed $\frac{1}{2}$ as much as Kym, you can represent these relationships as follows:

$$T = \frac{1}{2} K$$

$$B = \frac{1}{2} K$$

Now, substitute variables so that you can solve the equation.

$$K + T + B = K + \frac{1}{2} K + \frac{1}{2} K$$

$$K + \frac{1}{2} K + \frac{1}{2} K = \$5,200$$

$$2K = \$5,200$$

$$K = \$2,600 \text{ Choice (K)}$$

If you choose to tackle the problem, look for the fastest method.

EXAMPLE

53. Jenna is now x years old, and Amy is 3 years younger than Jenna. In terms of x, how old will Amy be in 4 years?

A. $x - 1$
B. x
C. $x + 1$
D. $x + 4$
E. $2x + 1$

Imagine a dialogue between Jenna and Amy:

Jenna: This is an easy problem. If my age is x, then your age, Amy, is $x - 3$ since you're three years younger than me. Therefore, in four years, you'll be $(x - 3) + 4$ or $x + 1$.

Amy: You may be right, but there's a much easier way to figure it out. Let's say you're 10 years old now. That makes me 7, since I'm three years younger. In four years, I'll be 11. Now let's just substitute your age, 10, for x in all the answer choices and see which answer gives us 11. Once you try all the answers, you see that only choice (C), $x + 1$, works.

Jenna: That's so much extra work. Why not just do the algebra?

Amy: Shut up, algebra head, I'll do it my own way.

Before this degenerates any further, let's get to the point: **Know your strengths and make decisions about how to approach Math problems accordingly!**

Some people "get" algebra. Some people have a harder time with it. The same is true for geometry, word problems, etc. There is often more than one way to do a particular problem. The "best" method is the method that will get you the correct answer accurately and quickly.

The lesson here is that you have to know your own strengths. Again, in case you missed the point, know your strengths and use them to your advantage.

Make an Educated Guess

Don't Underestimate the Value of Guessing

Remember, there's no penalty for wrong answers. Even if you guess randomly, you have a 1 in 5 chance of guessing correctly.

Don't leave any answers blank on the SHSAT. Since there's no penalty for wrong answers, there is no harm in guessing when you don't know the answer.

Of course, you should still guess strategically whenever possible. Remember, every answer choice you eliminate increases your odds of guessing correctly.

EXAMPLE

54. What is the greatest common factor of 95 and 114?

   F.   1
   G.   5
   H.   6
   J.   19
   K.   38

Note What You Skip

When you skip a question, circle it so that it will be easy to spot if you have time to go back.

If you looked at this problem and either could not remember how to find greatest common factor or were running out of time and wanted to save your time for other questions, you should be able to eliminate at least one answer choice pretty easily. Do you see which one?

Since all multiples of 5 end in either 5 or 0, 5 cannot be a factor of 114, and so choice (G) must be incorrect.

BACKDOOR METHODS

Reminder

Remember that the SHSAT is not a math test—it's an admissions exam. You don't have to do the math the "right" way. You just need to get the right answer.

You have to know math to do well at the Science high schools. No one is disputing this—and if you are really uncomfortable with math, you may want to consider why you're applying to these schools. However, the main thing to remember here is that this test is just a standardized admissions test. The timing is tight, and no one is going to check your math. If a backdoor method gets you the answer more quickly, use it.

There are two backdoor methods that are likely to serve you well on the test—**picking numbers** and **backsolving**.

Picking Numbers

Sometimes a math problem can seem more difficult than it actually is because it's general or abstract. You can make a question like this more concrete—and easier—by substituting numbers for the variables in the question. If you find that you often have difficulty with algebra problems, you may find that picking numbers helps make the math easier.

EXAMPLE

55. $3a(2b + 2) =$

    A. $2b + 3a$

    B. $5ab + 2b$

    C. $5ab + 2a + 1$

    D. $6ab + 2a$

    E. $6ab + 6a$

The algebra in this question is pretty straightforward. According to the distributive property, $3a(2b + 2) = (3a)(2b) + (3a)(2) = 6ab + 6$ or choice (E). Most test takers will probably do the algebra to solve the question.

However, if you have trouble with algebra—or simply find it takes you a long time—you can approach this problem another way. Pick simple numbers for a and b and plug them into the equation. If $a = 2$ and $b = 3$, then $3a(2b + 2) = (3)(2)[2(3) + 2] = 6(6 + 2) = 48$. Now you know that if $a = 2$ and $b = 3$, the equation equals 48.

Once you know this, simply plug 2 in for a and 3 in for b in each of the answer choices. The one that adds up to 48 is the correct answer.

    A. $2b + 3a = 2(3) + 3(2) = 12$

    B. $5ab + 2b = 5(2)(3) + 2(3) = 36$

    C. $5ab + 2a + 1 = 5(2)(3) + 2(2) + 1 = 35$

    D. $6ab + 2a = 6(2)(3) + 2(2) = 40$

    E. $6ab + 6a = 6(2)(3) + 6(2) = 48$

Choice (E) is the answer that gives you 48 when you plug 2 in for a and 3 for b. Therefore, it must be the correct answer.

If two or more answer choices had come out to 48, then you would have had to do a little more work. Under those circumstances, you have to pick new numbers for a and b, come up with a new value, and then plug those numbers into the answer choices that came out the same the first time. In other words, if choices (B) and (E) had both equaled 48, you could have made $a = 3$ and $b = 4$, discovered that the total was 90, and then plugged 3 and 4 into only choices (B) and (E) to determine which one equaled 90.

Pick Easy Numbers!

Pick small numbers that are easy to use. This method is supposed to make the problem *easier*.

Be Wary of 0 and 1

Although 0 and 1 are small, easy numbers, picking them increases the chance that more than one answer choice will yield the same value.

Word Problems

Picking numbers can be extremely helpful when the answer choices to a word problem contain variables. Remember this problem?

EXAMPLE

53. Jenna is now x years old, and Amy is 3 years younger than Jenna. In terms of x, how old will Amy be in 4 years?

A. $x - 1$

B. x

C. $x + 1$

D. $x + 4$

E. $2x + 1$

As you saw earlier, there is more than one way to solve this problem. Some test takers will find it easier to solve this question by setting up algebraic equations. However, setting up the algebra may slow down other test takers. Picking a number for x may be faster and easier.

For example, if you say that $x = 10$, then Jenna is 10 years old, and Amy is 7 since she is three years younger. In four years, Amy will be 11. Once you have this value, plug 10 in for x in each of the answer choices to see which one equals 11.

(A) $10 - 1 = 9$

(B) 10

(C) $10 + 1 = \mathbf{11}$

(D) $10 + 4 = 14$

(E) $2(10) + 1 = 21$

Only choice (C) adds up to 11, so it must be correct.

Percent Increase/Decrease Problems

If you see a problem on the SHSAT that deals with percents, picking 100 is the easiest and quickest way to solve the problem.

EXAMPLE

56. If the price of a stock decreases by 20 percent, and then by an additional 25 percent, by what percent has the price decreased from its original value?

A. 40

B. 45

C. 50

D. 55

E. 60

Make the original price of the stock $100. The initial 20% decrease brings the price down to $80 (20% of 100 is 20). Then 25% or $\frac{1}{4}$ of $80 is $20. Therefore, the price of the stock is decreased by an additional $20, bringing the final price down to $60. Since the price dropped from $100 to $60, the total decrease is $40 or 40% of the original price. (A) is the correct answer.

You may have been able to solve this problem by setting up algebraic equations, but picking 100 is easier and faster here.

100% Helpful

Always pick 100 for percent problems—it will help you find the answer quickly and accurately!

Backsolving

All of the answers in the Math Section of the SHSAT are multiple-choice. One way that you will be able to use this to your advantage is by backsolving. What this means is that sometimes it's helpful to work backwards from the answer choices.

Here's how it works. When answer choices are numbers—i.e., not variables—you can expect them to be arranged from small to large or large to small. The test maker does not get creative with the order of the answer choices. What you do is to start with the middle answer choice and plug it directly into the problem. If it works, you're set. If it doesn't, you can usually figure out whether to try a larger or smaller answer choice. If this seems confusing, take a look at the following problem and explanation.

Remember

You can backsolve only if your answer choices are all numbers.

EXAMPLE

57. Three consecutive multiples of 20 have a sum of 300. What is the **greatest** of these numbers?

A. 60
B. 80
C. 100
D. 120
E. 140

Begin with the middle answer choice. If 100 is the greatest of the three numbers, the three numbers must be 100, 80, and 60. We know that 100 + 80 + 60 = 240. The correct three numbers will add up to 300, so the **greatest** of these numbers must be greater than 100. Try answer choice (D). If 120 is the greatest, the three numbers must be 120, 100, and 80; 120 + 100 + 80 = 300. Answer (D) is correct.

It's worth noting that if (D) had also given you a sum less than 300, you would not have to check choice (E). Think about it. If the numbers are arranged from small to large and the second-largest number gives you an answer that is too small, you know that the largest number has to be correct.

Time Tip

Always start with the middle answer choice when solving a word problem by backsolving.

A Word about Calculators

This is an easy one. You cannot use a calculator on the SHSAT. Leave your calculator home. End of story.

The rest of this section in this book will deal with Math content review. Some of this will be familiar; some may be less familiar. Take a look at all of it, but spend more time with the subjects that are less familiar. Even if you do not need to review a particular subject too much, make sure you do the practice set. There's no harm in practicing extra problems.

8

Arithmetic Review

.... Highlights ....

- Get an Overview of What Will Be on the Test

- Review the Arithmetic Content Review You Need to Know

- Practice Set

OVERVIEW

On the SHSAT, **arithmetic** means more than addition and subtraction. **Arithmetic** is the umbrella term for a wide range of math concepts, including **number properties, factors, divisibility, fractions, decimals, exponents, radicals, percents, averages, ratios, proportions, rates,** and **probability**. These concepts are summarized in items 1–51 in 100 Essential Math Concepts in the Resource Section. This chapter will review these concepts and give you a chance to practice problems dealing with them.

First, take a look at a few definitions:

Number Type	Definition	Examples
Integers	*Whole numbers, including 0 and negative whole numbers.*	$-900, -3, 0, 1, 54$
Fractions	*A **fraction** is a number that is written in the form $\frac{A}{B}$, where A is the numerator and B is the denominator.*	$-\frac{5}{6}, -\frac{3}{17}, \frac{1}{2}, \frac{899}{901}$
	*An **improper fraction** is a number that is greater than 1 (or less than -1) that is written in the form of a fraction. Improper fractions can be converted to a **mixed number**.*	$\frac{-65}{64}, \frac{9}{8}, \frac{57}{10}$ $-1\frac{1}{64}, 1\frac{1}{8}, 5\frac{7}{10}$
Positive/Negative	*Numbers greater than 0 are positive numbers; numbers less than 0 are negative. The number 0 is neither positive nor negative.*	Positive: $\frac{7}{8}, 1, 5, 900$ Negative: $-64, -40, -11, -\frac{6}{13}$
Even/Odd	*An even number is an integer that is a multiple of 2.*	Even numbers: $-8, -2, 0, 4, 12, 188$
	An odd number is an integer that is not a multiple of 2	Odd numbers: $-17, -1, 3, 9, 457$
Prime Number	*A prime number is an integer greater than 1 that has no factors other than 1 and itself.* *The number 2 is the only even prime number.*	$2, 3, 5, 7, 11, 59, 83$
Consecutive Numbers	*These are numbers that follow one after another, in order, without skipping any.*	Consecutive integers: $3, 4, 5, 6$ Consecutive even integers: $2, 4, 6, 8, 10$ Consecutive multiples of 9: $9, 18, 27, 36$
Factor	*A factor is a positive integer that divides evenly into a given number with no remainder.*	The complete list of factors of 12: $1, 2, 3, 4, 6, 12$
Multiple	*A multiple is a number that a given number will divide into with no remainder.*	Some multiples of 12: $0, 12, 24, 60$

Odds and Evens

Even ± Even = Even

Even ± Odd = Odd

Odd ± Odd = Even

Even × Even = Even

Even × Odd = Even

Odd × Odd = Odd

Positives and Negatives

There are few things to remember about positives and negatives. You will not see many problems that focus specifically on positives and negatives, but you must know the basics because these concepts will show up as part of harder problems.

Adding a negative number is basically subtraction.

6 + (−4) is really 6 − 4 or 2.

4 + (−6) is really 4 − 6 or −2.

Subtracting a negative number is basically addition.

6 − (−4) is really 6 + 4 or 10.

−6 − (−4) is really −6 + 4 or −2.

Multiplying and **Dividing** positives and negatives is like all other multiplication and division, with one catch. To figure out whether your product is positive or negative, simply count the number of negatives you had to start. If you had an odd number of negatives, the product is negative. If you had an even number of negatives, the product is positive.

6 × (−4) = −24 (1 negative → negative product)

(−6) × (−4) = 24 (2 negatives → positive product)

(−1) × (−6) × (−4) = −24 (3 negatives → negative product)

Similarly,

−24 ÷ 6 = (−1) × (−6) × (−4) (1 negative → negative quotient)

−24 ÷(−4) = 6 (2 negatives → positive quotient)

> ### Dividing Positives and Negatives
>
> Negative ÷ negative = positive
>
> Positive ÷ negative = negative

Absolute Value

To find the **absolute value** of a number, simply strip the number within the vertical lines of its sign.

|4| = 4

|−4| = 4

When absolute value expressions contain different arithmetic operations, perform the operation and then strip the sign from the result.

|−6 + 4| = |−2| = 2

|(−6) × 4| = |−24| = 24

> ### Finding the Absolute Value
>
> To find the absolute value of a number, simply strip it of its sign.

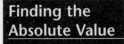

Exercise

i. $\left|-11.8\right| =$ ____

ii. $\left|5-6\right| =$ ____

iii. $\left|-3.5+1\right| - \left|-15-17\right| =$ ____

Factors and Multiples

To find the **prime factorization** of a number, keep breaking it down into factors of the number until you are left with only prime numbers.

To find the prime factorization of 168:

$$168 = 4 \times 42$$
$$= 4 \times 6 \times 7$$
$$= 2 \times 2 \times 2 \times 3 \times 7$$

To find the **greatest common factor** (**GCF**) of two integers, break down both integers into their prime factorizations and mulitply all prime factors they have in common.

If you're looking for the greatest common factor of 40 and 130, first identify the prime factors of each integer.

$$40 = 4 \times 10$$
$$= 2 \times 2 \times 2 \times 5$$

$$140 = 10 \times 14$$
$$= 2 \times 5 \times 2 \times 7$$
$$= 2 \times 2 \times 5 \times 7$$

Next, see what prime factors the two numbers have in common and then multiply these common factors.

Both integers share two 2s and 5, so the GCF is $2 \times 2 \times 5$ or 20.

If you need to find a **common multiple** of two integers, you can always multiply them. However, you can use prime factors to find the **least common multiple** (**LCM**). To do this, multiply all of the prime factors of each integer as many times as they appear. This may sound confusing, but is pretty clear once it's demonstrated. Take a look at the example to see how it works.

Common multiple of 20 and 16:
$$20 \times 16 = 320$$

So 320 is a common multiple of 20 and 16, but it is not the least common multiple.

The prime factorizations of 20 and 16 are as follows:

$$20 = 2 \times 2 \times 5 = 2^2 \times 5$$
$$16 = 2 \times 2 \times 2 \times 2 = 2^4$$

Therefore, the prime factors of both of these numbers are 2 and 5, and the greatest power of each of these numbers is 4 and 1 respectively, so the least common multiple is

$$2^4 \times 5 = 16 \times 5 = 80$$

The Order of Operations

You need to remember the order in which arithmetic operations must be performed. **PEMDAS** (or Please Excuse My Dear Aunt Sally) may help you remember the order.

<u>Pl</u>ease = Parentheses
<u>Ex</u>cuse = Exponents
<u>My</u> <u>D</u>ear = Multiplication and Division (from left to right)
<u>A</u>unt <u>S</u>ally = Addition and Subtraction (from left to right)

$$3^3 - 8(4-2) + 60 \div 4$$
$$= 3^3 - 8(2) + 60 \div 4$$
$$= 27 - 8(2) + 60 \div 4$$
$$= 27 - 16 + 15$$
$$= 11 + 15$$
$$= 26$$

Divisibility Rules

If you've forgotten—or never learned—divisibility rules, spend a little time with this chart. Even if you know the rules, take a moment to refresh your memory. Remember, there are no easy divisibility rules for 7 and 8.

Divisible by	The Rule	Example: 558
2	*The last digit is even.*	a multiple of 2 because 8 is even
3	*The sum of the digits is a multiple of 3.*	a multiple of 3 because $5 + 5 + 8 = 18$, which is a multiple of 3
4	*The last 2 digits comprise a 2-digit multiple of 4.*	NOT a multiple of 4 because 58 is not a multiple of 4
5	*The last digit is 5 or 0.*	NOT a multiple of 5 because it doesn't end in 5 or 0
6	*The last digit is even AND the sum of the digits is a multiple of 3.*	a multiple of 6 because it's a multiple of both 2 and 3
9	*The sum of the digits is a multiple of 9.*	a multiple of 9 because $5 + 5 + 8 = 18$, which is a multiple of 9
10	*The last digit is 0.*	not a multiple of 10 because it doesn't end in 0

The Divisibility Test

Don't confuse the divisibility tests. To test for 2, 4, 5, or 10, just look at the last digit or two. To test for 3 or 9, add all the digits.

Exercise

iv.   What are the following numbers divisible by?

1,455 ___1,5___

50,022 ___1,2,___

0 ___0___

Fractions and Decimals

Generally, it's a good idea to **reduce fractions** when solving math questions. To do this, simply cancel all factors that the numerator and denominator have in common.

$$\frac{28}{36} = \frac{4 \times 7}{4 \times 9} = \frac{7}{9}$$

To **add fractions**, get a common denominator and then add the numerators.

$$\frac{1}{4} + \frac{1}{3} = \frac{3}{12} + \frac{4}{12} = \frac{3+4}{12} = \frac{7}{12}$$

To **subtract fractions**, get a common denominator and then subtract the numerators.

$$\frac{1}{4} - \frac{1}{3} = \frac{3}{12} - \frac{4}{12} = \frac{3-4}{12} = -\frac{1}{12}$$

To **multiply fractions**, multiply the numerators and multiply the denominators.

$$\frac{1}{4} \times \frac{1}{3} = \frac{1 \times 1}{4 \times 3} = \frac{1}{12}$$

To **divide fractions**, invert the second fraction and multiply. In other words, multiply the first fraction by the reciprocal of the second fraction.

$$\frac{1}{4} \div \frac{1}{3} = \frac{1}{4} \times \frac{3}{1} = \frac{1 \times 3}{4 \times 1} = \frac{3}{4}$$

Dividing by Fractions

Dividing by a fraction is the same as multiplying by its reciprocal.

To **compare fractions**, multiply the numerator of the first fraction by the denominator of the second fraction to get a product. Then, multiply the numerator of the second fraction by the denominator of the first fraction to get a second product. If the first product is greater, the first fraction is greater. If the second product is greater, the second fraction is greater.

Compare $\frac{2}{3}$ and $\frac{5}{8}$.

$$2 \times 8 = 16$$

$$5 \times 3 = 15$$

Because 16 is greater than 15, $\frac{2}{3}$ is greater than $\frac{5}{8}$.

To **convert a fraction to a decimal**, divide the denominator into the numerator.

To convert $\frac{8}{25}$ to a decimal, divide 25 into 8.

$$\frac{8}{25} = 0.32$$

To **convert a decimal to a fraction**, first set the decimal over 1. Then, move the decimal over as many places as it takes until it is immediately to the right of the units digit. Count the number of places that you moved the decimal. Then add that many 0s to the 1 in the denominator.

$$0.3 = \frac{0.3}{1} = \frac{3.0}{10} \text{ or } \frac{3}{10}$$

$$0.32 = \frac{0.32}{1} = \frac{32.0}{100} \text{ or } \frac{8}{25}$$

Exercise

v. Reduce the following fractions and expressions to lowest terms:

$$\frac{39}{72} = \underline{\qquad} \quad \frac{13}{\cancel{3}} \quad \frac{13}{24}$$

$$\frac{248}{504} = \frac{124}{252} \quad \frac{62}{\cancel{126}21}$$

$$\frac{5}{9} + \frac{2}{6} = \underline{\qquad} \frac{8}{9} \quad \frac{6}{18} + \frac{10}{18}$$

$$\frac{1}{2} - \frac{3}{7} = \frac{1}{14} \qquad \frac{7}{14} - \cancel{c}$$

vi. Convert the following fractions to decimals:

$$\frac{11}{16} = \underline{\qquad} \qquad \frac{11}{16} = \frac{4}{160} \qquad \frac{16\ 4}{1100}$$

$$\frac{5}{8} = \underline{\qquad} .1245$$

vii. Convert the following decimals to fractions:

$$0.15 = \underline{\frac{15}{100}}$$

$$0.64 = \underline{\qquad} \frac{64}{100} \quad \frac{32}{50}$$

Common Percent Equivalencies

Familiarity with the relationships among percents, decimals, and fractions can save you time on test day. Don't worry about memorizing the following chart. Simply use it to refresh your recollection of relationships you already know (e.g., $50\% = 0.50 = \frac{1}{2}$) and to familiarize yourself with some that you might not already know. To convert a fraction or decimal to a percent, multiply by 100%. To convert a percent to a fraction or decimal, divide by 100%.

Fraction	Decimal	Percent	Fraction	Decimal	Percent
$\frac{1}{20}$	0.05	5%	$\frac{2}{5}$	0.40	40%
$\frac{1}{10}$	0.10	10%	$\frac{1}{2}$	0.50	50%
$\frac{1}{8}$	0.125	12.5%	$\frac{3}{5}$	0.60	60%
$\frac{1}{6}$	$0.16\overline{6}$	$16\frac{2}{3}$%	$\frac{2}{3}$	$0.66\overline{6}$	$66\frac{2}{3}$%
$\frac{1}{5}$	0.20	20%	$\frac{3}{4}$	0.75	75%
$\frac{1}{4}$	0.25	25%	$\frac{4}{5}$	0.80	80%
$\frac{1}{3}$	$0.33\overline{3}$	$33\frac{1}{3}$%	$\frac{5}{6}$	$0.83\overline{3}$	$83\frac{1}{3}$%
$\frac{3}{8}$	0.375	37.5%	$\frac{7}{8}$	0.875	87.5%

Rounding

You might be asked to estimate or round off a number on the SHSAT. There are a few simple rules to rounding. Look at the digit to the right of the number in question. If it is 4 or less, leave the number as it is and replace all numbers to the right with 0s.

For example, round the number 765,432 to the nearest hundreds digit. The hundreds digit is 4, but the important digit to pay attention to is the number to its right, the tens digit. Because this digit is less than 5 (it is 3), you should round to the nearest hundred below this number, or 765,400 (rather than rounding up to 765,500).

If the digit to the right of number in question is 5 or greater, increase the number in question by 1 and replace all numbers to the right with 0s.

For example, 765,553 rounded to the nearest 100 would be 765,600.

Exponents and Roots

Exponents are the small raised numbers written to the right of a variable or number. They indicate the number of times that variable or number is to be used as a factor. On the SHSAT, you'll usually deal with numbers or variables that are squared, but you could see a few other concepts involving exponents.

To **add** or **subtract** terms consisting of a coefficient (the number in front of the variable) multiplied by a power (a power is a base raised to an exponent), both the base and the exponent must be the same. As long as the base and the exponents are the same, you can add the coefficients.

$$x^2 + x^2 = 2x^2$$
$$3x^4 - 2x^4 = x^4$$
$$x^2 + x^3 \text{ cannot be combined.}$$

To **multiply** terms consisting of coefficients multiplied by powers having the same base, multiply the coefficients and add the exponents.

$$2x^5 \times 8x^7 = (2 \times 8)(x^{5+7}) = 16x^{12}$$

To **divide** terms consisting of coefficients multiplied by powers having the same base, divide the coefficients and subtract the exponents.

$$6x^7 \div 2x^5 = (6 \div 2)(x^{7-5}) = 3x^2$$

To **raise a power to an exponent**, multiply the exponents.

$$(x^2)^4 = x^{2 \times 4} = x^8$$

A **square root** is a number that, when multiplied by itself, produces the given quantity. The radical sign " $\sqrt{}$ " is used to represent the positive square root of a number, so $\sqrt{25} = 5$, since $5 \times 5 = 25$.

To **add** or **subtract** radicals, make sure the numbers under the radical sign are the same. If they are, you can add or subtract the coefficients outside the radical signs.

$$2\sqrt{2} + 3\sqrt{2} = 5\sqrt{2}$$
$$\sqrt{2} + \sqrt{3} \text{ cannot be combined.}$$

To **simplify** radicals, factor out the perfect squares under the radical, unsquare them, and put the result in front of the radical sign.

$$\sqrt{32} = \sqrt{16 \times 2} = 4\sqrt{2}$$

To **multiply** or **divide** radicals, multiply (or divide) the coefficients outside the radical. Multiply (or divide) the numbers inside the radicals.

$$\sqrt{x} \times \sqrt{y} = \sqrt{xy}$$
$$3\sqrt{2} \times 4\sqrt{5} = 12\sqrt{10}$$
$$\frac{\sqrt{x}}{\sqrt{y}} = \sqrt{\frac{x}{y}}$$
$$12\sqrt{10} \div 3\sqrt{2} = 4\sqrt{5}$$

To **take the square root of a fraction**, break the fraction into two separate roots and take the square root of the numerator and the denominator.

$$\sqrt{\frac{16}{25}} = \frac{\sqrt{16}}{\sqrt{25}} = \frac{4}{5}$$

Multiplying Powers

To multiply powers with the same base, add exponents. To raise a power to an exponent, multiply exponents.

Perfect Square

Learn to recognize perfect squares.

Exercise

viii.   Simplify the following expressions.

$$x^5 + 2x^5 = \underline{3x^5}$$
$$2x(x^2 + 3y) = \underline{2x^3 + 6\,xy}$$
$$(x^4)^3 = \underline{x^{12}}$$
$$\sqrt{49} - \sqrt{16} = \underline{3}$$
$$\sqrt{2} \times \sqrt{10} = \underline{\sqrt{20}}$$
$$\sqrt{\frac{25}{64}} = \underline{\frac{5}{64}} = \frac{5}{8}$$

Scientific Notation

The exponent of a power of 10 indicates how many zeros the number would contain if it were written out. For example, $10^4 = 10{,}000$ (4 zeros) since the product of four factors of 10 is equal to 10,000.

When multiplying a number by a power of 10, move the decimal point to the right the same number of places as the number of zeros in that power of 10.

$$0.0123 \times 10^4 = 123$$

When dividing by a power of 10, move the decimal point to the left.

$$43.21 \div 10^3 = 0.04321$$

Multiplying by a number with a negative exponent is the same as dividing by a positive exponent. Therefore, when you multiply by a number with a positive exponent, move the decimal to the right. When you multiply by a number with a negative exponent, move the decimal to the left.

Percents

Remember this formula: $Part = Percent \times Whole$ or $Percent = \dfrac{Part}{Whole}$.

To find **part, percent,** or **whole,** plug the values you have into the equation and solve.

From Fraction to Percent

To change a fraction to a percent, multiply by 100%.

$$44\% \text{ of } 25 = 0.44 \times 25 = 11$$

42 is what percent of 70?
$$42 \div 70 = 0.6$$
$$0.6 \times 100\% = 60\%$$

To **increase or decrease a number by a given percent,** take that percent of the original number and add it to or subtract it from the original number.

To increase 25 by 60%, first find 60% of 25.

$$25 \times 0.6 = 15$$

Then add the result to the original number.

$$25 + 15 = 40$$

To decrease 25 by the same percent, subtract the 15.

$$25 - 15 = 10$$

Exercise

ix. Of the 64 cookies on the tray, 16 are chocolate chip. What percent are NOT chocolate chip? ___75%___

x. 3% of 42 equals 42% of ___12___.

Shortcut

A handy shortcut:

x% of y = y% of x.

Average, Median, and Mode

Remember this formula: *Average = Sum of the terms/Number of the terms.*

The average (arithmetic mean) of 15, 18, 15, 32 and 20 = $\dfrac{15 + 18 + 15 + 32 + 20}{5} = \dfrac{100}{5} = 20$.

When there is an odd number of terms, the median of a group of terms is the value of the middle term with the terms arranged in increasing order.

First, put the terms in order from small to large: 15, 15, 18, 20, 32.

Then, identify the middle term. The middle term is 18.

When there is an even number of terms, the median is the average of the two middle terms with the terms arranged in increasing order.

The mode is the value of the term that occurs most.

In the above list, 15 occurs twice, so it is the mode.

Exercise

xi. There are five children whose ages are 11, 5, 8, 5, and 6.

What is the average age? ___7___

What is the median age? ___6___

Which age is the mode? ___5___

Ratios, Proportions, and Rates

Ratios can be expressed in two forms.

The first form is $\frac{a}{b}$.

If you have 15 dogs and 5 cats, the ratio of dogs to cats is $\frac{15}{5}$. (The ratio of cats to dogs is $\frac{5}{15}$.) As with any other fraction, this ratio can be reduced: $\frac{15}{5}$ can be reduced to $\frac{3}{1}$. In other words, for every 3 dogs, there is 1 cat.

The second form is $a{:}b$.

The ratio of dogs to cats is 15:5 or 3:1. The ratio of cats to dogs is 5:15 or 1:3.

Make sure that you pay attention to what ratio is specified in the problem. Remember that the ratio of dogs to cats is different from the ratio of cats to dogs.

To solve a **proportion**, cross multiply and solve for the variable.

$$\frac{x}{6} = \frac{2}{3}$$

$$3x = 12$$

$$x = 4$$

A **rate** is a ratio that compares quantities measured in different units. The most common example is miles per hour. Use the following formula for such problems:

Distance = Rate × Time

Remember that although not all rates are speeds, this formula can be adapted to any rate.

Exercise

xii.   There are 18 white marbles and 6 red marbles in a bag. What is the ratio of red marbles to white marbles? __1:4__

xiii. $\frac{36}{8} = \frac{9}{y}$. What is the value of y? __2__

xiv.   If it took Michael three hours to bike 48 miles, what was his average speed in miles per hour? __~~B~~ 16__

Probability

An event is a collection or set of outcomes. For example, suppose that a die with faces numbered 1, 2, 3, 4, 5, and 6 is rolled. All the possible outcomes are 1, 2, 3, 4, 5, and 6. Let *A* be the event that a 1, 3, or 5 is rolled. The event *A* is made up of the outcomes 1, 3, and 5; that is, {*A* = 1, 3, 5} The event *A* can also be described by saying that the number is odd. A possible outcome is the elementary building block from which events are made up. An event is a set of possible outcomes. Of course, it is possible for an event to consist of a single possible outcome. For example, suppose that $B = \{4\}$; that is, the event B is the result that a 4 is rolled. An event consisting of a single possible outcome is called an elementary event. Thus, B, which is $\{4\}$, is an elementary event. However, in general, an outcome is more elementary than an event, with an event being a set of possible outcomes. For example, the event $C = \{1, 2, 4, 6\}$ consists of possible outcomes 1, 2, 4, and 6. Note that C is not an elementary event.

To find the probability that a **single event** will occur, use the formula:

$$Probability = \frac{Number\ of\ desirable\ outcomes}{total\ number\ of\ possible\ outcomes}$$

If there are 12 books on a shelf and 9 of them are mysteries, what is the probability of picking a mystery?

$\frac{9}{12} = \frac{3}{4}$. This probability can also be expressed as 0.75 or 75%.

To find the probability that **two events** will both occur, find the probability that the first event occurs and multiply this by the probability that the second event occurs given that the first event occurs.

If there are 12 books on a shelf and 9 of them are mysteries, what is the probability of picking a mystery first and a nonmystery second if exactly two books are selected?

Probability of picking a mystery: $\frac{9}{12} = \frac{3}{4}$.

Probability of picking a nonmystery: $\frac{3}{11}$. (Originally there were 9 mysteries and 3 nonmysteries. After the mystery is selected, there are 8 mysteries and 3 nonmysteries, or 11 books remaining.)

Probability of picking both books: $\frac{3}{4} \times \frac{3}{11} = \frac{9}{44}$.

Strange Symbolism and Terminology

Some math problems will be confusing because you're unfamiliar with the math concept being tested. Other problems will seem confusing because the math has literally been made up just for the purposes of the test. The test makers make up math symbols and terminology to test your ability to deal with unfamiliar concepts.

These problems are not as hard as they sound. When a strange symbol appears in a math problem, the problem will **always** tell you what the symbol means. Similarly, if you see strange terminology, it will **always** be defined. The problems are essentially about following directions, so do not panic when you see them. All you have to do is slow down, read the problem, and follow the directions.

Look for Quotes

Made up terminology will most likely be in quotes.

If $x<<>>y = \sqrt{x+y}$, what is $9<<>>16$?

All you have to do here is to plug $9<<>>16$ into the defining equation: $\sqrt{9+16} = \sqrt{25} = 5$.

To "chomp" a number, take the sum of the digits of that number and divide this value by the number of digits. What value do you get when you "chomp" 43,805?

$$4 + 3 + 8 + 0 + 5 = 20$$

$$20 \div 5 = 4$$

The following 46 problems address the range of topics covered in this chapter. As you solve these problems, think about the content you've just reviewed and the Kaplan strategies. Make sure you check the answers and read the explanations at the end of the chapter.

PRACTICE SET

1. Which of the following is not even?

    A. 330
    B. 436
    C. 752
    D. 861
    E. 974   Ⓐ Ⓑ Ⓒ Ⓓ Ⓔ

2. What is the least prime number greater than 50?

    F. 51
    G. 53
    H. 55
    J. 57
    K. 59   Ⓕ Ⓖ Ⓗ Ⓙ Ⓚ

3. Which of the following is a multiple of 2?

    A. 271
    B. 357
    C. 463
    D. 599
    E. 756   Ⓐ Ⓑ Ⓒ Ⓓ Ⓔ

4. $\dfrac{15 \times 7 \times 3}{9 \times 5 \times 2} =$ *90*

    F. $\dfrac{2}{7}$

    G. $\dfrac{3}{5}$

    H. $3\dfrac{1}{2}$

    J. 7

    K. $7\dfrac{1}{2}$ Ⓕ Ⓖ Ⓗ Ⓙ Ⓚ

5. What is the least common multiple of 18 and 24?

    A. 6
    B. 54
    C. 72
    D. 96
    E. 432   Ⓐ Ⓑ Ⓒ Ⓓ Ⓔ

6. Which of the following is a multiple of 3?

    F. 115
    G. 370
    H. 465
    J. 589
    K. 890   Ⓕ Ⓖ Ⓗ Ⓙ Ⓚ

7. $-6(3 - 4 \times 3) =$

    A.   −66

    B.   −54

    C.   −12

    D.   18

    E.   54   Ⓐ Ⓑ Ⓒ Ⓓ Ⓔ

8. Which of the following is a multiple of 10?

    F.   10,005

    G.   10,030

    H.   10,101

    J.   100,005

    K.   101,101   Ⓕ Ⓖ Ⓗ Ⓙ Ⓚ

9. Which of the following is a multiple of both 5 and 2?

    A.   2,203

    B.   2,342

    C.   1,005

    D.   7,790

    E.   9,821   Ⓐ Ⓑ Ⓒ Ⓓ Ⓔ

10. Which of the following is a multiple of both 3 and 10?

    F.   103

    G.   130

    H.   210

    J.   310

    K.   460   Ⓕ Ⓖ Ⓗ Ⓙ Ⓚ

11. Which of the following is a multiple of 2, 3, and 5?

    A.   165

    B.   235

    C.   350

    D.   420

    E.   532   Ⓐ Ⓑ Ⓒ Ⓓ Ⓔ

12. Which of the following is an even multiple of both 3 and 5?

    F.   135

    G.   155

    H.   250

    J.   350

    K.   390   Ⓕ Ⓖ Ⓗ Ⓙ Ⓚ

13. Professor Jones bought a large carton of books. She gave 3 books to each student in her class and there were no books left over. Which of the following could be the number of books she distributed?

    A.   133

    B.   143

    C.   252

    D.   271

    E.   332   Ⓐ Ⓑ Ⓒ Ⓓ Ⓔ

14. Two teams are having a contest in which the prize is a box of candy that the members of the winning team will divide evenly. If team A wins, each player will get exactly 3 pieces of candy, and if team B wins, each player will get exactly 5 pieces of candy. Which of the following could be the number of pieces of candy in the box?

    F.   153

    G.   325

    H.   333

    J.   425

    K.   555   Ⓕ Ⓖ Ⓗ Ⓙ Ⓚ

15. Three consecutive multiples of 4 have a sum of 60. What is the greatest of these numbers?

    A.   8

    B.   12

    C.   16

    D.   20

    E.   24   Ⓐ Ⓑ Ⓒ Ⓓ Ⓔ

16. Sheila cuts a 60 foot wire cable in equal strips of $\frac{4}{5}$ of a feet each. How many strips does she make?

    F.   48

    G.   51

    H.   60

    J.   70

    K.   75   Ⓕ Ⓖ Ⓗ Ⓙ Ⓚ

17. Which of the following is **not** odd?

    A.   349

    B.   537

    C.   735

    D.   841

    E.   918   Ⓐ Ⓑ Ⓒ Ⓓ Ⓔ

18. Which of the following can be the sum of two negative numbers?

    F. 4
    G. 2
    H. 1
    J. 0
    K. −1   Ⓕ Ⓖ Ⓗ Ⓙ Ⓚ

19. Which of the following is **not** a prime number?

    A. 2
    B. 7
    C. 17
    D. 87
    E. 101   Ⓐ Ⓑ Ⓒ Ⓓ Ⓔ

20. All of the following can be the product of a negative integer and positive integer **except**

    F. 1
    G. −1
    H. −2
    J. −4
    K. −6   Ⓕ Ⓖ Ⓗ Ⓙ Ⓚ

21. Susie and Dennis are training for a marathon. On Monday, they both run 3.2 miles. On Tuesday, Susie runs $5\frac{1}{5}$ miles and Dennis runs 3.6 miles. On Wednesday, Susie runs 4.8 miles and Dennis runs $2\frac{2}{5}$ miles. During those 3 days, how many more miles does Susie run than Dennis?

    A. 4.8
    B. 4.0
    C. 3.2
    D. 3.0
    E. 2.4   Ⓐ Ⓑ Ⓒ Ⓓ Ⓔ

22. Which number is a multiple of 60?

    F. 213
    G. 350
    H. 540
    J. 666
    K. 1,060   Ⓕ Ⓖ Ⓗ Ⓙ Ⓚ

23. Two odd integers and one even integer are multiplied together. Which of the following could be their product?

    A. 1.5
    B. 3
    C. 6
    D. 7.2
    E. 15   Ⓐ Ⓑ Ⓒ Ⓓ Ⓔ

24. If the number 9,899,399 is increased by 2,082, the result will be

    F. 9,902,481
    G. 9,901,481
    H. 9,901,471
    J. 9,891,481
    K. 901,481   Ⓕ Ⓖ Ⓗ Ⓙ Ⓚ

25. What is the sum of 5 consecutive integers if the middle one is 13?

    A. 55
    B. 60
    C. 65
    D. 70
    E. 75   Ⓐ Ⓑ Ⓒ Ⓓ Ⓔ

26. $\dfrac{4x^4}{2x^2} =$

    F. $2x^2$
    G. $2x^3$
    H. $2x^4$
    J. $4x^2$
    K. $4x^3$ Ⓐ Ⓑ Ⓒ Ⓓ Ⓔ

27. $-2^3(1-2)^3 + (-2)^3 =$

    A. −12
    B. −4
    C. 0
    D. 4
    E. 12   Ⓕ Ⓖ Ⓗ Ⓙ Ⓚ

28. n is an odd integer and $10 < n < 19$. What is the mean of all possible values of n ?

    F. 13
    G. 13.5
    H. 14
    J. 14.5
    K. 15.5   Ⓐ Ⓑ Ⓒ Ⓓ Ⓔ

29. $a \triangle b = 3\left(\frac{a}{b}\right)$. What is $\frac{14}{32} \triangle 1\frac{3}{4}$?

A. $\frac{1}{4}$

B. $\frac{1}{3}$

C. $\frac{1}{2}$

D. $\frac{3}{4}$

E. $\frac{49}{64}$ Ⓕ Ⓖ Ⓗ Ⓙ Ⓚ

30. Jon works 4.5 hours a day, 3 days each week after school. He is paid $7.25 per hour. How much is his weekly pay (rounded to the next highest cent)?

F. $13.50

G. $19.13

H. $21.45

J. $94.50

K. $97.88   Ⓐ Ⓑ Ⓒ Ⓓ Ⓔ

31. Zim buys a calculator that is marked 30% off. If he pays $35, what was the original price?

A. $24.50

B. $45.50

C. $47.00

D. $50.00

E. $62.50   Ⓕ Ⓖ Ⓗ Ⓙ Ⓚ

32. A museum records 16 visitors to an exhibit on Monday, 21 on Tuesday, 20 on Wednesday, 17 on Thursday, 19 on Friday, 21 on Saturday, and 17 on Sunday. What is the median number of visitors for the week?

F. 18.5

G. 18.75

H. 19

J. 19.5

K. 19.75   Ⓐ Ⓑ Ⓒ Ⓓ Ⓔ

33. A bag contains 8 white, 4 red, 7 green, and 5 blue marbles. Then 8 marbles are withdrawn randomly. How many of the withdrawn marbles were white if the chance of drawing a white marble is now $\frac{1}{4}$?

A. 0

B. 3

C. 4

D. 5

E. 6   Ⓕ Ⓖ Ⓗ Ⓙ Ⓚ

34. $\sqrt{1,500} =$

F. $10 + \sqrt{15}$

G. $10\sqrt{15}$

H. 25

J. $100 + \sqrt{15}$

K. $10\sqrt{150}$ Ⓐ Ⓑ Ⓒ Ⓓ Ⓔ

35. $2(3 \times 2)^2 - 27(6 \div 2) + 3^2 =$

A. 72

B. 9

C. 3

D. 0

E. −24   Ⓕ Ⓖ Ⓗ Ⓙ Ⓚ

36. Which of the following numbers is closest to the product 48.9×21.2?

F. 10,000

G. 8,000

H. 1,000

J. 100

K. 70   Ⓐ Ⓑ Ⓒ Ⓓ Ⓔ

37. $|16 - 25| + \sqrt{25 - 16} =$

A. −12

B. −6

C. 0

D. 6

E. 12   Ⓕ Ⓖ Ⓗ Ⓙ Ⓚ

38. Which of the following is 81,455 rounded to the nearest 100?

F. 81,000

G. 81,400

H. 81,500

J. 82,000

K. 90,000   Ⓐ Ⓑ Ⓒ Ⓓ Ⓔ

39. If 35% of x is 7, what is x% of 35?

A. 7

B. 20

C. 28

D. 35

E. 42   Ⓕ Ⓖ Ⓗ Ⓙ Ⓚ

40. A number is considered "blue" if the sum of its digits is equal to the product of its digits. Which of the following numbers is "blue"?

F. 111
G. 220
H. 321
J. 422
K. 521

Ⓐ Ⓑ Ⓒ Ⓓ Ⓔ

To "fix" a number, you must perform the following four steps:

Step 1: Raise the number to the 3rd power.
Step 2: Divide the result by 2.
Step 3: Take the absolute value of the result of Step 2.
Step 4: Round off this result to the nearest whole number.

41. When you "fix" −3, you get

A. −13
B. 4
C. 5
D. 13
E. 14

Ⓕ Ⓖ Ⓗ Ⓙ Ⓚ

42. When D is divided by 15, the result is 6 with a remainder of 2. What is the remainder when D is divided by 6?

F. 0
G. 1
H. 2
J. 3
K. 4

Ⓐ Ⓑ Ⓒ Ⓓ Ⓔ

43. For any two numbers a and b, $a ? b = (a + b)(a − b)$. For example, $10 ? 5 = (10 + 5)(10 − 5) = (15)(5) = 75$. The value of $7 ? 5$ is

A. 2
B. 12
C. 24
D. 36
E. 48

Ⓕ Ⓖ Ⓗ Ⓙ Ⓚ

44. What is the **greatest** integer less than $\frac{71}{6}$?

F. 9
G. 10
H. 11
J. 12
K. 13

Ⓐ Ⓑ Ⓒ Ⓓ Ⓔ

45. Which of the following is **not** less than 0.25?

A. $\frac{2}{9}$

B. $\frac{3}{14}$

C. $\frac{16}{64}$

D. $\frac{19}{80}$

E. $\frac{2}{9}$

Ⓕ Ⓖ Ⓗ Ⓙ Ⓚ

46. If the average of 5 consecutive odd numbers is 11, then the **largest** number is

F. 17
G. 15
H. 13
J. 11
K. 9

Ⓐ Ⓑ Ⓒ Ⓓ Ⓔ

Exercise Answers

i. 11.8

ii. 1

iii. −29.5

iv. 3, 5

2, 3, 6, 9

0 is divisible by every nonzero integer.

v. $\frac{13}{24}, \frac{31}{63}, \frac{8}{9}, \frac{1}{14}, \frac{1}{15}, 1$

vi. 0.6875, 0.625

vii. $\frac{3}{20}, \frac{16}{25}$

viii. $3x^5, 2x^3 + 6xy, x^{12}, 3, 2\sqrt{5}, \frac{5}{8}$

ix. 75%

x. 3

xi. 7, 6, 5

xii. 1:3

xiii. $y = 2$

xiv. 16 mph

Practice Set Explanations

1. **D** The way to tell if a number is even is to look at the last digit to the right—in the ones column. If that digit is divisible by 2, or is 0, the number is even. Looking at the choices, only (D) ends in a number that isn't 0 and isn't divisible by 2, so only it is not even.

2. **G** A prime number is one that is divisible by only itself and 1. Of the choices, only (G), 53, and (K), 59, are prime. You want the least prime number greater than 50, so (G) is correct. Using the divisibility rules would quickly show you that 51 and 57 are divisible by 3, while 55 is divisible by 5.

3. **E** If the ones digit of a number can be divided by 2, the number is divisible by 2. All of the answer choices except (E) end in an odd number, so only choice (E) is a multiple of 2.

4. **H** Before multiplying these expressions out, begin by checking if there are any common factors between the numerator and the denominator. In the numerator, 15 is the same as 5 times 3 and 9 is the same as 3 times 3, so this expression can be rewritten as $\frac{5 \times 3 \times 7 \times 3}{3 \times 3 \times 5 \times 2}$. Common factors of the numerator and the denominator are both the 3s and the 5, resulting in $\frac{\cancel{5} \times \cancel{3} \times 7 \times \cancel{3}}{\cancel{3} \times \cancel{3} \times \cancel{5} \times 2} = \frac{7}{2}$. This method is much simpler than multiplying everything out and then trying to factor after the fact.

5. **C** The least common multiple (LCM) of two integers is the product of their prime factors, each raised to the highest power with which it appears. The prime factorization of 18 is $2 \cdot 3^2$ and that of 24 is $2^3 \cdot 3$. So their LCM is $2^3 \cdot 3^2 = 8 \cdot 9 = 72$. You could also find their LCM by checking out the multiples of the larger integer until you find the one that's also a multiple of the smaller. Check out the multiples of 24: 24? No. 48? No. 72? Yes.

6. **H** If a number is divisible by 3, the sum of its digits will be divisible by 3. Checking the answer choices, only (H), 465, works since $4 + 6 + 5 = 15$, which is divisible by 3.

7. **E** According to PEMDAS, start in the parentheses. As per PEMDAS, perform multiplication before subtraction: $-6(3 - 12)$. After the subtraction: $-6 (-9)$. Since a negative times a negative is a positive, the answer is 54, (E).

8. **G** If a number is divisible by 10, its last digit will be a 0. Only (G) fits this criterion.

9. **D** If a number is divisible by both 5 and 2, then it must also be divisible by $5 \cdot 2$ or 10. Since a number divisible by 10 must have a 0 as its last digit, (D) is correct.

10. **H** For a number to be divisible by 3 and 10, it must satisfy the divisibility rules of both: Its last digit must be 0 (which automatically eliminates (F)), and the sum of its digits must be divisible by 3. Checking the rest of the answer choices, only (H) is also divisible by 3, since $2 + 1 + 0 = 3$.

11. **D** For a number to be a multiple of both 2 and 5 it must also be a multiple of $2 \cdot 5 = 10$. This means it must have a 0 as its last digit, which eliminates all but choices (C) and (D). To be a multiple of 3, the number's digits must sum to a multiple of 3. Choice (D) is the only of the two that fits this requirement, since $4 + 2 + 0 = 6$.

12. **K** Since an even number is divisible by 2, the question is asking for a number that is divisible by 2, 3, and 5. If the number is divisible by 2 and 5, it must also be divisible by 10, so its last digit must be 0. To be a multiple of 3, its digits must sum to a multiple of 3. Eliminate (F) and (G) since they don't end in 0. Of the remaining choices, only (K) is a multiple of 3, since $3 + 9 + 0 = 12$.

13. **C** If Professor Jones was able to distribute all the books in groups of 3 without any left over, the number of books she started with was divisible by 3. Whichever choice is divisible by 3 must therefore be correct. For a number to be divisible by 3, the sum of its digits must also be divisible by 3. Only (C) fits this requirement: $2 + 5 + 2 = 9$.

14. **K** The problems tells you that the number of pieces of candy in the box can be evenly divided by 3 and 5. So the correct answer is the choice that has a 0 or 5 as its last digit and whose digits sum to a number divisible by 3. Eliminate (F) and (H) since they don't end in either 0 or 5. Of the remaining choices, only (K) is also divisible by 3, since $5 + 5 + 5 = 15$.

15. **E** Use the answer choices to help find the solution. When backsolving, start with the middle choice, since checking it out can often tell if the correct answer must be greater or less than it. In this case it's 16. The sum of 16 and two numbers that are each smaller than 16 has to be less than $3 \cdot 16$ or 48, so it is obviously too small. Therefore, choices (A) and (B) must also be too small, and you can eliminate all three. Try (D), 20. Again 20 plus two numbers smaller than 20 will be less than $3 \cdot 20$ or 60, so it is not correct. The only choice remaining is (E), 24, so it must be correct. To prove it, 24 plus the two preceding consecutive multiples of 4, which are 16 and 20, do indeed sum to 60: $16 + 20 + 24 = 60$.

16. **K** When you're asked how many strips $\frac{4}{5}$ of a foot long can be cut from a 60-foot piece of wire, the question is really asking how many times $\frac{4}{5}$ goes into 60 or, What is $60 \div \frac{4}{5}$? Before you even do the division, you can eliminate some unreasonable answer choices. Since $\frac{4}{5}$ is less than 1, $\frac{4}{5}$ must go into 60 more than 60 times. Eliminate (F), (G), and (H) because they are all less than or equal to 60. Dividing by a fraction is the same as multiplying by its inverse, so $60 \div \frac{4}{5} = 60 \times \frac{5}{4} = 75$.

38. **H** To round a number off to the nearest hundred, consider the tens digit. If the tens digit is 5 or greater, round the hundreds digit up 1. If the tens digit is 4 or less, keep the same hundreds digit. Here the tens digit is 5, so round the hundreds digit up to 5. To the nearest 100, 81,455 is 81,500.

39. **A** This problem is a snap if you remember that $a\%$ of $b = b\%$ of a. In this case 35% of $x = x\%$ of 35, or 7. You could have solved for x if you didn't remember this. Percent • whole = part, so $\frac{35}{100} = \frac{7}{x}$ and 20% of 35 is 7.

40. **H** In this type of problem, you're given a rule or definition you've never heard before and then asked a question involving the new rule. In this particular example, you're given a definition of the term "blue": A number is "blue" if the sum of its digits is equal to the product of its digits. To solve this, simply try each answer until you find the one that fits the definition of "blue." When you do so, you see that only (H) is "blue," because $3 + 2 + 1 = 3 • 2 • 1 = 6$.

41. **E** This is another invented rule question. This time all you have to do is follow directions. To "fix" −3, you first raise it to the 3rd power: $(-3)^3 = -27$. Then divide this result by 2: $-27 \div 2 = -13.5$. Next take the absolute value of −13.5, which is just 13.5. Finally, round off this result to the nearest integer: 13.5 rounds up to 14.

42. **H** First figure out what D is. You're told that $D \div 15 = 6$ with a remainder of 2. This means that $D = (15 • 6) + 2$. So, $D = 90 + 2$, or 92. Now that you know the value of D, just divide it by 6 and see what the remainder is: $92 \div 6 = 15$ with a remainder of 2.

43. **C** This is another "follow the instructions" problem. Just replace a with 7 and b with 5. So 7 ? 5 = (7 + 5)(7 − 5) = (12)(2), or 24.

44. **H** We know that $\frac{71}{6} = 11\frac{5}{6}$, so the greatest integer less than $\frac{71}{6}$ is 11.

45. **C** We know that $0.25 = \frac{1}{4}$, so just find which choice is NOT less than $\frac{1}{4}$. Choice (C), $\frac{16}{64}$, reduces to $\frac{1}{4}$ so it is equal to, not less than, 0.25.

46. **G** The average of a series of consecutive numbers is equal to the middle term. Since 11 is the average of these five consecutive odd numbers, 11 is the third and middle term. So the five numbers are 7, 9, 11, 13, 15, and 15. The largest number is 15.

9

Algebra Review: The Basics

Highlights

- Get an Overview

- Review the Algebra Concepts You Need to Know

- Practice Set

OVERVIEW

Algebra problems will appear in two forms on the SHSAT: as regular math problems and as word problems. Word problems are a little more heavily represented and will be dealt with in the following chapter. This chapter will give you a chance to review the basic algebra concepts that you'll see on the test. The Word Problems chapter will build on these concepts and introduce word problem–specific skills.

ALGEBRA CONCEPTS

Before diving into the content review, turn to 100 Essential Math Concepts in the Resources Section of this book and review items 52–68.

Expressions

An algebraic **expression** on the SHSAT is likely to look something like this:

$$(11 + 3x) - (5 - 2x) =$$

It would, of course, be followed by five answer choices. In addition to algebra, this problem tests your knowledge of odds and evens and the order of operations (PEMDAS). It's not uncommon for algebra problems to contain elements of arithmetic, but there are certain algebraic concepts you need to know for the test.

The main thing that you need to remember about **expressions** on the SHSAT exam is that you can combine only "like terms."

For example, to combine monomials or polynomials, simply add or subtract the coefficients of terms that have the exact same variable. When completing the addition or subtraction, do not change the variables.

$$6a + 5a = 11a$$

$$8b - 2b = 6b$$

$$3a + 2b - 8a = 3a - 8a + 2b = -5a + 2b \text{ or } 2b - 5a$$

Remember, you cannot combine

$$6a + 5a^2$$

or

$$3a + 2b$$

Now, try the following sample problem.

Exercise

i. $(11 + 3x) - (5 - 2x) =$

    a. $6 + x$
    b. $6 + 5x$
    c. $13 + 6x$
    d. $14 + x$
    e. $16 + 5x$

Watch Out

Make sure you combine only like terms.

Multiplying and dividing monomials is a little different. In addition and subtraction, you can combine only like terms. With multiplication and division, you can multiply and divide terms that are different. When you multiply monomials, multiply the coefficients of each term. (In other words, multiply the numbers that come before the variables.) Add the exponents of like variables. Multiply different variables together.

$$(6a)(4b) =$$
$$= (6 \times 4)(a \times b)$$
$$= 24ab$$

$$(6a)(4ab) =$$
$$= (6 \times 4)(a \times a \times b)$$
$$= (6 \times 4)(a^{1+1} \times b)$$
$$= 24\, a^2 b$$

Use the FOIL method to multiply and divide binomials. FOIL stands for First, **Outer**, **Inner**, Last.

$$(y+1)(y+2) = (y \times y) + (y \times 2) + (1 \times y) + (1 \times 2)$$
$$= y^2 + 2y + y + 2$$
$$= y^2 + 3y + 2$$

× MULTIPLY ×

Exercise

ii. $5a + 2b - 3(b + 3a)$

  -1b -3a   2a-1b

iii. $-3a + (+2a)$

  -1a

iv. $6xy \div 2x$

  3y

v. $(m+2)(m+8)$ *m²+16+8m+2m+16   m²+10m+16*

vi. $(n-6)(n+3)$ *n²+3n+6n-18*

  n²-3n-18

Equations

The key to **solving equations** is to do the same thing to both sides of the equation until you have your variable isolated on one side of the equation and all of the numbers on the other side of the equation.

$$12a + 8 = 23 - 3a$$

First, subtract 8 from each side so that the left side of the equation has only variables.

$$12a + 8 - 8 = 23 - 3a - 8$$
$$12a = 15 - 3a$$

Then, add $3a$ to each side so that the right side of the equation has only numbers.

$$12a + 3a = 15 - 3a + 3a$$
$$15a = 15$$

Don't Forget

Always do the same thing to both sides to solve for a variable in an equation.

Finally, divide both sides by 15 to isolate the variable.

$$\frac{15a}{15} = \frac{15}{15}$$

$$a = 1$$

Sometimes you are given an equation with two variables and asked to **solve for one variable in terms of the other**. This means that you must isolate the variable for which you are solving on one side of the equation and put everything else on the other side. In other words, when you're done, you'll have x (or whatever the variable is) on one side of the equation and an expression on the other side.

Solve $7x + 2y = 3x + 10y - 16$ for x in terms of y.

Since you want to isolate x on one side of the equation, begin by subtracting $2y$ from both sides.

$$7x + 2y - 2y = 3x + 10y - 16 - 2y$$
$$7x = 3x + 8y - 16$$

Then, subtract $3x$ from both sides to get all the x's on one side of the equation.

$$7x - 3x = 3x + 8y - 16 - 3x$$
$$4x = 8y - 16$$

Finally, divide both sides by 4 to isolate x.

$$\frac{4x}{4} = \frac{8y - 16}{4}$$

$$x = 2y - 4$$

Exercise

vii. $5a - 6 = -11$ $-1 = a$

viii. $6y + 3 = y + 38$ $35 \cdot y = 7$

ix. $18 = -6x + 4(3x - 3)$ -6 $6x + 2$ $x = 5$

x. If $5a = b$, what is a in terms of b? $\frac{1}{5}b$

xi. If $2xy = 8y$, what is x in terms of y? $\frac{1}{4}$ of y.

Substitution

If a problem gives you the value for a variable, just plug the value into the equation and solve. Make sure that you follow the rules of PEMDAS and are careful with your calculations.

If $x = 15$ and $y = 10$, what is the value of $4x(x - y)$?

Plug 15 in for x and 10 in for y.

$$4(15)(15 - 10) =$$

Then solve.

$$(60)(5) = 300$$

Picking Numbers

You read about Kaplan's backdoor method of **picking numbers** in the Introducing SHSAT Math chapter of this book. You should remember that the picking numbers strategy is particularly helpful on algebra problems. Reread the passage to refresh your recollection of this strategy.

Some typical questions that can be solved by picking numbers are these:

- Age stated in terms of variables
- Remainder problems
- Percentages or fractions of variables
- Even/odd variables calculations
- Questions with algebraic expressions as answers

Take Your Pick

Don't be afraid to pick numbers out of thin air if the answer choices contain variables.

Inequalities

Solve **inequalities** as you would any other equation. Isolate the variable for which you are solving on one side of the equation and everything else on the other side of the equation.

$$4a + 6 > 2a + 10$$
$$4a - 2a > 10 - 6$$
$$2a > 4$$
$$a > 2$$

The only difference here is that instead of finding a specific value for *a*, you get a range of values for *a*. The rest of the math is the same.

There is, however, one **crucial** difference between solving equations and inequalities. **When you multiply or divide an inquality by a negative number, you must change the direction of the sign.**

$$-5a > 10$$
$$a < -2$$

If this seems confusing, think about the logic. You're told that −5 times something is greater than 10. This is where your knowledge of positives and negatives comes into play. You know that negative × positive = negative and negative × negative = positive. Since −5 is negative and 10 is positive, −5 has to be multiplied by something negative to get a positive product. Therefore *a* has to be *less* than −2, not *greater* than it. If *a* > −2, then any value for *a* that is greater than −2 should make −5*a* greater than 10. Say *a* is 20, −5*a* would be −100, which is certainly *not* greater than 10.

The point here is that, while it's a good idea to memorize that you need to flip the sign if you multiply or divide by a negative, the math makes sense if you think about it.

Exercise

xii. Solve for y in each of the following inequalities.

$y + 2 > 10$
$10 + 2a - 3 < 4 - a$
$6y < -20 + y$
$18 - 6y > 12$
$3(y + 10) - 4 > 2 + 5(2y - 3)$

PRACTICE SET

1. What is the value of $a(b - 1) + \dfrac{bc}{2}$ if $a = 3$, $b = 6$, and $c = 5$?
    A. 0
    B. 15
    C. 30
    D. 45
    E. 60   Ⓐ Ⓑ Ⓒ Ⓓ Ⓔ

2. If $\dfrac{c}{d} = 3$ and $d = 1$, then $3c + d =$
    F. 3
    G. 4
    H. 6
    J. 7
    K. 10   Ⓕ Ⓖ Ⓗ Ⓘ Ⓚ

3. What is the value of x in the equation $5x - 7 = y$, if $y = 8$?
    A. −1
    B. 1
    C. 2
    D. 3
    E. 70   Ⓐ Ⓑ Ⓒ Ⓓ Ⓔ

4. What is the value of $x(y - 2) + xz$, if $x = 2$, $y = 5$, and $z = 7$?
    F. 12
    G. 20
    H. 22
    J. 28
    K. 32   Ⓕ Ⓖ Ⓗ Ⓘ Ⓚ

5. If $x = \sqrt{3}$, $y = 2$, and $z = \frac{1}{2}$, then $x^2 - 5yz + y^2 =$
   A. 1
   B. 2
   C. 4
   D. 7
   E. 8

   Ⓐ Ⓑ Ⓒ Ⓓ Ⓔ

6. If $x + y = 7$, what is the value of $2x + 2y - 2$?
   F. 5
   G. 9
   H. 12
   J. 14
   K. 16

   Ⓕ Ⓖ Ⓗ Ⓙ Ⓚ

7. What is the value of a in the equation $3a - 6 = b$, if $b = 18$?
   A. 4
   B. 6
   C. 8
   D. 10
   E. 18

   Ⓐ Ⓑ Ⓒ Ⓓ Ⓔ

8. If $\frac{x}{y} = \frac{2}{5}$ and $x = 10$, $y =$
   F. 4
   G. 10
   H. 15
   J. 20
   K. 25

   Ⓕ Ⓖ Ⓗ Ⓙ Ⓚ

9. $-5n(3m - 2) =$
   A. $-15mn + 10n$
   B. $15mn - 10n$
   C. $-8mn + 7n$
   D. $8mn + 7n$
   E. $-2mn - 7n$

   Ⓐ Ⓑ Ⓒ Ⓓ Ⓔ

10. What is the value of $(a + b)^2$, when $a = -1$ and $b = 3$?
    F. 2
    G. 4
    H. 8
    J. 10
    K. 16

    Ⓕ Ⓖ Ⓗ Ⓙ Ⓚ

11. If $s - t = 5$, what is the value of $3s - 3t + 3$?

    A. 2
    B. 8
    C. 11
    D. 12
    E. 18

    Ⓐ Ⓑ Ⓒ Ⓓ Ⓔ

12. $(3d - 7) - (5 - 2d) =$

    F. $d - 12$
    G. $5d - 2$
    H. $5d + 12$
    J. $5d - 12$
    K. $8d + 5$

    Ⓕ Ⓖ Ⓗ Ⓙ Ⓚ

13. What is the value of $xyz + y(z - x) + 2x$ if $x = -2$, $y = 3$ and $z = 1$?

    A. -13
    B. -7
    C. -1
    D. 7
    E. 19

    Ⓐ Ⓑ Ⓒ Ⓓ Ⓔ

14. If $3x + 7 = 14$, then $x =$

    F. -14

    G. 0

    H. $\dfrac{7}{3}$

    J. 3

    K. 7

    Ⓕ Ⓖ Ⓗ Ⓙ Ⓚ

15. If x is an integer, which of the following expressions is **always** even?

    A. $2x + 1$
    B. $3x + 2$
    C. $4x + 3$
    D. $5x + 4$
    E. $6x + 2$

    Ⓐ Ⓑ Ⓒ Ⓓ Ⓔ

16. If $4z - 3 = -19$, then $z =$

    F. -16

    G. $-5\frac{1}{2}$

    H. -4

    J. 0

    K. 4 Ⓕ Ⓖ Ⓗ Ⓙ Ⓚ

17. If $3ab = 6$, what is the value of a in terms of b?

    A. 2

    B. $\frac{2}{b}$

    C. $\frac{2}{b^2}$

    D. $2b$

    E. $2b^2$ Ⓐ Ⓑ Ⓒ Ⓓ Ⓔ

18. If x and y are integers, in which equation **must** x be negative?

    F. $xy = -1$

    G. $xy^2 = -1$

    H. $x^2y = -1$

    J. $x^2y^2 = 1$

    K. $xy^2 = 1$ Ⓕ Ⓖ Ⓗ Ⓙ Ⓚ

19. If n is an odd number, which of the following expressions is **always** odd?

    A. $2n + 4$

    B. $3n + 2$

    C. $3n + 5$

    D. $5n + 5$

    E. $5n + 7$ Ⓐ Ⓑ Ⓒ Ⓓ Ⓔ

20. If $5p + 12 = 17 - 4\left(\frac{p}{2} + 1\right)$, what is the value of p?

    F. $\frac{1}{7}$

    G. $\frac{1}{3}$

    H. $\frac{6}{7}$

    J. $1\frac{2}{7}$

    K. 2 Ⓕ Ⓖ Ⓗ Ⓙ Ⓚ

21. If $\frac{2x}{5y} = 6$, what is the value of y, in terms of x?

    A. $\frac{x}{15}$

    B. $\frac{x}{2}$

    C. $\frac{15}{x}$

    D. $15x$

    E. $\frac{30}{x}$ Ⓐ Ⓑ Ⓒ Ⓓ Ⓔ

22. If x is an odd integer and y is an even integer, which of the following expressions **must** be odd?

    F. $2x + y$

    G. $2(x + y)$

    H. $x^2 + y^2$

    J. $xy + y$

    K. $2x + y^2$ Ⓕ Ⓖ Ⓗ Ⓙ Ⓚ

23. If $100 \div x = 10n$, then which of the following is equal to nx?

    A. 10

    B. $10x$

    C. 100

    D. $10xn$

    E. $1,000$ Ⓐ Ⓑ Ⓒ Ⓓ Ⓔ

24. For what value of y is $4(y - 1) = 2(y + 2)$?

    F. 0

    G. 2

    H. 4

    J. 6

    K. 8 Ⓕ Ⓖ Ⓗ Ⓙ Ⓚ

$$\frac{3}{4} + x = 8.3$$

25. What is the value of x in the equation above?

    A. 4.9

    B. 6.75

    C. 7.55

    D. 8.0

    E. 9.05 Ⓐ Ⓑ Ⓒ Ⓓ Ⓔ

26. If $2(a + m) = 5m - 3 + a$, what is the value of a, in terms of m?

    F. $\frac{3m}{2}$

    G. 3

    H. $5m$

    J. $4m + 33$

    K. $3m - 3$ Ⓕ Ⓖ Ⓗ Ⓙ Ⓚ

Exercise Answers

i. **B** $(11 + 3x) - (5 - 2x) =$

$11 + 3x - 5 + 2x =$

$11 - 5 + 3x + 2x = 6 + 5x$

ii. $-4a - b$

iii. $-a$

iv. $3y$

v. $m^2 + 10m + 16$

vi. $n^2 - 3n - 18$

vii. $a = -1$

viii. $y = 7$

ix. $x = 5$

x. $a = \dfrac{b}{5}$

xi. $x = 4$

xii. $y > 8$

$y < -3$

$y < -4$

$y < 1$

$y < \dfrac{39}{7}$

Practice Set Explanations

1. **C** Plug in $a = 3$, $b = 6$, and $c = 5$.

$$3(6 - 1) + \frac{6 \times 5}{2}$$

$$3(5) + \frac{30}{2}$$

$$15 + 15$$

$$30$$

2. **K** Since we are told the value of d, we can plug it into the equation $\frac{c}{d} = 3$ to find the value of c. We are told that $d = 1$, so $\frac{c}{d} = 3$ can be rewritten as $\frac{c}{1} = 3$. Since $\frac{c}{1}$ is the same as c, we can rewrite the equation again as $c = 3$. Now we can plug the values of c and d into the expression: $3(3) + 1 = 10$.

3.   **D**   We are told that $y = 8$, so first we will replace the y in the equation with 8, and then we can solve for x.

$$5x - 7 = y$$
$$5x - 7 = 8$$

Now we can add 7 to both sides:

$$5x - 7 + 7 = 8 + 7$$
$$5x = 15$$

Next we divide both sides by 5:

$$\frac{5x}{5} = \frac{15}{5}$$
$$x = 3$$

4.   **G**   Here we have three values to plug in. Remember, xz means x times z. After we plug in the values of x, y, and z, we will do the operations in PEMDAS order—Parentheses, Exponents, Multiplication and Division, Addition and Subtraction.

$$
\begin{aligned}
x(y - 2) + xz &= 2(5 - 2) + 2 \cdot 7 \\
&= 2(3) + 2 \cdot 7 \\
&= 6 + 14 \\
&= 20
\end{aligned}
$$

5.   **B**   This is another "plug-in" question. Remember, $5yz$ means $5 \cdot y \cdot z$. First we will replace x, y, and z with the values given. Then we will carry out the indicated operations using the PEMDAS order of operations—Parentheses, Exponents, Multiplication and Division, Addition and Subtraction.

$$
\begin{aligned}
x^2 - 5yz + y^2 &= (\sqrt{3})^2 - 5 \cdot 2 \cdot \frac{1}{2} + 2^2 \\
&= 3 - 5 \cdot 2 \cdot \frac{1}{2} + 4 \\
&= 3 - 5 + 4 \\
&= -2 + 4 \\
&= 2
\end{aligned}
$$

6.   **H**   If you look carefully at the expression $2x + 2y - 2$, you should see some similarity to $x + y = 7$. If we ignore the -2 for a moment, $2x + 2y$ is really just twice $x + y$. If it helps to make it clearer, we can factor out the 2, making $2x + 2y$ into $2(x + y)$. Since $x + y = 7$, $2(x + y)$ must equal $2(7)$, or 14. If we replace $2x + y$ with 14, the expression $2x + 2y - 2$ becomes $14 - 2$, which equals 12, or choice (H).

7.   **C**   Plug in 18 for b in the equation:

$$3a - 6 = 18$$

Isolate a on one side of the equation:

$$3a = 18 + 6$$
$$3a = 24$$

Divide both sides by 3 to find the value of a:

$$a = 8$$

8.   **K**   Substitute 10 for x in the equation:

$$\frac{10}{y} = \frac{2}{5}$$

Cross multiply:

$$(10)(5) = (2)(y)$$
$$50 = 2y$$

Divide both sides by 2 to find the value of y:

$$\frac{50}{2} = \frac{2y}{2}$$
$$25 = y$$

9.   **A**   Distribute $-5n$ to each term within the parentheses:

$$-5n(3m - 2) = (-5n)(3m) + (-5n)(-2)$$

Multiply through:

$$= -15mn + 10n$$

Note that $(-5n)(-2) = +10n$, because a negative times a negative is a positive.

10.   **G**   Plug $a = -1$ and $b = 3$ into the expression:

$$(-1 + 3)^2 =$$
$$(2)^2 = 4$$

11.   **E**   The expression can be rewritten as

$$3(s - t) + 3$$

Plug in 5 for $s - t$:

$$3(5) + 3$$
$$= 15 + 3$$
$$= 18$$

12. J Perform the operations:
$$3d - 7 - 5 - (-2d)$$

Combine like terms:
$$= 3d - (-2d) - 7 - 5$$
$$= 5d - 12$$

Note that $3d$ minus $-2d$ equals $+5d$, because subtracting a negative is the same as adding a positive.

13. C Plug in $x = -2$, $y = 3$, and $z = 1$:
$$(-2)(3)(1) + 3[(1 - (-2)] + 2(-2)$$
$$= -6 + 3(3) - 4$$
$$= -6 + 9 - 4$$
$$= 3 - 4$$
$$= -1$$

14. H To solve this problem, we have to rearrange the equation until the x is alone on one side of the = sign. Remember, when you do something to one side of the equation, you must do the same thing to the other side.

First we will take away the 7 from both sides:
$$3x + 7 = 14$$
$$3x + 7 - 7 = 14 - 7$$
$$3x = 7$$
$$\frac{3x}{3} = \frac{7}{3}$$
$$x = \frac{7}{3}$$

15. E This is another question for which we have to try each answer choice until we find one that represents an even number. Notice that the question asks which expression is always even. (E), $6x + 2$, is correct. Since 6 is even, the product of 6 and any integer is even. The sum of two even numbers is an even number, so $6x + 2$ is even.

16. H In this question, we must rearrange the equation until the z is alone on one side of the = sign. Anything we do to one side of the equation we must also do to the other side.

First we will add 3 to both sides:
$$4z - 3 = -19$$
$$4z - 3 + 3 = -19 + 3$$
$$4z = -16$$

Next we divide both sides by 4:
$$\frac{4z}{4} = \frac{16z}{4}$$
$$z = -4$$

17. **B** To solve this problem, we have to rearrange the equation until we have the variable alone on one side of the = sign.

$$3ab = 6$$
$$\frac{3ab}{3} = \frac{6}{3}$$
$$ab = 2$$
$$\frac{ab}{b} = \frac{2}{b}$$
$$a = \frac{2}{b}$$

18. **G** For this question we will have to try each answer choice until we find the correct one.

   F. $xy = -1$. If the product of two integers is negative, then one of the two integers must be negative. In this case x could be negative, but it is also possible that y is negative and x is positive. We are looking for an equation where x will always have to be negative, so this is not the correct answer.

   G. $xy^2 = -1$. The exponent here applies only to the y, not to the x. The square of any nonzero number is positive, so whatever y is, y^2 must be positive. (We know that y isn't zero; if it were, then the product xy^2 would also be zero.) Since y^2 is positive and the product of y^2 and x is negative, x must be negative. (G) is the correct answer.

19. **B** In this question we are told that n is odd, so we don't have to check to see what happens if n is even. We do have to try each answer to see which one represents an odd number. Let's say $n = 3$ and replace all the n's with 3s.

   A. $2n + 4$. $2(3) + 4 = 6 + 4 = 10$. 10 is even.
   B. $3n + 2$. $3(3) + 2 = 9 + 2 = 11$. 11 is odd, so (B) is the correct answer.

20 **F** This equation takes a few more steps than the previous ones, but it follows the same rules.

   First we multiply using the distributive law:

$$5p + 12 = 17 - 4\left(\frac{p}{2} + 1\right)$$
$$5p + 12 = 17 + \left(-4 \cdot \frac{p}{2}\right) + (-4) \cdot 1$$
$$5p + 12 = 17 + \left(-\frac{4p}{2}\right) + (-4)$$

$\frac{4p}{2}$ is equal to $2p$, so

$$5p + 12 = 17 - 2p - 4$$

Now we can combine the integers on the right side:
$$5p + 12 = 13 - 2p$$

We can add $2p$ to each side to get all the p's on one side:
$$5p + 2p + 12 = 13 - 2p + 2p$$
$$7p + 12 = 13$$

Now we will subtract 12 from both sides:
$$7p + 12 - 12 = 13 - 12$$
$$7p = 1$$

And lastly, we divide both sides by 7:
$$\frac{7p}{7} = \frac{1}{7}$$
$$p = \frac{1}{7}$$

21. **A** We want to rearrange the equation until y is alone one side of the = sign. There's more than one way to do this, but here's one way:

$$\frac{2x}{5y} = 6$$

$$(5y)\,\frac{2x}{5y} = 6(5y)$$

$$2x = 30y$$

$$\frac{x}{15} = y$$

22. **H** This is another "try each answer" problem. We are told that x is odd and y is even. Let's say that $x = 3$ and $y = 4$.

F. $2x + y$. $2(3) + 4 = 6 + 4 = 10$. 10 is even, so this is not the correct choice.

G. $2(x + y)$. $2(3 + 4) = 2(3 + 4) = 2(7) = 14$. 14 is even.

H. $x^2 + y^2$. $3^2 + 4^2 = 9 + 16 = 25$. 25 is odd, so (H) is correct.

23. **A** This problem looks harder than it really is. If
$$100 \div x = 10n \text{ then}$$
$$10n \cdot x = 100 \text{ or}$$
$$10nx = 100$$
$$nx = 10, \text{ choice (A)}.$$

24.　　**H**　　Multiply through and solve for y by isolating it on one side of the equation:

$$4(y - 1) = 2(y + 2)$$

$$4y - 4 = 2y + 4$$

$$4y - 4 - 2y + 4 = 2y + 4 - 2y + 4$$

$$\frac{2y}{2} = \frac{8}{2}$$

$$y = 4$$

25.　　**C**　　Isolate x on one side of the equation:

$$\frac{3}{4} + x = 8.3$$

$$\frac{3}{4} + x - \frac{3}{4} = 8.3 - \frac{3}{4}$$

$$x = 8.3 - \frac{3}{4}$$

Then $\frac{3}{4}$ can be rewritten as 0.75, so subtracting 0.75 from 8.3 gives you 7.55.

26.　　**K**　　Multiply through and then find a in terms of m by isolating a on one side of the equation:

$$2(a + m) = 5m - 3 + a$$

$$2a + 2m = 5m - 3 + a$$

$$2a + 2m - a - 2m = 5m - 3 + a - 2m - a$$

$$a = 3m - 3$$

10

Algebra: Word Problems

- Get an Overview of What Will Be on the Test

- Learn How to Translate Word Problems

- Practice with Backdoor Strategies for Getting the Right Answer

OVERVIEW

Word Problems

Two simple words that evoke more fear and loathing than most other math concepts or question types combined.

When the subject of word problems arises, many students envision the following nightmare:

> Two trains are loaded with equal amounts of rock salt and ball bearings. Train *A* leaves Frogboro at 10:00 A.M. carrying 62 passengers. Train *B* leaves Toadville at 11:30 A.M. carrying 104 passengers. If Train *A* is traveling at a speed of 85 mph and makes 4 stops and Train *B* is traveling at an average speed of 86 mph and makes 3 stops and the trains both arrive at Lizard Hollow at 4:30 P.M., what is the average weight of the passengers on Train *B*?

… or something along these lines.

The good news is that you will **not** see anything this ugly. SHSAT word problems are pretty straightforward. Generally, all you have to do is translate the prose to math and solve.

The bad news is that you can expect to see a lot of word problems on the test. You just have to practice and get comfortable with them. Keep in mind that, while word problems are generally algebra problems, they can contain other math concepts.

TRANSLATION

Often, word problems seem tricky because it's hard to figure out precisely what they're asking. It can be difficult to translate English into math. The following table lists some common words and phrases that turn up in word problems, along with their mathematical translations.

When you see:	Think:
sum, plus, more than, added to, combined total	+
minus, less than, difference between, decreased by	−
is, was, equals, is equivalent to, is the same as, adds up to	=
times, product, multiplied by, of, twice, double, triple	×
divided by, over, quotient, per, out of, into	÷
what, how much, how many, a number	$x, n,$ etc.

Exercise

Now, try translating the following phrases from English to math.

English	Math
y is 5 more than x.	$y = x + 5$
r equals half of s.	$r = \frac{1}{2}s$
x is twice as great as y.	$x = 2y$
Two less than m is equivalent to n.	$n = m - 2$
The product of a and b is 3 more than their sum.	

Sift Through the Fiction— Find the Math!

In some questions, the translation will be embedded within a "story." Don't be put off by the details of the scenario—it's the numbers that matter. Focus on the math and translate.

i. In a certain class there are twice as many boys as girls. If the total number of students in the class is 36, how many boys are there?

    A. 9

    B. 12

    C. 18

    D. 24

    E. 27

ii. Paul developed a roll of film containing 36 pictures. If he made 2 prints each of half of the pictures, and 1 print of each of the rest, how many prints did he make in all?

F. 18
G. 27
H. 36

J. 54
K. 72

Symbolism Word Problems

Word problems, by definition, require you to translate English to math. Some word problems contain an extra level of translation. If you have not looked at the section on Strange Symbolism and Terminology in the Arithmetic Review chapter, take a look at it now.

Symbolism word problems are like any other word problems. You just need to translate the English and the symbols into math and then solve.

Assume that the notation $\Delta(w, x, y, z)$ means "Divide the sum of w and x by y and multiply by z." What is the value of

$$\Delta(10, 4, 7, 8) + \Delta(2, 6, 4, 5)?$$

First, translate the English/symbols into math.

$$\Delta(w, x, y, z) \text{ means } \frac{w + x}{y} \times z$$

Next, plug the values into the equation.

$$\Delta(10, 4, 7, 8) + \Delta(2, 6, 4, 5) = \left(\frac{10 + 4}{7} \times 8\right) + \left(\frac{2 + 6}{4} \times 5\right) = 16 + 10 = 26$$

Now try a testlike question.

Exercise

iii. Assume that the notation $a - b$ means "Subtract 12 from the product of ab and then round the result to the nearest 10." What is the value of $14 - 10$?

A. 120
B. 128
C. 125
D. 130
E. 140

Word Problems with Formulas

Some of the more difficult word problems may involve translations with mathematical formulas. For example, you might see questions dealing with averages, rates, or areas of geometric figures. Since the SHSAT does not provide formulas for you, you have to know these going in.

If a truck travels at 50 miles per hour for $6\frac{1}{2}$ hours, how far will the truck travel?

To answer this question, you need to remember the distance formula:

$Distance = Rate \times Time$

Once you note the formula, you can just plug in the numbers.

$D = 50 \times 6.5$
$D = 325$ miles

Now try a couple of these on your own.

Exercise

iv. If the average weight of a group of 6 children is 71 pounds, what is the total weight, in pounds, of the children?

A. 331
B. 348
C. 366
D. 396

E. 426

v. If a machine produces 150 widgets in 30 minutes, how many widgets will the machine produce in 4 hours?

F. 500
G. 600
H. 750
J. 900
K. 1,200

BACKDOOR STRATEGIES

Word problems are extraordinarily susceptible to the backdoor strategies detailed in chapter 7. Here's a quick recap of Kaplan's **picking numbers** and **backsolving strategies**.

Kaplan's 3-Step Method for Picking Numbers

Step 1: Pick simple, easy-to-use numbers for each variable.

Step 2. Solve the problem using the numbers you pick.

Step 3. Plug your numbers into each answer choice. The choice that gives you the same numerical solution you arrived at in Step 2 is correct.

A Few Things to Remember:

- You can pick numbers only when the answer choices contain variables.

- Pick easy numbers rather than realistic numbers. Keep the numbers small and manageable, but try to avoid 0 and 1.

- Remember that you have to try all the answer choices. If more than one works, pick another set of numbers.

- Don't pick the same number for more than one variable.

- When picking a number for a remainder problem, add the remainder to the number you're dividing by.

- Always pick 100 for percent questions.

Try picking numbers for the following problem.

Exercise

vi. The average of four numbers is n. If three of the numbers are $n + 3$, $n + 5$, and $n - 2$, what is the value of the fourth number?

 F. $n - 6$

 G. $n - 4$

 H. n

 J. $n + 2$

 K. $n + 4$

Backsolving

- You can backsolve when the answer choices contain only numbers.

- Always start with the middle answer choice, (C) or (H).

- If the middle answer choice is not correct, you can usually eliminate two more choices simply by determining whether the value must be higher or lower.

Exercise

vii. Mike has n Hawaiian shirts, and Adam has 3 times as many Hawaiian shirts. If Adam gives Mike 6 Hawaiian shirts, they would have an equal number of Hawaiian shirts. How many Hawaiian shirts does Mike have?

 A. 3

 B. 6

 C. 9

 D. 15

 E. 18

PRACTICE SET

1. After the announcement of a sale, a bookstore sold $\frac{1}{2}$ of all its books in stock. On the following day, this bookstore sold 4,000 more books. Now only $\frac{1}{10}$ of the number of books in stock before the sale remain in the store. How many books were in stock before the announcement of the sale?
   A. 8,000
   B. 10,000
   C. 12,000
   D. 15,000
   E. 20,000   Ⓐ Ⓑ Ⓒ Ⓓ Ⓔ

2. Brad bought a radio on sale at a 20% discount from its regular price of $118. If there is an 8% sales tax that is calculated on the sale price, how much did Brad pay for the radio?
   F. $23.60
   G. $86.85
   H. $94.40
   J. $101.95
   K. $127.44   Ⓕ Ⓖ Ⓗ Ⓙ Ⓚ

3. Sheila charges $5.00 per haircut during the weekdays. On Saturday, she charges $7.50 per haircut. If Sheila has 6 customers each day of the week except Sunday, how much money does she earn in the five weekdays and Saturday?
   A. $150.00
   B. $175.00
   C. $180.00
   D. $195.00
   E. $210.00   Ⓐ Ⓑ Ⓒ Ⓓ Ⓔ

4. The original price of a television decreases by 20 percent. By what percent must the price increase to reach its original value?
   F. 15%
   G. 20%
   H. 25%
   J. 30%
   K. 40%   Ⓕ Ⓖ Ⓗ Ⓙ Ⓚ

5. Ed has 100 dollars more than Robert. After Ed spends 20 dollars on groceries, Ed has 5 times as much money as Robert. How much money does Robert have?
   A. $20
   B. $30
   C. $40
   D. $50
   E. $120   Ⓐ Ⓑ Ⓒ Ⓓ Ⓔ

6. A worker earns $15.00 an hour for the first 40 hours he works each week, and one and a half times this much for every hour over 40 hours. If he earned $667.50 for one week's work, how many hours did he work?
   F. 40
   G. 41
   H. 42
   J. 43
   K. 44
   F G H J K

7. Liza has 40 less than three times the number of books that Janice has. If B is equal to the number of books that Janice has, which of the following expressions shows the total number of books that Liza and Janice have together?
   A. $3B - 40$
   B. $3B + 40$
   C. $4B - 40$
   D. $4B$
   E. $4B + 40$
   A B C D E

8. If $a \infty b = \dfrac{ab}{a - b}$, which of the following does $3 \infty 2$ equal?
   F. $2 \infty 3$
   G. $6 \infty 1$
   H. $6 \infty 2$
   J. $6 \infty 3$
   K. $8 \infty 4$
   F G H J K

9. If William divides the amount of money he has by 5, and adds $8, the result will be $20. If X is equal to the number of dollars that William has, which of the following equations shows this relationship?
   A. $(X \div 8) + 5 = 20$
   B. $(X \div 5) + 8 = 20$
   C. $(X + 8) \div 5 = 20$
   D. $(X + 5) \div 8 = 20$
   E. $8(X + 5) = 20$
   A B C D E

10. If a six-sided pencil with a trademark on one of its sides is rolled on a table, what is the probability that the side with the trademark is **not** touching the surface of the table when the pencil stops?
    F. $\dfrac{1}{6}$
    G. $\dfrac{1}{3}$
    H. $\dfrac{1}{2}$
    J. $\dfrac{2}{3}$
    K. $\dfrac{5}{6}$
    F G H J K

11. Team *A* had 4 times as many losses as it had ties in a season. If Team *A* won none of its games, which could be the total number of games it played that season?

    A. 12
    B. 15
    C. 18
    D. 21
    E. 26
                            Ⓐ Ⓑ Ⓒ Ⓓ Ⓔ

12. On a field trip, 587 people are travelling by bus. If each bus seats 48 people and all the buses are filled to capacity except one, how many people sit in the unfilled bus?

    F. 37
    G. 36
    H. 12
    J. 11
    K. 7
                            Ⓕ Ⓖ Ⓗ Ⓙ Ⓚ

13. Rose has finished $\frac{5}{6}$ of her novel after one week of reading. If she reads an additional tenth of the novel during the next 2 days, what part of the novel will she have read?

    A. $\frac{1}{10}$

    B. $\frac{7}{15}$

    C. $\frac{4}{5}$

    D. $\frac{14}{15}$

    E. $\frac{29}{30}$
                            Ⓐ Ⓑ Ⓒ Ⓓ Ⓔ

14. A farmer has $4\frac{2}{3}$ acres of land for growing corn, and $2\frac{1}{2}$ times as many acres for growing wheat. How many acres does she have for wheat?

    F. $2\frac{2}{3}$

    G. $4\frac{1}{2}$

    H. $8\frac{1}{6}$

    J. $10\frac{1}{2}$

    K. $11\frac{2}{3}$
                            Ⓕ Ⓖ Ⓗ Ⓙ Ⓚ

15. Joyce baked 42 biscuits for her 12 guests. If 6 biscuits remain uneaten, what is the average number of biscuits that the guests ate?

    A. 2
    B. 3
    C. 4
    D. 6
    E. 12
                            Ⓐ Ⓑ Ⓒ Ⓓ Ⓔ

16. The average weight of Jake, Ken, and Larry is 60 kilograms. If Jake and Ken both weigh 50 kilograms, how much, in kilograms, does Larry weigh?

    F. 40
    G. 50
    H. 60
    J. 70
    K. 80   Ⓕ Ⓖ Ⓗ Ⓘ Ⓚ

17. If 3 added to 4 times a number is 11, the number must be

    A. 1
    B. 2
    C. 3
    D. 4
    E. 5   Ⓐ Ⓑ Ⓒ Ⓓ Ⓔ

18. If the sum of 8 and a certain number, b, is equal to 20 minus the same number, then $b = $?

    F. 2
    G. 4
    H. 6
    J. 10
    K. 14   Ⓕ Ⓖ Ⓗ Ⓘ Ⓚ

19. Liz worked 3 less than twice as many hours as Rachel did. If W is the number of hours Rachel worked, which of the following expressions shows the total number of hours worked by Liz and Rachel together?

    A. $2W - 3$
    B. $2W + 3$
    C. $3W - 3$
    D. $3W + 3$
    E. $4W - 2$ Ⓐ Ⓑ Ⓒ Ⓓ Ⓔ

20. The area of a circle is πr^2 where r is the radius. If the circumference of a circle is $h\pi$, what is the area of the circle, in terms of h?

    F. $h^2 r^2$

    G. $\dfrac{h^2\pi}{4}$

    H. $\dfrac{h^2\pi}{2}$

    J. $h^2\pi$

    K. $4h^2\pi$ Ⓕ Ⓖ Ⓗ Ⓘ Ⓚ

21. If $m \neq 0$ and $m \neq 1$, $m \ddagger = \dfrac{m}{m^2 - m}$. What is the value of $6 \ddagger - (-5)\ddagger$?

    A. $\dfrac{1}{30}$

    B. $\dfrac{1}{20}$

    C. $\dfrac{1}{4}$

    D. $\dfrac{11}{30}$

    E. $\dfrac{9}{20}$

    Ⓐ Ⓑ Ⓒ Ⓓ Ⓔ

22. Five less than 3 times a certain number is equal to twice the original number plus 7. What is the original number?

    F. 2

    G. $2\dfrac{2}{5}$

    H. 6

    J. 11

    K. 12

    Ⓕ Ⓖ Ⓗ Ⓙ Ⓚ

23. The volume of a sphere is $\dfrac{4}{3}\pi r^3$, where r is the radius. What is the volume of a sphere with a radius of 3?

    A. 4π

    B. 8π

    C. 16π

    D. 36π

    E. 72π

    Ⓐ Ⓑ Ⓒ Ⓓ Ⓔ

Exercise Answers

Translation exercise

$$y = x + 5$$
$$r = \frac{s}{2} \text{ or } 2r = s$$
$$x = 2y$$
$$n = m - 2$$
$$ab = (a + b) + 3$$

i.   **D** $2g = b$

$$g + b = 36$$
$$g + 2g = 36$$
$$3g = 36$$
$$g = 12$$
$$12 + b = 36$$
$$b = 24$$

ii.   **J** $36 \div 2 = 18$

$$(18 \times 2) + (18 \times 1) =$$
$$36 + 18 = 54$$

iii.   **D** $14 - 10 = (14)(10) - 12$ (rounded to nearest 10)
$$= 140 - 12$$
$$= 128 \text{ rounded} = 130$$

iv.   **K** $\text{Average} = \dfrac{\text{Sum of terms}}{\text{Number of terms}}$

$$71 = \frac{x}{6}$$
$$x = 71 \times 6$$
$$x = 426$$

v.   **E** $\text{Total widgets} = \text{Rate} \times \text{Time}$

$$\text{Total widgets} = \frac{150}{30 \text{ min}} \times 4 \text{ hours}$$

$$\text{Total widgets} = \frac{150}{\frac{1}{2} \text{ hr}} \times 4 \text{ hours}$$

$$\text{Total widgets} = 1{,}200$$

vi.   **F**   Pick an easy number for n, such as 10. If the average of four numbers is 10, the sum of the four numbers is 40 ($4 \times 10 = 40$). If three of the numbers are $n + 3$, $n + 5$, and $n - 2$, then those three numbers are $10 + 3$, $10 + 5$, and $10 - 2$ or 13, 15, and 8. Then $13 + 15 + 8 = 36$. The sum of the four numbers must equal 40, so the remaining number is 4. If you plug 10 in for n in each of the answer choices, only (F) gives you 4.

vii.   **B**   Start with the middle answer choice—9. If Mike has 9 shirts, then Adam has three times as many, or 27. If Adam gives Mike 6 shirts, Adam now has 21, and Mike has 15. This is not equal, so (C) is not correct. Since Adam was left with too many shirts when Mike had 9, Mike must have fewer than 9. Try answer choice (B). If Mike has 6 shirts, then Adam has 18. If Adam gives Mike 6, then they both have 12 shirts.

Practice Set Explanations

1.   **B**   After two days of the sale, $\frac{1}{10}$ of the original number of books in stock is left. This means that altogether, $\frac{9}{10}$ of the original number of books have been sold. Of the books, $\frac{1}{2}$ were sold on the first day; $\frac{1}{2}$ can also be called $\frac{5}{10}$. If $\frac{9}{10}$ were sold in two days, and $\frac{5}{10}$ were sold on the first day, then on the second day $\frac{4}{10}$ must have been sold. You are told that 4,000 books were sold on the second day, so 4,000 must be $\frac{4}{10}$ of the original number of books. Now you need to determine what number 4,000 is $\frac{4}{10}$ of. Call the number N. If $\frac{4}{10} N = 4{,}000$, then $N = \frac{10}{4}(4{,}000) = 10(1{,}000) = 10{,}000$.

2.　**J**　This problem needs to be done in several steps. First find out what the sale price of the radio was. The discount was 20%, so the sale price was 80% of the original price.

> Percent • Whole = Part
> 80% • \$118 = Sale Price
> 0.80 • \$118 = Sale Price
> \$94.40 = Sale Price

Now figure out how much tax Brad paid. The tax was 8% of the sale price.

> Percent • Whole = Part
> 8% • \$94.40 = Tax
> 0.08 • \$94.40 = Tax
> \$7.5520 = Tax
> \$7.55 = Tax

Now just add the tax to the sale price.

> \$94.40 + 7.55 = \$101.95

3.　**D**　Each weekday Sheila earns

> \$5.00 • 6 haircuts = \$30 per weekday

Each Saturday Sheila earns

> \$7.50 • 6 haircuts = \$45 per Saturday

In 5 weekdays she earns 5 • \$30 = \$150.
In 1 Saturday she earns \$45.
So in 5 weekdays plus 1 Saturday, Sheila earns \$150 + \$45, or \$195.

4.　**H**　The key is that while the value of the TV decreases and increases by the same amount, it doesn't increase and decrease by the same percent. Let's pick \$100 for the price of the television. If the price decreases by 20%, then since 20% of \$100 is \$20, the price decreases by \$20. The new price is \$100 − \$20, or \$80. For the new price to reach the original price (\$100), it must be increased by \$20. Then \$20 is $\frac{1}{4}$80, or 25% of \$80. The new price must be increased by 25%, choice (H).

5.　**A**　Translate to get two equations. Let E be the amount Ed has and R be the amount Robert has.

"Ed has \$100 more than Robert," becomes $E = R + 100$.
"Ed spends \$20," means he'll have \$20 less, or $E - 20$.
"5 times as much as Robert," becomes $5R$. Therefore, $E - 20 = 5R$.
Substitute $R + 100$ for E in the second equation and solve for R:

$$(R + 100) - 20 = 5R$$
$$R + 80 = 5R$$
$$80 = 4R$$
$$20 = R$$

So Robert has \$20.

6.   J   Run the answer choices through the information given in the stem, to see which gives a total of $667.50. Since the answer choices are in numerical order, start with the middle choice, (H). If he works for 42 hours, he earns $15 per hour for the first 40 hours, or $600. He earns $1\frac{1}{2}$ times his normal rate for the two extra hours, and $\frac{3}{2}$ times $15 is $22.50 per hour. Since he worked 2 hours at that rate, he made an additional $45. The total is $645, which is not enough. Now you know that not only is answer choice (H) too small, but so are (F) and (G). Now try choice (J). He still earns $600 for the first 40 hours, but now you have to multiply the overtime rate, $22.50, by 3, which gives you $67.50. The total is $667.50, which means that answer choice (J) is correct.

7.   C   This is a simple translation problem. You're told that Janice has B books. Liza has 40 less than 3 times the number of books Janice has, which you can translate as $L = 3B - 40$. The total number they have together equals $B + (3B - 40)$, or $4B - 40$, which is choice (C).

8.   J   Plug in the given values to solve. Then try the values in each answer choice until you find the one that produces the same result. Plugging in 3 and 2 gives you $\frac{(3)(2)}{3 - 2} = \frac{6}{1} = 6$. So you're looking for the answer choice that produces a result of 6. Only (J) does, so it is correct.

9.   B   This problem asks you to translate from English sentences into math.

The amount of money William has: X
This amount divided by 5: $X \div 5$
Add 8 dollars: $X \div 5 + 8$
The result is 20 dollars: $(X \div 5) + 8 = 20$, choice (B).

Since division comes before addition in the order of operations, the parentheses aren't really necessary.

10.   K   The probability of an event happening is the ratio of the number of desired outcomes possible to the total number of possible outcomes, or

$$\text{Probability} = \frac{\text{Sum of the terms}}{\text{Number of the terms}}$$

If one side of the pencil has the trademark on it, then the other 5 sides are blank. When any one of these 5 blank sides is touching the surface of the table, the marked side cannot be touching the table. So there are 5 different ways for the pencil to lie on the table without the marked side touching the surface. The total number of possible sides for the pencil to lie on is 6. The probability that the trademark will not be touching the surface of the table when the pencil stops rolling is $\frac{5}{6}$, choice (K).

11.   **B**   Let the number of ties Team A had $= x$. It lost 4 times as many games as it tied, or $4x$ games. It had no wins, so the total number of games played by Team A is $x + 4x = 5x$. So the number of games played must be a multiple of 5; the only choice that is a multiple of 5 is (B), 15.

12.   **J**   There are a total of 587 people traveling, and each bus holds 48 people. Then $587 \div 48 = 12$ with a remainder of 11. So 12 buses are full, and 11 people remain to ride in the unfilled bus.

13.   **D**   Rose read $\frac{5}{6}$ of the novel and plans to read another $\frac{1}{10}$, which will result in her having read $\frac{5}{6} + \frac{1}{10}$ of the novel. Add these two fractions, using 30 as the common denominator:

$$\frac{5}{6} + \frac{1}{10} = \frac{25}{30} + \frac{3}{30} = \frac{28}{30} = \frac{14}{15}$$

14.   **K**   The farmer has $4\frac{2}{3} \times 2\frac{1}{2}$ acres for growing wheat. Change these mixed numbers to fractions in order to multiply:

$$\frac{14}{3} \times \frac{5}{2} = \frac{35}{3} = 11\frac{2}{3}$$

15.   **B**   If 6 biscuits remained, $42 - 6 = 36$ were eaten by the 12 guests.

Average $= \dfrac{\text{Sum of the terms}}{\text{Number of the terms}}$, so the average number of biscuits eaten by the guests was $\frac{36}{12} = 3$.

16.   **K**   Average $= \dfrac{\text{Number of desired outcomes}}{\text{Number of possible outcomes}}$, so

$$60 \times 3 = \text{Total weight}$$
$$180 = \text{Total weight}$$

Jake and Ken each weigh 50 pounds, so $50 + 50 +$ Larry's weight $= 180$ pounds, and Larry must weigh 80 pounds.

17.   **B**   Let the number be x. Translating gives you $3 + 4x = 11$, $4x = 8$, and $x = 2$.

18.   **H**   Translate from English to math. The sum of 8 and b is simply $8 + b$. The question states that this is equal to 20 minus the same number, or $20 - b$. So your equation is $8 + b = 20 - b$, and you can solve for b:

$$8 + b = 20 - b$$
$$2b = 12$$
$$b = 6$$

19.   **C**   Rachel worked W hours, and Liz worked 3 less than twice as many hours as Rachel, or $2W - 3$. Add these expressions to find the total number of hours worked by Liz and Rachel together:

$$W + 2W - 3 = 3W - 3, \text{ choice (C)}$$

20.   G   The circumference of a circle is π times diameter, so a circumference of $h\pi$ means a diameter of h. The radius is half the diameter, or $\frac{h}{2}$. Plug $\frac{h}{2}$ into the area formula:

$$\pi\left(\frac{h}{2}\right)^2 = \pi\left(\frac{h^2}{4}\right) = \left(\frac{h^2\pi}{4}\right)$$

21.   D   Just plug into the expression that defines the symbol ‡:

$$6‡ - (-5)‡ = \frac{6}{6^2 - 6} - \frac{-5}{(-5)^2 - (-5)}$$
$$= \frac{6}{36 - 6} - \frac{-5}{25 + 5}$$
$$= \frac{3}{60} - \frac{-5}{3C}$$
$$= \frac{6}{30} + \frac{5}{30} = \frac{11}{30}$$

Note that at two points in your calculation, it is crucial to remember that subtracting a negative is the same as adding a positive.

22.   K   Call the unknown number x. Then 5 less than three times the number, or $3x - 5$, equals twice the original number plus 7, or $2x + 7$. So $3x - 5 = 2x + 7$. Solve for x:

$$3x - 5 = 2x + 7$$
$$x - 5 = 7$$
$$x = 12$$

23.   D   All you need to do is plug the value of $r = 3$ into the formula you're given and simplify:

$$\text{volume} = \frac{4}{3}\pi(3)^3$$
$$= \frac{4}{3}\pi(27)$$
$$= 36\pi$$

11

Geometry Review

- Get an Overview of What Will Be on the Test

- Review the Geometry Content You Need to Know

- Practice Set

OVERVIEW

You'll definitely see some geometry on the SHSAT. Like the rest of the math you'll see on the test, SHSAT geometry will range from straightforward to difficult and tricky. You can count on seeing questions that test your knowledge of lines and angles, triangles, circles, and other assorted geometric figures. Additionally, you'll see a little coordinate geometry. Remember that diagramless geometry can also show up as word problems.

The most helpful thing you can do is review geometry content and practice a whole bunch of geometry problems. Before moving forward, you should turn to the Resources Section in the back of the book and review 100 Essential Math Concepts items 69–100. Next, read through this chapter, spending more time with the subjects that are less familiar to you. Make certain that you do all of the problems in the practice set, even if you feel comfortable with the geometry problems presented.

A major point to remember is that you should not assume that diagrams are drawn to scale. Keep this in mind so that you do not carelessly "eyeball" diagrams and reach false conclusions.

Don't Let Your Eyes Fool You

Figures are **not** necessarily drawn to scale. Don't "eyeball" unless specifically told the diagram is drawn to scale.

GEOMETRY CONTENT REVIEW

Lines and Angles

Line Segments

Some of the most basic geometry problems on the SHSAT deal with line segments. A **line segment** is a piece of a line, and it has an exact measurable length. Questions will give you a segment divided into several pieces, give you the measurements of some of these pieces, and ask you for the measurement of a particular piece.

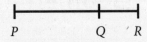

If $PR = 12$ and $QR = 4$, $PQ =$

$PQ = PR - QR$

$PQ = 12 - 4$

$PQ = 8$

The point exactly in the middle of a line segment, halfway between the endpoints, is called the **midpoint** of the line segment. To *bisect* means to cut in half, so the midpoint of a line segment bisects that line segment.

Midpoint

The midpoint of a line segment bisects that line segment.

 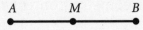

M is the midpoint of AB, so $AM = MB$.

Exercise

i. If points A, D, B, and C lie on a line in that order, and $AB = 8$, $DC = 16$, and D is the midpoint of AB, then $AC = ?$

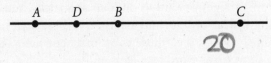

20

Angles

Rule to Remember

A straight angle contains 180°.

A **right angle** measures 90 degrees and is usually indicated in a diagram by a little box. The figure above is a right angle. Lines that intersect to form right angles are said to be **perpendicular.**

Angles that form a straight line add up to 180 degrees. In the figure above, $a + b = 180$.

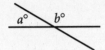

When two lines intersect, **adjacent angles are supplementary,** meaning they add up to 180 degrees. In the figure above, $a + b = 180$.

Angles around a point add up to 360 degrees. In the figure above, $a + b + c + d + e = 360$.

Recall

Angles around a point add up to 360º.

When lines intersect, angles across the vertex from each other are called **vertical angles** and **are equal to each other.** Above, $a = c$ and $b = d$.

Exercise
In the following figures, find x:

ii.

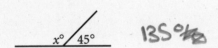

135%

iii.

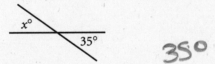

35°

iv.

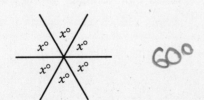

60°

Parallel Lines

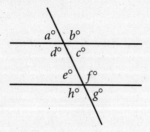

When parallel lines are crossed by a transversal,

- **Corresponding angles are equal (for example, $a = e$).**
- **Alternate interior angles are equal ($d = f$).**
- **Same side interior angles are supplementary ($c + f = 180$).**
- **All four acute angles are equal, as are all four obtuse angles.**

Triangles

Triangles in General

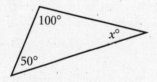

The three interior angles of any triangle **add up to 180°**. In this figure, $x + 50 + 100 = 180$, so $x = 30$.

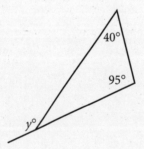

An exterior angle of a triangle is equal to the **sum of the remote interior angles**. In this figure, the exterior angle labeled $y°$ is equal to the sum of the remote angles: $y = 40 + 95 = 135$.

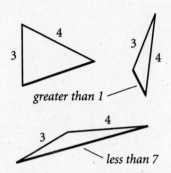

greater than 1

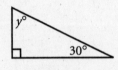

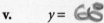

less than 7

Don't Forget

The length of one side of a triangle must be greater than the
positive difference and less than
the sum of the lengths of the
other two sides.

The length of one side of a triangle must be **greater than the positive difference** and **less than the sum** of the lengths of the other two sides. For example, if it is given that the length of one side is 3 and the length of another side is 4, then you know that the length of the third side must be greater than $4 - 3 = 1$ and less than $4 + 3 = 7$.

Exercise

v. $y = 68$

vi.   If two sides of a triangle are 5 and 8, which of the following could be the length of its third side? (circle all that are possible)

3   5   9   13   15

Triangles—Area and Perimeter

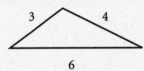

The **perimeter** of a triangle is the sum of the lengths of its sides.

The **perimeter** of the triangle in the figure above is
     $3 + 4 + 6 = 13$

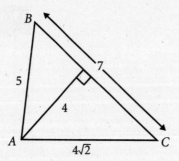

Area of triangle $= \frac{1}{2}$(**base**)(**height**)

The height is the perpendicular distance between the side that's chosen as the base and the opposite vertex. In this triangle, 4 is the height when the 7 is chosen as the base.

$$\text{Area} = \frac{1}{2}\,bh = \frac{1}{2}(7)(4) = 14$$

Exercise

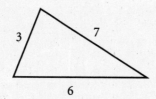

vii.   Perimeter = 16

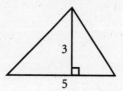

viii.   Area = 7.5

Similar Triangles

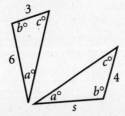

Similar triangles have the same shape: **corresponding angles are equal,** and **corresponding sides are proportional**. The triangles above are similar because they have the same angles. The 3 corresponds to the 4 and the 6 corresponds to the s.

$$\frac{3}{4} = \frac{6}{s}$$
$$3s = 24$$
$$s = 8$$

Special Triangles

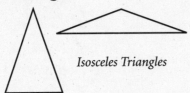

Isosceles Triangles

An isosceles triangle is a triangle that has **two equal sides**. Not only are two sides equal, but the angles opposite the equal sides, called base angles, are also equal.

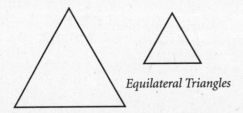

Equilateral Triangles

Equilateral triangles are triangles in which **all three sides are equal**. Since all the sides are equal, all the angles are also equal. All three angles in an equilateral triangle measure 60 degrees, regardless of the lengths of sides.

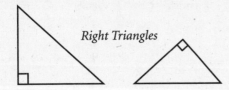

Right Triangles

A right triangle is a triangle with a **right angle**. Every right triangle has exactly two acute angles. The sides opposite the acute angles are called the **legs**. The side opposite the right angle is called the hypotenuse. Since it's opposite the largest angle, the hypotenuse is the longest side of a right triangle.

Right Triangles

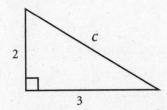

The Pythagorean Theorem:

$$(\text{leg}_1)^2 + (\text{leg}_2)^2 = (\text{hypotenuse})^2$$

If one leg is 2 and the other leg is 3, and the hypotenuse is c, then

$$2^2 + 3^2 = c^2$$

$$c^2 = 4 + 9$$

$$c = \sqrt{13}$$

Exercise

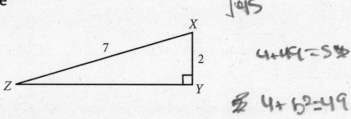

ix.   In right triangle XYZ, what is the length of YZ?

Pythagorean "Triplets"

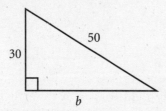

If a right triangle's leg-to-leg ratio is 3:4, or if the leg-to-hypotenuse ratio is 3:5 or 4:5, it's a 3-4-5 triangle, and you don't need to use the Pythagorean theorem to find the third side. Just figure out what multiple of 3-4-5 it is. In this right triangle, one leg is 30, and the hypotenuse is 50. This is 10 times 3-4-5. The other leg is 40.

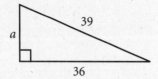

If a right triangle's leg-to-leg ratio is 5:12, or if the leg-to-hypotenuse ratio is 5:13 or 12:13, then it's a **5-12-13 triangle**, and you don't need to use the Pythagorean theorem to find the third side. Just figure out what multiple of 5-12-13 it is. Here, one leg is 36, and the hypotenuse is 39. This is 3 times 5-12-13. The other leg is 15.

Exercise

Find the missing side in each of the following triangles:

x.

xi.

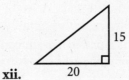

xii.

Side-Angle Ratios

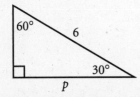

The sides of a 30-60-90 triangle are in a ratio of $x : x\sqrt{3} : 2x$. You don't need to use the Pythagorean theorem. If the hypotenuse is 6, then the shorter leg is half that, or 3; the longer leg is equal to the short leg times $\sqrt{3}$, or $3\sqrt{3}$.

Time-Saving Tip

Be on the lookout for "special" right triangles. Recognizing them can save you time and gain you points on the SHSAT.

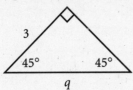

The sides of a 45-45-90 triangle are in a ratio of $x : x : x\sqrt{2}$.

If one leg is 3, then the other leg is also 3, and the hypotenuse is equal to a leg times $\sqrt{2}$, or $3\sqrt{2}$.

Quadrilaterals

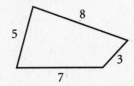

The **perimeter** of a polygon is the sum of the lengths of its sides.

The perimeter of the quadrilateral in the figure above is $5 + 8 + 3 + 7 = 23$.

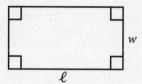

A **rectangle** is a parallelogram containing four right angles. Opposite sides are equal. The formula for the area of a rectangle is

Area = (Length)(Width)

In the diagram above, ℓ = length and w = width, so area = ℓw.

Perimeter = 2(ℓ + w)

A **square** is a rectangle with four equal sides. The formula for the area of a square is

Area = (Side)^2

In the diagram above, s = the length of a side, so area = s^2.

Perimeter = 4s

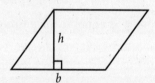

A **parallelogram** is a quadrilateral with two sets of parallel sides. Opposite sides are equal, as are opposite angles. The formula for the area of a parallelogram is

Area = (base)(height)

In the diagram above, h = height and b = base, so area = bh.

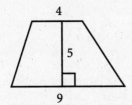

A **trapezoid** is a quadrilateral with one pair of parallel sides.

The formula for the area of a trapezoid is

$$\text{Area} = \frac{1}{2}\,(\text{Sum of the lengths of the parallel sides})(\text{Height})$$

In the diagram above, the area of the trapezoid is $\frac{1}{2}\,(4 + 9)(5) = 32.5$.

If **two polygons are similar**, then corresponding angles are equal, and corresponding sides are in proportion.

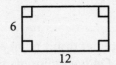

In the two rectangles above, the angles are all the same (all rectangles have four 90° angles), and the sides of the larger are 1.5 times the sides of the smaller. Therefore, these two rectangles are similar.

Exercise

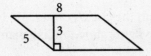

xiii. What is the area of the parallelogram above?

24

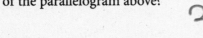

xiv. What is the area of the trapezoid above?

24

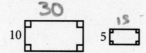

xv. The rectangles above are similar. If the area of the larger rectangle is 300, what is the area of the smaller rectangle?

~~150~~ 75

Circles

A **circle** is a figure each point of which is an equal distance from its center. In the diagram, O is the center of the circle.

The **radius** of a circle is the straight-line distance from its center to any point on the circle. All radii of one circle have equal lengths. In the figure above, OA is a radius of circle O.

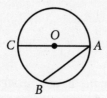

A **chord** is a line segment that connects any two points on a circle. Segments AB and AC are both chords. The largest chord that may be drawn in a circle will be a diameter of that circle.

A **diameter** of a circle is a chord that passes through the circle's center. All diameters are the same length and are equal to twice the radius. In the figure above, AC is a diameter of circle O.

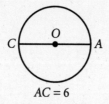

$AC = 6$

The **circumference** of a circle is the distance around it. It is equal to πd, or $2\pi r$. In this example, Circumference $= \pi d = 6\pi$.

The **area** of a circle equals π times the square of the radius, or πr^2. In this example, since AC is the diameter, $r = \frac{6}{2} = 3$, and

$$\text{Area} = \pi r^2 = \pi(3^2) = 9\pi$$

Exercise

xvi.   Radius = 3

Diameter = 6

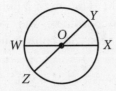

xvii. $OZ = 4$

$WX = 8$

$OX = 4$

xviii.   Radius = 8

Circumference = 50.24

xix.   Area = 16π

Radius = 4

Estimating π

π is approximately 3.14, but all you need to remember is that it's a little more than 3.

Coordinate Geometry

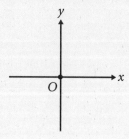

The diagram above represents the coordinate axes—the perpendicular "number lines" in the coordinate plane. The horizontal line is called the **x-axis**. The vertical line is called the **y-axis**. In a coordinate plane, the point O at which the two axes intersect is called the origin.

The pair of numbers, written inside parentheses, that specifies the location of a point in the coordinate plane is called **coordinates**. The first number is the x-coordinate, and the second number is the y-coordinate. The origin is the zero point on both axes, with coordinates (0, 0).

Starting at the origin:

to the right:	x is positive
to the left:	x is negative
up:	y is positive
down:	y is negative

The two axes divide the coordinate plane into four quadrants. When you know what quadrant a point lies in, you know the signs of its coordinates. A point in the upper left quadrant, for example, has a negative x-coordinate and a positive y-coordinate.

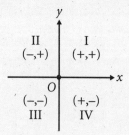

Plotting Points

If you were asked to graph the point $(2, -3)$ you would start at the origin and count 2 units to the right and 3 down. To graph $(-4, 5)$, you would start at the origin and go 4 units to the left and 5 units up.

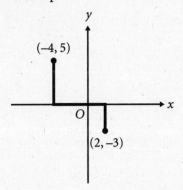

Slope of a Line

To **use two points to find the slope of a line**, use the following formula:

$$\text{Slope} = \frac{\text{Change in } y}{\text{Change in } x} = \frac{\text{rise}}{\text{run}}$$

In general, the slope of a line connecting the points (x_1, y_1) and (x_2, y_2) is

$$\frac{y_2 - y_1}{x_2 - x_1}$$

The slope of a line that contains the points $A(4, 6)$ and $B(0, -3)$ is calculated as follows:

$$\frac{y_2 - y_1}{x_2 - x_1} = \frac{-3 - 6}{0 - 4} = \frac{-9}{-4} = \frac{9}{4}$$

To **use an equation of a line to find the slope**, put the equation into the **slope-intercept form**:

$y = mx + b$, where the slope is m.

To find the slope of the equation $5x + 3y = 6$, rearrange it:

$$5x + 3y = 6$$

$$3y = -5x + 6$$

$$y = \frac{-5x}{3} + 2$$

The slope is $-\frac{5}{3}$.

Finding Lengths

When a line segment is **parallel to the x-axis** in the coordinate plane, its length is the absolute value of the difference of its x-coordinates.

When a line segment is **parallel to the y-axis** in the coordinate plane, its length is the absolute value of the difference of its y-coordinates.

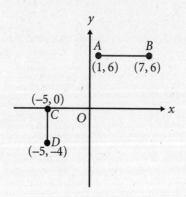

In the figure above, the length of segment AB is $|7 - 1| = 6$. The length of segment CD is $|0 - (-4)| = 4$.

Exercise

xx. Find the slopes of the lines that contain the following points:

(0, 3) and (4, 5)   ½ ~~2~~

(−1, 2) and (9, 8)   3/5

xxi. Find the slopes of the following lines:

$y = 2x - 3$ 2

$y = -\frac{1}{5}x + 2$ −1/5

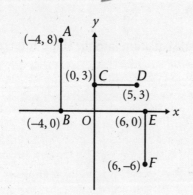

xxii. Find the lengths of the line segments graphed above:

1. $AB =$ 8

2. $CD =$ ~~5~~ 5

3. $EF =$ −6

PRACTICE SET

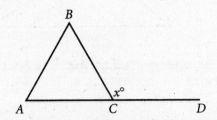

1. In the figure above, segments *AB, BC, CD,* and *AC* are all equal. What is the value of *x*?

    A. 30
    B. 45
    C. 60
    D. 90
    E. 120   Ⓐ Ⓑ Ⓒ Ⓓ Ⓔ

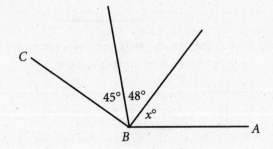

2. If the measure of angle *ABC* is 145°, what is the value of *x*?

    F. 39
    G. 45
    H. 52
    J. 55
    K. 62   Ⓕ Ⓖ Ⓗ Ⓙ Ⓚ

3. If the perimeter of a square is 32 meters, then what is the area of the square, in square meters?

    A. 16
    B. 32
    C. 48
    D. 56
    E. 64   Ⓐ Ⓑ Ⓒ Ⓓ Ⓔ

4. In triangle *XYZ*, the measure of angle *Y* is twice the measure of angle *X*, and the measure of *Z* is three times the measure of angle *X*. What is the measure of angle *Y*?

    F. 15
    G. 30
    H. 45
    J. 60
    K. 90   Ⓕ Ⓖ Ⓗ Ⓙ Ⓚ

5. The perimeter of triangle *ABC* is 24. If *AB* = 9 and *BC* = 7, then *AC* =

    A. 6
    B. 8
    C. 10
    D. 15
    E. 17   Ⓐ Ⓑ Ⓒ Ⓓ Ⓔ

6. If the perimeter of an equilateral triangle is 150, what is the length of one of its sides?

    F. 15
    G. 35
    H. 50
    J. 75
    K. 100   Ⓕ Ⓖ Ⓗ Ⓙ Ⓚ

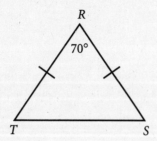

7. In triangle *RST*, if *RS* = *RT*, what is the degree measure of angle *S*?

   A. 40
   B. 55
   C. 70
   D. 110
   E. Cannot be determined from the information
      given.   Ⓐ Ⓑ Ⓒ Ⓓ Ⓔ

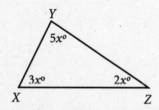

8. In triangle *XYZ*, what is the measure of angle *YXZ*?

   F. 18
   G. 36
   H. 54
   J. 72
   K. 90   Ⓕ Ⓖ Ⓗ Ⓙ Ⓚ

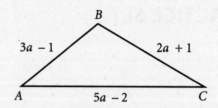

9. If the perimeter of triangle *ABC* is 18, what is the length
   of *AC*?

   A. 2
   B. 4
   C. 5
   D. 6
   E. 8   Ⓐ Ⓑ Ⓒ Ⓓ Ⓔ

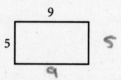

10. What is the area, in square units, of a square that has the
    same perimeter as the rectangle above?

    F. 25
    G. 36
    H. 49
    J. 64
    K. 81   Ⓕ Ⓖ Ⓗ Ⓙ Ⓚ

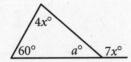

11. What is the value of *a* in the figure above?

    A.   20

    B.   40

    C.   60

    D.   80

    E.   140   Ⓐ Ⓑ Ⓒ Ⓓ Ⓔ

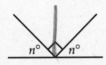

12. In the figure above, what is the value of *n* ?

    F.   30

    G.   60

    H.   45

    J.   90

    K.   135   Ⓕ Ⓖ Ⓗ Ⓙ Ⓚ

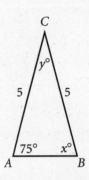

13. In the figure above, what is the value of $x - y$?

    A.   30

    B.   45

    C.   75

    D.   105

    E.   150   Ⓐ Ⓑ Ⓒ Ⓓ Ⓔ

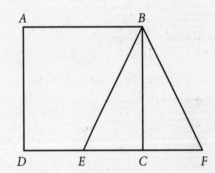

14. A square and a triangle are drawn together as shown above. The perimeter of the square is 64, and $DC = EF$. What is the area of triangle *BEF* ?

    F.   32

    G.   64

    H.   128

    J.   256

    K.   It cannot be determined from the information given.   Ⓕ Ⓖ Ⓗ Ⓙ Ⓚ

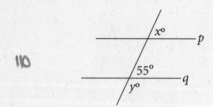

15. If line p is parallel to line q, what is the value of $x + y$?

A. 90

B. 110

C. 125

D. 180

E. 250

Ⓐ Ⓑ Ⓒ Ⓓ Ⓔ

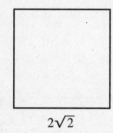

$2\sqrt{2}$

16. What is the area of the square above?

F. 4

G. 8

H. $4\sqrt{2}$

J. 16

K. 24

Ⓕ Ⓖ Ⓗ Ⓙ Ⓚ

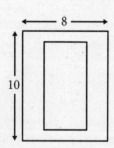

17. What is the area of the frame in the above diagram if the inside picture has a length of 8 and a width of 4?

A. 4

B. 8

C. 16

D. 24

E. 48

Ⓐ Ⓑ Ⓒ Ⓓ Ⓔ

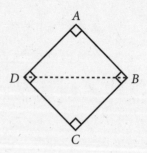

18. In the diagram above, $ABCD$ is a square and the area of triangle ABD is 8. What is the area of square $ABCD$?

F. 2

G. 4

H. 8

J. 16

K. 64

Ⓕ Ⓖ Ⓗ Ⓙ Ⓚ

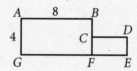

19. In the above diagram, $ABFG$ and $CDEF$ are rectangles, C bisects BF, and EF has a length of 2. What is the area of the entire figure?

A. 4

B. 16

C. 32

D. 36

E. 72

Ⓐ Ⓑ Ⓒ Ⓓ Ⓔ

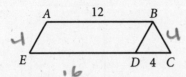

20. In the above diagram, *ABDE* is a parallelogram, and *BCD* is an equilateral triangle. What is the perimeter of *ABCE*?

    F. 12
    G. 16
    H. 24
    J. 32
    K. 36   Ⓕ Ⓖ Ⓗ Ⓙ Ⓚ

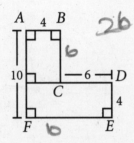

21. In the above diagram, what is the perimeter of *ABCDEF*?

    A. 14
    B. 24
    C. 28
    D. 38
    E. 40   Ⓐ Ⓑ Ⓒ Ⓓ Ⓔ

22. If the shaded regions are 4 rectangles, what is the area of the unshaded region?

    F. 9
    G. 12
    H. 16
    J. 19
    K. 20   Ⓕ Ⓖ Ⓗ Ⓙ Ⓚ

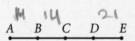

23. In the figure above, *AB* is twice the length of *BC*, *BC* = *CD* and *DE* is triple the length of *CD*. If *AE* = 49, what is the length of *BD*?

    A. 14
    B. 20
    C. 22
    D. 24.5
    E. 29   Ⓐ Ⓑ Ⓒ Ⓓ Ⓔ

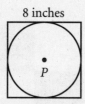

8 inches

24. In the figure above, circle *P* is inscribed in a square with sides length 8 inches. What is the area of the circle?

    F. 4π square inches

    G. 6π square inches

    H. 8π square inches

    J. 16π square inches

    K. 32π square inches   Ⓕ Ⓖ Ⓗ Ⓙ Ⓚ

25. What is the radius of a circle whose circumference is 36π?

    A. 3

    B. 6

    C. 8

    D. 18

    E. 36   Ⓐ Ⓑ Ⓒ Ⓓ Ⓔ

26. If the perimeter of the square is 36, what is the circumference of the circle?

    F. 6π

    G. 9π

    H. 12π

    J. 15π

    K. 18π   Ⓕ Ⓖ Ⓗ Ⓙ Ⓚ

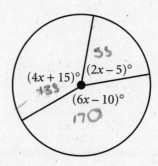

27. In the figure above, what is the value of *x*?

    A. 15

    B. 30

    C. 55

    D. 70

    E. 135   Ⓐ Ⓑ Ⓒ Ⓓ Ⓔ

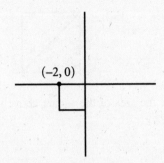

28. In the figure above, a square is graphed on the coordinate plane. If the coordinates of one corner are (−2, 0), what is the area of the square?

    F. $\frac{1}{4}$

    G. 0

    H. 2

    J. 4

    K. 16   Ⓕ Ⓖ Ⓗ Ⓙ Ⓚ

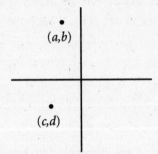

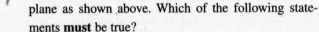

29. Points (a, b) and (c, d) are graphed in the coordinate plane as shown above. Which of the following statements **must** be true?

    A. $bd > ac$

    B. $c > ad$

    C. $b > acd$

    D. $bc > ad$

    E. It cannot be determined from the information given.   Ⓐ Ⓑ Ⓒ Ⓓ Ⓔ

30. What is the distance from the point (0, 6) to the point (0, 8) in a standard coordinate plane?

    F. 2

    G. 7

    H. 10

    J. 12

    K. 14

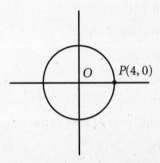

31. Circle O above has its center at the origin. If point P lies on circle O, what is the area of circle O ?

    A. 4π

    B. 8π

    C. 10π

    D. 12π

    E. 16π

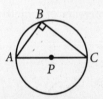

32. In the figure above, right triangle ABC is inscribed in circle P, with AC passing through center P. If AB = 6, and BC = 8, what is the area of the circle?

    F. 10π

    G. 14π

    H. 25π

    J. 49π

    K. 100π Ⓕ Ⓖ Ⓗ Ⓙ Ⓚ

33. In the figure above, a circle is inscribed within a square. If the area of the circle is 25π, what is the perimeter of the shaded region?

   A. $40 + 5\pi$

   B. $40 + 10\pi$

   C. $100 + 10\pi$

   D. $100 + 25\pi$

   E. $40 + 50\pi$ Ⓐ Ⓑ Ⓒ Ⓓ Ⓔ

34. What is the slope of the line that contains points $(3, -5)$ and $(-1, 7)$?

   F. -3

   G. $\dfrac{1}{3}$

   H. $-\dfrac{1}{4}$

   J. $\dfrac{1}{3}$

   K. 3 Ⓕ Ⓖ Ⓗ Ⓙ Ⓚ

35. If the circumference of a circle is 16π, what is its area?

   A. 8π

   B. 16π

   C. 32π

   D. 64π

   E. 256π Ⓐ Ⓑ Ⓒ Ⓓ Ⓔ

36. What is the area of the square above with diagonals of length 6?

   F. 9

   G. 12

   H. $9\sqrt{2}$

   J. 15

   K. 18 Ⓕ Ⓖ Ⓗ Ⓙ Ⓚ

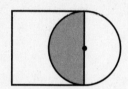

37. A square and a circle are drawn as shown above. The area of the square is 64. What is the area of the shaded region?

   A. 4π

   B. 8π

   C. 16π

   D. 32π

   E. It cannot be determined from the information given.   Ⓐ Ⓑ Ⓒ Ⓓ Ⓔ

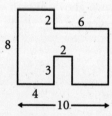

38. What is the area of the polygon above if each corner of the polygon is a right angle?

   F. 40

   G. 62

   H. 68

   J. 74

   K. 80 Ⓕ Ⓖ Ⓗ Ⓙ Ⓚ

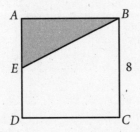

39. *ABCD* is a square. If *E* is the midpoint of *AD*, what is the area of the shaded region?

    A. 8

    B. 12

    C. 16

    D. 24

    E. 32   Ⓐ Ⓑ Ⓒ Ⓓ Ⓔ

40. Circle *A* has radius $r + 1$. Circle *B* has radius $r + 2$. What is the positive difference between the circumference of circle *B* and the circumference of circle *A* ?

    F. 1

    G. 2π

    H. $2\pi + 3$

    J. $2\pi r + 3$

    K. $2\pi(2r + 3)$ Ⓕ Ⓖ Ⓗ Ⓙ Ⓚ

41. Erica has 8 squares of felt, each with area 16. For a certain craft project, she cuts the largest circle possible from each square of felt. What is the combined area of the excess felt left over after cutting out all the circles?

    A. $4(4 - \pi)$

    B. $8(4 - \pi)$

    C. $8(\pi - 2)$

    D. $32(4 - \pi)$

    E. $8(16 - \pi)$ Ⓐ Ⓑ Ⓒ Ⓓ Ⓔ

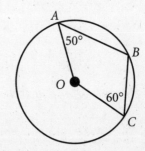

42. In the figure above, points *A*, *B*, and *C* lie on the circumference of the circle centered at *O*. If $\angle OAB$ measures 50° and $\angle BCO$ measures 60°, what is the degree measure of $\angle AOC$?

    F. 110

    G. 125

    H. 140

    J. 250

    K. It cannot be determined from the information given.   Ⓕ Ⓖ Ⓗ Ⓙ Ⓚ

Exercise Answers

i. $AC = 20$

ii. $x = 135$

iii. $x = 35$

iv. $x = 60$

v. $y = 60$

vi.   5, 9 (The third side must be greater than 3 and less than 13.)

vii.   16

viii. $\dfrac{15}{2}$

ix. $\sqrt{45}$ or $3\sqrt{5}$

x.   12

xi.   10

xii.   25

xiii.   24

xiv.   24

xv.   75

xvi.   Diameter = 6

xvii. $WX = 8$, $OX = 4$

xviii. Circumference = 16π

xix.   Radius = 4

xx. $\dfrac{1}{2}, \dfrac{3}{5}$

xxi. $2, -\dfrac{1}{5}$

xxii. $AB = 8$, $CD = 5$, $EF = 6$

Practice Set Explanations

1. **E** Since $AB = BC = AC$, triangle ABC is equilateral. Therefore, all of its angles are 60°. Since angle BCD, or x, is supplementary to angle BCA, a 60° angle, the value x is $180 - 60$ or 120.

2. **H** Since the degree measure of angle ABC is 145, $45 + 48 + x = 145$, $93 + x = 145$, and $x = 52$.

3. **E** A square has 4 equal sides, so its perimeter is equal to $4s$, where s is a side of the square. Its perimeter is 32, so its side length is $\frac{32}{4} = 8$. The area of a square is equal to s^2, so the area of the square is 8^2, or 64.

4. **J** In any triangle, the measures of the three interior angles sum to 180°, so $X + Y + Z = 180$. Since the measure of angle Y is twice the measure of angle X, $Y = 2X$. Similarly, $Z = 3X$. So $X + 2X + 3X = 180$, $6X = 180$, and $X = 30$. Since $Y = 2X$, the measure of angle Y is $2 \times 30 = 60$.

5. **B** The perimeter of a triangle is the sum of the lengths of its sides, in this case, $AB + BC + AC$. The perimeter of triangle ABC is 24, so plugging in the given values, $9 + 7 + AC = 24$, $16 + AC = 24$, and $AC = 8$.

6. **H** In an equilateral triangle, all three sides have equal length. The perimeter of a triangle is equal to the sum of its three sides. Since all three sides are equal, each side must be $\frac{1}{3}$ of 150, or 50.

7. **B** Since RS and RT are equal, the angles opposite them must be equal. Therefore, angle $T =$ angle S. Since the degree measures of the three interior angles of a triangle sum to 180, $70 +$ angle $S +$ angle $T = 180$ and angle $S +$ angle $T = 110$. Since the two angles, S and T, are equal, each must be half of 110, or 55.

8. **H** The three interior angles of a triangle sum to 180 degrees, so $2x + 3x + 5x = 180$, $10x = 180$ and $x = 18$. Angle YXZ has a degree measure of $3x = 3(18) = 54$.

9. **E** The perimeter of triangle ABC is 18, so $AB + BC + AC = 18$. Plug in the algebraic expression given for the length of each side:

$$(3a - 1) + (2a + 1) + (5a - 2) = 18$$
$$10a - 2 = 18$$
$$10a = 20$$
$$a = 2$$

The length of AC is represented by the expression $5a - 2$, so $AC = 5(2) - 2 = 8$.

10. **H** The perimeter of a rectangle is $2(\ell + w)$, where ℓ represents its length and w its width. The perimeter of this rectangle is $2(9 + 5) = 28$. A square has 4 equal sides, so a square with a perimeter of 28 has sides of length 7. The area of a square is equal to the length of a side squared, so the area of a square with a perimeter of 28 is 7^2 or 49.

11. **B** The exterior angle of a triangle is equal to the sum of the measures of the two remote interior angles. So $7x = 4x + 60$, $3x = 60$, and $x = 20$. The angle marked $7x°$ has degree measure $7(20) = 140$. Angle a is supplementary to this angle, so its measure is $180 - 140 = 40$.

12. **H** The angle between the two angles of measure n degrees is a right angle, so it contains 90°. A straight angle contains 180°, so $2n + 90 = 180$, $2n = 90$, and $n = 45$.

13. **B** Since $AC = CB$, the angles opposite these sides are equal as well. So angle CAB = angle CBA, and $x = 75$. The three interior angles of a triangle sum to 180 degrees, so $2(75) + y = 180$ and $y = 30$. The question asks for the value of $x - y$, or $75 - 30 = 45$.

14. **H** The area of a triangle is equal to $\frac{1}{2}(b \times h)$. In triangle BEF, the height is BC, and the base is EF. The square's perimeter is 64, so each of its sides is a fourth of 64, or 16. Therefore, $BC = 16$. The question also states that $DC = EF$, so $EF = 16$ as well. Plugging into the formula, the area of triangle BEF is $\frac{1}{2}(16 \times 16) = 128$.

15. **D** When parallel lines are crossed by a transversal, all acute angles formed are equal, and all acute angles are supplementary to all obtuse angles. So in this diagram, obtuse angle y is supplementary to the acute angle of 55°. Angle x is an acute angle, so it is equal to 55°. Therefore, angle x is supplementary to angle y, and the two must sum to 180°.

16. **G** The area of a square is equal to one of its sides squared. In this case, the square has a side length of $2\sqrt{2}$, so its area is $(2\sqrt{2})^2$ or $2 \times 2 \times \sqrt{2} \times \sqrt{2}$ or $4 \times 2 = 8$.

17. **E** To find the area of the frame, find the area of the frame and picture combined (the outer rectangle) and subtract from it the area of the picture (the inner rectangle). The outer rectangle has area $10 \times 8 = 80$ and the inner rectangle has area $8 \times 4 = 32$, so the area of the frame is $80 - 32 = 48$.

18. **J** Diagonal BD divides square $ABCD$ into two identical triangles. If the area of triangle ABD is 8, the area of the square must be twice this, or 16.

19. **D** The area of the entire figure is equal to the area of rectangle $ABFG$ plus the area of rectangle $CDEF$. The area of $ABFG$ is $8 \times 4 = 32$. So the area of the entire figure must be greater than 32, and at this point you could eliminate (A), (B), and (C). Since BF has length 4 and C bisects BF, CF has length 2. The question states that EF has length 2, so $CDEF$ is actually a square, and its area is 2^2 or 4. The area of the entire figure is $32 + 4 = 36$, choice (D).

20. **K** The perimeter of $ABCE$ is equal to $AB + BC + CD + DE + EA$. Since triangle BCD is equilateral, $BC = CD = BD = 4$. Because $ABDE$ is a parallelogram, $AB = DE = 12$ and $BD = EA = 4$. Therefore, the perimeter of $ABCE$ is $12 + 4 + 4 + 12 + 4 = 36$, choice (K).

21. E Simply add the six sides of the L-shaped figure. Four of them are labeled, and you can use these to figure out the remaining two. The length of side EF must be $4 + 6 = 10$. The length of side BC is $10 - 4 = 6$. This makes the perimeter:

$$10 + 10 + 4 + 6 + 6 + 4 = 40$$

22. F Each of the shaded segments has a side of length 3 as its segment contributing to the inside region. Hence, the unshaded region, a square, has an area of $3^2 = 9$.

23. A Let $BC = x$. AB has twice the length of BC, so it is $2x$. $BC = CD$, so $CD = x$. DE is three times the length of CD, or $3x$. Since $AE = 49$, $2x + x + x + 3x = 49$, $7x = 49$, and $x = 7$. BD is composed of segments BC and CD, so its length is $7 + 7 = 14$.

24. J Since circle P is inscribed within the square, you can see that its diameter is equal in length to a side of the square. Since the circle's diameter is 8, its radius is half this, or 4. Area of a circle $= \pi r^2$, where r is the radius of the circle, so the area of the circle P is $\pi(4)^2 = 16\pi$.

25. D Circumference of a circle $= 2\pi r$, where r is the radius of the circle. So, a circle with a circumference of 36π has a radius of $\frac{36\pi}{2\pi} = 18$.

26. G The perimeter of the square is 36, and since all four sides are equal, one side has length 9. Since the circle is inscribed in the square, its diameter is equal in length to a side of the square, or 9. Circumference is πd, where d represents the diameter, so the circumference of the circle is 9π.

27. B A circle contains 360°, so

$$\begin{aligned}
(4x + 15) + (2x - 5) + (6x - 10) &= 360 \\
4x + 2x + 6x + 15 - 5 - 10 &= 360 \\
12x &= 360 \\
x &= 30
\end{aligned}$$

28. J The area of a square is equal to the length of one of its sides squared. Since one of the vertices (corners) of the square lies on the origin at $(0, 0)$ and another vertex lies on the point $(-2, 0)$, the length of a side of the square is $|-2 - 0| = |-2| = 2$. Therefore, the area of the square is $2^2 = 4$.

29. C While there is no way to determine the numerical values of a, b, c, and d from their positions on the coordinate plane, you do know that a is negative, b is positive, c is negative, and d is negative. Bearing in mind that a negative times a negative is a positive, consider each answer choice. Choice (C) is indeed true: b, which is positive, is greater than acd, which is negative.

30. F The points $(0, 6)$ and $(0, 8)$ have the same x-coordinate. That means that the segment that connects them is parallel to the y-axis and that all you have to do to figure out the distance is subtract the y-coordinates: $|8 - 6| = 2$. So the distance between the points is 2.

31.　　E　　OP is the radius of the circle. Since O has coordinates $(0, 0)$, the length of OP is $|4 - 0| = |4| = 4$. The area of a circle is πr^2, where r is the radius, so the area of circle O is $\pi(4)^2 = 16\pi$.

32.　　H　　Right triangle ABC has legs of 6 and 8, so its hypotenuse must be 10. Notice that the hypotenuse is also the diameter of the circle. To find the area of the circle, we need its radius. Radius is half the diameter, so the radius of circle P is 5. The area of a circle is πr^2, so the area of circle P is $\pi(5)^2 = 25\pi$.

33.　　B　　Note that the perimeter of the shaded region is in fact equal to the perimeter of the square plus the perimeter—or circumference—of the circle. The area of a circle is πr^2, where r is the radius, and since the area of the circle is 25π, its radius is 5. Circumference is equal to $2\pi r$, or $2\pi(5) = 10\pi$. Only choices (B) and (C) contain 10π, so you could eliminate choices (A), (D), and (E). Since the circle is inscribed within the square, its diameter is equal to a side of the square. The diameter of the circle is $2r$ or 10, so a side of the square is 10 and its perimeter is $4(10) = 40$. Therefore, the perimeter of the shaded region is $40 + 10\pi$, choice (B).

34.　　F　　Slope of a line is defined by the formula $\dfrac{y_2 - y_1}{x_2 - x_1}$, where (x_1, y_1) and (x_2, y_2) represent two points on the line. Plug the given points into the formula (it doesn't matter which you designate as point 1 or point 2):

$$\text{Slope} = \frac{y_2 - y_1}{x_2 - x_1} = \frac{7 - (-5)}{-1 - 3} = \frac{12}{-4} = -3$$

35.　　D　　The circumference of a circle is $2\pi r$, where r is the radius, so a circle whose circumference is 16π has a radius of $\dfrac{16\pi}{2\pi} = 8$. The area of a circle is defined by the formula πr^2, where r is the radius. So in this case the area is $\pi(8)^2 = 64\pi$, choice (D).

36.　　K　　It might help to sketch a diagram:

Since all sides of a square are equal, notice that the diagonal of the square is also the hypotenuse of an isosceles right triangle. Use this information to determine the length of a side of the square, marked s in the diagram. The ratio of the sides in such a triangle is $1:1:\sqrt{2}$. Since the hypotenuse is 6, each leg is $\dfrac{6}{\sqrt{2}}$ (because $\dfrac{6}{\sqrt{2}} \times \sqrt{2} = 6$). The area of a square is equal to the length of one side squared, or $\left(\dfrac{6}{\sqrt{2}}\right)^2 = \dfrac{36}{2} = 18$.

37.　　B　　The shaded region represents one-half the area of the circle. Find the length of the radius to determine this area. Notice that the diameter of the circle is equal to a side of the square. Since the area of the square is 64, it has a side length of 8. So the diameter of the circle is 8, and its radius is 4. The area of a circle is πr^2, where r is the radius, so the area of this circle is $\pi(4)^2 = 16\pi$. This isn't the answer though; the shaded region is only half the circle, so its area is 8π.

38.　　G　　Think of the figure as a rectangle with two rectangular bites taken out of it. Sketch in lines to make one large rectangle (see diagram below):

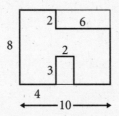

The area of a rectangle is length times width. If we call the length of the large rectangle 10, then its width is 8, so its area is $10 \times 8 = 80$. The rectangular bite taken out of the top right corner has dimensions 6 and 2, so its area is 6×2 or 12. The bite taken out of the bottom has dimensions 2 and 3, so its area is $2 \times 3 = 6$. To find the area of the polygon, subtract the areas of the two bites from the area of the large rectangle: $80 - (12 + 6) = 80 - 18 = 62$, choice (G).

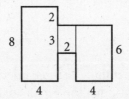

39.　　C　　Since *ABCD* is a square, all four sides have the same length, and the corners meet at right angles. The area you're looking for is that of a triangle, and since all corners of the square are right angles, angle *EAB* is a right angle, which makes triangle *EAB* a right triangle. The area of a right triangle is $\frac{1}{2}(\text{leg}_1)$ (leg_2). The diagram shows that *BC* has length 8, so $AB = AD = 8$. Point *E* is the midpoint of *AD*, so *AE* is 4. Now that you have the lengths of both legs, you can plug into the formula: $\frac{1}{2}(AB)(AE) = \frac{1}{2}(8)(4) = 16$, choice (C).

40.　　G　　The circumference of a circle is equal to $2\pi r$, where *r* is the radius. The circumference of circle *A* is $2\pi(r + 1) = 2\pi r + 2\pi$. The circumference of circle *B* is $2\pi(r + 2) = 2\pi r + 4\pi$. So the positive difference between the two circumferences is simply 2π, choice (G).

41.　　D　　A square with area 16 has sides of length 4. Therefore, the largest circle that could possibly be cut from such a square would have a diameter of 4.

Such a circle would have a radius of 2, making its area $\pi(2)^2 = 4\pi$. So the amount of felt left after cutting such a circle from one of the squares of felt would be $16 - 4\pi$, or $4(4 - \pi)$. There are 8 such squares, so the total area of the leftover felt is $8 \times 4(4 - \pi) = 32(4 - \pi)$, choice (D).

42.   **H**   The key to solving this problem is to draw in *OB*:

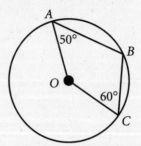

Because *OA*, *OB*, and *OC* are all radii of the same circle, triangle *AOB* and triangle *BOC* are both isosceles triangles, each therefore having equal base angles:

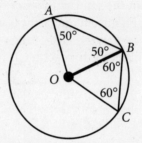

Using the fact that the three interior angles of a triangle add up to 180°, you can figure out that the vertex angles measure 80° and 60° as shown:

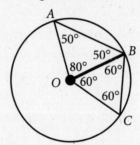

Angle *AOC* measures 80 + 60 = 140, choice (H).

Ready, Set, Go!

12

Countdown to the Test

Highlights

- Review the Information You Need to Know About the Test to Avoid Surprises

- What to Do the Week Before the Test, the Night Before the Test, and the Morning Before the Test

Is it starting to feel as though your whole life is a buildup to the SHSAT? You really want to go to a certain school, and you know your parents want you to as well. You've worried about the test for months and spent at least a few hours in solid preparation for it. As the test gets closer, you may find your anxiety is on the rise. You shouldn't worry. After the preparation you've received from this book, you're in good shape for the test.

REVIEW

The Timing of Each Section Is Flexible

Be aware of your time. If you need a few extra minutes on the Verbal Section, you can take them. If you finish the section early, you can get a jump on the Math Section. This flexibility can be helpful, but it can also get you into trouble. No one will stop you from spending an hour and a half or two hours on the Verbal Section. However, you cannot get the time back to spend on the Math Section. Therefore, make sure that you are aware of your time since, ultimately, you are responsible for managing it.

No Calculators

Leave your calculator at home! If you did not realize that you could not use a calculator on the test and have been practicing with one, make sure you do some practice without a calculator.

You'll See Fewer Verbal Questions Than Math Questions

Remember that the Verbal Section contains 45 questions while the Math contains 50. This is because Scrambled Paragraphs are weighted more heavily than other question types. Math and Verbal count the same toward your overall score.

You'll See Questions You Do Not Know How to Answer

This is going to happen because the SHSAT is hard. The moral of this story: Don't panic if you do not know something. You don't have to get everything correct to do well on the test. When you see something you don't know, see if you can quickly eliminate answers that cannot be correct and then guess. Save your energy for the stuff you know and don't worry about the stuff you don't know.

Do Not Leave Any Answers Blank

If you leave an answer blank, you have a 0 percent chance of getting the question right. If you guess, you have at least a 20 percent chance of getting the right answer. Go with the odds.

Your Value as a Human Being Does Not Depend on Your Performance on the Specialized High Schools Admissions Test

We hope you know this already. The point here is that you are probably feeling a lot of pressure as the test draws near. Some of it may be self-inflicted. Some may be coming from your parents. The test is certainly important and has the potential to affect your future. But ultimately, it's just a test. Have faith in the preparation that you've completed and give yourself a break.

COUNTDOWN TO THE TEST

To calm any pretest jitters you may have, this chapter leads you through a sane itinerary for the last week.

The Week Before the Test

- Focus on strategy and backup plans.

- Practice strategies you had the best success rate with.

- Decide and know **exactly** how you are going to approach each section and question type.

- Sit down and do practice problems in the Practice Sets or complete extra drills you might have skipped the first time through.

- Start practicing waking up early and eating breakfast so that you will be alert in the morning on test day.

Two Days Before the Test

Do your last studying—a few more practice problems—and call it quits.

The Night Before the Test

Don't study. Get together the following items:

- Your admission/registration ticket

- Your ID

- A watch (choose one that is easy to read)

- Slightly dull No. 2 pencils (so they fill in the ovals faster)

- Pencil sharpener

- Erasers

- Clothes you will wear (Dress in layers! The climate at the test location may vary, as may your body temperature. Make sure you can warm up or cool down easily.)

- Snacks (easy to open or partially unwrapped)

- Money

- Packet of tissues

Know exactly where you're going and exactly how you're getting there.

Relax the night before the test. Read a good book, take a bubble bath, or watch TV. Get a good night's sleep. Go to bed at a reasonable hour and leave yourself extra time in the morning.

The Morning of the Test

Eat breakfast. Make it something substantial and nutritious, but don't deviate too much from your everyday pattern.

Dress in layers so that you can adjust to the temperature of the test room.

Read a newspaper or a magazine to warm up your brain before the test starts.

Be sure to get there early. Leave enough time to allow for traffic, mass transit delays, your dad getting lost en route, and any other snag that could slow you down.

During the Test

Don't be shaken. If you find your confidence slipping, remind yourself how well you've prepared. You know the structure of the test; you know the instructions; you've studied for every question type.

Even if something goes really wrong, don't panic. If the test booklet is defective—two pages are stuck together or the ink has run—try to stay calm. Raise your hand and tell the proctor you need a new book. If you accidentally misgrid your answer page or put the answers in the wrong section, again don't panic. Raise your hand and tell the proctor. He or she might be able to arrange for you to regrid your test after it's over, when it won't cost you any time.

ONCE THE TEST IS OVER . . .

Put it out of your mind! Start thinking about more interesting things. Do something fun and relaxing that day. You might walk out of the SHSAT thinking that you blew it. You probably didn't. You tend to remember the questions that stumped you, not the many that you knew.

If you want more help, want to know more about the SHSAT, or want to find out about Kaplan prep courses for the PSAT, SAT, and ACT, give us a call at 1-800-KAP-TEST. We're here to answer your questions and help you in any way we can. You can also check out our website at **kaptest.com**.

13

Stress Management

Highlights

- Learn How to Tame Test Stress

- Find Out How to Prepare for Success

The countdown has begun. Your date with THE TEST is looming on the horizon. Anxiety is on the rise. The butterflies in your stomach have gone ballistic. Perhaps you feel as though the last thing you ate has turned into a lead ball. Your thinking is getting cloudy. Maybe you think you won't be ready. Maybe you already know your stuff, but you're going into panic mode anyway. Worst of all, you're not sure of what to do about it.

Don't freak! It is possible to tame that anxiety and stress—before and during the test. We'll show you how. You won't believe how quickly and easily you can deal with that killer anxiety.

MAKE THE MOST OF YOUR PREP TIME

Lack of control is one of the prime causes of stress. A ton of research shows that if you don't have a sense of control over what's happening in your life, you can easily end up feeling helpless and hopeless. So just having concrete things to do and to think about—taking control—will help reduce your stress. This chapter shows you how to take control during the days leading up to taking the test.

Avoid Must-y Thinking

Let go of "must-y" thoughts, those notions that you must do something in a certain way—for example, "I must get a great score, or else!" or "I must meet Mom and Dad's expectations!"

IDENTIFY THE SOURCES OF STRESS

In the space provided, jot down anything you identify as a source of your test-related stress. The idea is to pin down that free-floating anxiety so that you can take control of it. Here are some common examples to get you started:

- I always freeze up on tests.

- I'm nervous about the Verbal/Math Section.

- I need a good/great score to go to Brooklyn Tech.

- My older brother/sister/best friend/girl- or boyfriend got in. I have to, too.

- My parents will be really disappointed if I don't get in.

- I'm afraid of losing my focus and concentration.

- I'm afraid I'm not spending enough time preparing.

- I study like crazy, but nothing seems to stick in my mind.

- I always run out of time and get panicky.

- I feel as though thinking is becoming like wading through thick mud.

Sources of Stress

I am not good at the testing process.

I need a good score

I work too fast.

Don't Do It in Bed

Don't study on your bed, especially if you have problems with insomnia. Your mind might start to associate the bed with work, making it even harder for you to fall asleep.

Take a few minutes to think about the things you've just written down. Then rewrite them in some sort of order. List the statements you most associate with your stress and anxiety first and put the least disturbing items last. Chances are, the top of the list is a fairly accurate description of exactly how you react to test anxiety, both physically and mentally. The later items usually describe your fears (disappointing Mom and Dad, looking bad, etc.). As you write the list, you're forming a hierarchy of items so you can deal first with the anxiety provokers that bug you most. Very often, taking care of the major items from the top of the list goes a long way toward relieving overall testing anxiety. You probably won't have to bother with the stuff you placed last.

STRENGTHS AND WEAKNESSES

Take one minute to list the areas of the test that you are good at. They can be general ("reading") or specific ("Logical Reasoning questions"). Put down as many as you can think of and, if possible, time yourself. Write for the entire time; don't stop writing until you've reached the one-minute stopping point.

Strong Test Subjects

Reading comprehension
Logical Reasoning
Angles
Ratios.

Next, take one minute to list areas of the test you're not so good at, just plain bad at, have failed at, or keep failing at. Again, keep it to one minute and continue writing until you reach the cutoff. Don't be afraid to identify and write down your weak spots! In all probability, as you do both lists, you'll find you are strong in some areas and not so strong in others. Taking stock of your assets and liabilities lets you know the areas you don't have to worry about and the ones that will demand extra attention and effort.

Weak Test Subjects

Area/Circumference
scrambled Paragraphs

Facing your weak spots gives you some distinct advantages. It helps a lot to find out where you need to spend extra effort. Increased exposure to tough material makes it more familiar and less intimidating. (After all, we mostly fear what we don't know and are probably afraid to face.) You'll feel better about yourself because you're dealing directly with areas of the test that bring on your anxiety. You can't help feeling more confident when you know you're actively strengthening your chances of earning a higher overall test score.

Think Good Thoughts

Create a set of positive but brief affirmations and mentally repeat them to yourself just before you fall asleep at night. (That's when your mind is very open to suggestion.) You'll find yourself feeling a lot more positive in the morning.

Periodically repeating your affirmations during the day makes them more effective.

Very Superstitious

Stress expert Stephen Sidcroff, PhD, tells of a client who always stressed out before, during, and even after taking tests. Yet, she always got outstanding scores. It became obvious that she was thinking superstitiously—subconsciously believing that the great scores were a result of her worrying. She also didn't trust herself and believed that if she didn't worry, she wouldn't study hard enough. Sideroff convinced her to take a risk and work on relaxing before her next test. She did, and her test results were still as good as ever—which broke her cycle of superstitious thinking.

Now, go back to the "good" list and expand on it for two minutes. Take the general items on that first list and make them more specific; take the specific items and expand them into more general conclusions. Naturally, if anything new comes to mind, jot it down. Focus all of your attention and effort on your strengths. Don't underestimate yourself or your abilities. Give yourself full credit. At the same time, don't list strengths you don't really have; you'll only be fooling yourself.

Expanding from general to specific might go as follows. If you listed "reading" as a broad topic you feel strong in, you would then narrow your focus to include areas of this subject about which you are particularly knowledgeable. Your areas of strength might include a strong sense of logical construction, ability to spot logical flaws, etc.

Whatever you know comfortably goes on your "good" list. Okay. You've got the picture. Now, get ready, check your starting time, and start writing down items on your expanded "good" list.

Strong Test Subjects: An Expanded List

Angles	Ratios
linear equations	slope
graphing	speed & distance
Mixtures	

After you've stopped, check your time. Did you find yourself going beyond the two minutes allotted? Did you write down more things than you thought you knew? Is it possible you know more than you've given yourself credit for? Could that mean you've found a number of areas in which you feel strong?

You just took an active step toward helping yourself. Notice any increased feelings of confidence? Enjoy them.

Here's another way to think about your writing exercise. Every area of strength and confidence you can identify is much like having a reserve of solid gold at Fort Knox. You'll be able to draw on your reserves as you need them. You can use your reserves to solve difficult questions, maintain confidence, and keep test stress and anxiety at a distance. The encouraging thing is that every time you recognize another area of strength, succeed at coming up with a solution, or get a good score on a test, you increase your reserves. And, there is absolutely no limit to how much self-confidence you can have or how good you can feel about yourself.

IMAGINE YOURSELF SUCCEEDING

This next little group of exercises is both physical and mental. They're a natural follow-up to what you've just accomplished with your lists.

First, get yourself into a comfortable sitting position in a quiet setting. Wear loose clothes. If you wear glasses, take them off. Then, close your eyes and breathe in a deep, satisfying breath of air. Really fill your lungs until your rib cage is fully expanded and you can't take in any more. Then, exhale the air completely. Imagine you're blowing out a candle with your last little puff of air. Do this two or three more times, filling your lungs to their maximum and emptying them totally. Keep your eyes closed, comfortably but not tightly. Let your body sink deeper into the chair as you become even more comfortable.

With your eyes shut you can notice something very interesting. You're no longer dealing with the worrisome stuff going on in the world outside of you. Now you can concentrate on what happens *inside* you. The more you recognize your own physical reactions to stress and anxiety, the more you can do about them. You might not realize it, but you've begun to regain a sense of being in control.

Let images begin to form on the "viewing screens" on the back of your eyelids. You're experiencing visualizations from the place in your mind that makes pictures. Allow the images to come easily and naturally; don't force them. Imagine yourself in a relaxing situation. It might be in a special place you've visited before or one you've read about. It can be a fictional location that you create in your imagination, but a real-life memory of a place or situation you know is usually better. Make it as detailed as possible and notice as much as you can.

Stay focused on the images as you sink farther back into your chair. Breathe easily and naturally. You might have the sensations of stress or tension draining from your muscles and flowing downward, out your feet, and away from you.

Take a moment to check how you're feeling. Notice how comfortable you've become. Imagine how much easier it would be if you could take the test feeling this relaxed and in this state of ease. You've coupled the images of your special place with sensations of comfort and relaxation. You've also found a way to become relaxed simply by visualizing your own safe, special place.

Now, close your eyes and start remembering a real-life situation in which you did well on a test. If you can't come up with one, remember a situation in which you did something (academic or otherwise) that you were really proud of—a genuine accomplishment. Make the memory as detailed as possible. Think about the sights, the sounds, the smells, even the tastes associated with this remembered experience. Remember how confident you felt as you accomplished your goal. Now start thinking about the upcoming test. Keep your thoughts and feelings in line with that successful experience. Don't make comparisons between them. Just imagine taking the upcoming test with the same feelings of confidence and relaxed control.

Counseling

Don't forget that your school probably has counseling available. If you can't conquer test stress on your own, make an appointment at the counseling center. That's what counselors are there for.

Take a Hike, Pal

When you're in the middle of studying and hit a wall, take a short, brisk walk. Breathe deeply and swing your arms as you walk. Clear your mind. (And, don't forget to look for flowers that grow in the cracks of the sidewalk.)

Play the Music

If you want to play music, keep it low and in the background. Music with a regular, mathematical rhythm—reggae, for example—aids the learning process. A recording of ocean waves is also soothing.

This exercise is a great way to bring the test down to earth. You should practice this exercise often, especially when the prospect of taking the exam starts to stress you out. The more you practice it, the more effective the exercise will be for you.

EXERCISE YOUR FRUSTRATIONS AWAY

Whether it is jogging, walking, biking, mild aerobics, pushups, or a pickup basketball game, physical exercise is a very effective way to stimulate both your mind and body and to improve your ability to think and concentrate. A surprising number of students get out of the habit of regular exercise, ironically because they're spending so much time prepping for exams. Also, sedentary people—this is a medical fact—get less oxygen to the blood and hence to the head than active people. You can live fine with a little less oxygen; you just can't think as well.

Any big test is a bit like a race. Thinking clearly at the end is just as important as having a quick mind early on. If you can't sustain your energy level in the last sections of the exam, there's too good a chance you could blow it. You need a fit body that can weather the demands any big exam puts on you. Along with a good diet and adequate sleep, exercise is an important part of keeping yourself in fighting shape and thinking clearly for the long haul.

There's another thing that happens when students don't make exercise an integral part of their test preparation. Like any organism in nature, you operate best if all your "energy systems" are in balance. Studying uses a lot of energy, but it's all mental. When you take a study break, do something active instead of raiding the fridge or vegging out in front of the TV. Take a 5- to 10-minute activity break for every 50 or 60 minutes that you study. The physical exertion gets your body into the act, which helps to keep your mind and body in sync. Then, when you finish studying for the night and hit the sack, you won't lie there, tense and unable to sleep because your head is overtired and your body wants to pump iron or run a marathon.

One warning about exercise, however: It's not a good idea to exercise vigorously right before you go to bed. This could easily cause sleep onset problems. For the same reason, it's also not a good idea to study right up to bedtime. Make time for a "buffer period" before you go to bed: For 30 to 60 minutes, just take a hot shower, meditate, simply veg out.

THE DANGERS OF DRUGS

Using drugs (prescription or recreational) specifically to prepare for and take a big test is definitely self-defeating. (And if they're illegal drugs, you can end up with a bigger problem than the SHSAT on your hands.) Except for the drugs that occur naturally in your brain, every drug has major drawbacks—and a false sense of security is only one of them.

You may have heard that popping uppers helps you study by keeping you alert. If they're illegal, definitely forget about it. They wouldn't really work anyway, since amphetamines make it hard to retain information. Mild stimulants, such as coffee, cola, or over-the-counter caffeine pills can sometimes help as you study, since they keep you alert. On the downside, they can also lead to agitation, restlessness, and insomnia. Some people can drink a pot of high-octane coffee and sleep like a baby. Others have one cup and start to vibrate. It all depends on your tolerance for caffeine. Remember, a little anxiety is a good thing. The adrenaline that gets pumped into your bloodstream helps you stay alert and think more clearly. But too much anxiety, and you can't think straight at all.

Instead, go for endorphins—the "natural morphine." Endorphins have no side effects and they're free—you've already got them in your brain. It just takes some exercise to release them. Running around on the basketball court, bicycling, swimming, aerobics, power walking—these activities cause endorphins to occupy certain spots in your brain's neural synapses. In addition, exercise develops staying power and increases the oxygen transfer to your brain. Go into the test naturally.

The Relaxation Paradox

Forcing relaxation is like asking yourself to flap your arms and fly. You can't do it, and every push and prod only gets you more frustrated. Relaxation is something you don't work at. You simply let it happen. Think about it. When was the last time you tried to force yourself to go to sleep and it worked?

TAKE A DEEP BREATH . . .

Here's another natural route to relaxation and invigoration. It's a classic isometric exercise that you can do whenever you get stressed out—just before the test begins, even *during* the test. It's very simple and takes just a few minutes.

Close your eyes. Starting with your eyes and—without holding your breath—gradually tighten every muscle in your body (but not to the point of pain) in the following sequence:

1. Close your eyes tightly.
2. Squeeze your nose and mouth together so that your whole face is scrunched up. (If it makes you self-conscious to do this in the test room, skip the face-scrunching part.)
3. Pull your chin into your chest, and pull your shoulders together.
4. Tighten your arms to your body, then clench your hands into tight fists.
5. Pull in your stomach.
6. Squeeze your thighs and buttocks together and tighten your calves.
7. Stretch your feet, then curl your toes (watch out for cramping in this part).

Enlightenment

A lamp with a 75-watt bulb is optimal for studying. But don't put it so close to your study material that you create a glare.

At this point, every muscle should be tightened. Now, relax your body, one part at a time, *in reverse order*, starting with your toes. Let the tension drop out of each muscle. The entire process might take five minutes from start to finish (maybe a couple of minutes during the test). This clenching and unclenching exercise should help you to feel very relaxed.

AND KEEP BREATHING

Conscious attention to breathing is an excellent way of managing test stress (or any stress, for that matter). The majority of people who get into trouble during tests take shallow breaths. They breathe using only their upper chests and shoulder muscles, and they may even hold their breath for long periods of time. Conversely, the test taker who by accident or design keeps breathing normally and rhythmically is likely to be more relaxed and in better control during the entire test experience.

So, now is the time to get into the habit of relaxed breathing. Do the next exercise to learn to breathe in a natural, easy rhythm. By the way, this is another technique you can use during the test to collect your thoughts and ward off excess stress. The entire exercise should take no more than three to five minutes.

With your eyes still closed, breathe in slowly and *deeply* through your nose. Hold the breath for a bit, and then release it through your mouth. The key is to breathe slowly and deeply by using your diaphragm (the big band of muscle that spans your body just above your waist) to draw air in and out naturally and effortlessly. Breathing with your diaphragm encourages relaxation and helps minimize tension. Try it and notice how relaxed and comfortable you feel.

QUICK TIPS FOR THE DAYS JUST BEFORE THE EXAM

- The best test takers do less and less as the test approaches. Taper off your study schedule and take it easy on yourself. You want to be relaxed and ready on the day of the test. Give yourself time off, especially the evening before the exam. By then, if you've studied well, everything you need to know is firmly stored in your memory banks.

- Positive self-talk can be extremely liberating and invigorating, especially as the test looms closer. Tell yourself things such as "I choose to take this test," rather than "I have to"; "I will do well," rather than "I hope things go well"; "I can," rather than "I cannot." Be aware of negative, self-defeating thoughts and images and immediately counter any you become aware of. Replace them with affirming statements that encourage your self-esteem and confidence. Create and practice visualizations that build on your positive statements.

- Get your act together sooner rather than later. Have everything (including choice of clothing) laid out days in advance. Most important, know where the test will be held and the easiest, quickest way to get there. You will gain great peace of mind if you know that all the little details—gas in the car, directions, etc.—are firmly in your control before the day of the test.

- Experience the test site a few days in advance. This is very helpful if you are especially anxious. If at all possible, find out what room your part of the alphabet is assigned to and try to sit there (by yourself) for a while. Better yet, bring some practice material and do at least a section or two, if not an entire practice test, in that room. In this situation, familiarity doesn't breed contempt; it generates comfort and confidence.

Dress for Success

On the day of the test, wear loose layers. That way, you'll be prepared no matter what the temperature of the room is. (An uncomfortable temperature will just distract you from the job at hand.)

And, if you have an item of clothing that you tend to feel "lucky" or confident in—a shirt, a pair of jeans, whatever—wear it. A little totem couldn't hurt.

- Forego any practice on the day before the test. It's in your best interest to marshal your physical and psychological resources for 24 hours or so. Even race horses are kept in the paddock and treated like royalty the day before a race. Keep the upcoming test out of your consciousness; go to a movie, take a pleasant hike, or just relax. Don't eat junk food or tons of sugar. And—of course—get plenty of rest the night before. Just don't go to bed too early. It's hard to fall asleep earlier than you're used to, and you don't want to lie there thinking about the test.

HANDLING STRESS DURING THE TEST

The biggest stress monster will be the test itself. Fear not; there are methods of quelling your stress during the test.

- Keep moving forward instead of getting bogged down in a difficult question. You don't have to get everything right to achieve a fine score. The best test takers skip difficult material temporarily in search of the easier stuff. They mark the questions that require extra time and thought. This strategy buys time and builds confidence so you can handle the tough stuff later.

- Don't be thrown if other test takers seem to be working more furiously than you are. Continue to spend your time patiently thinking through your answers; it's going to lead to better results. Don't mistake the other people's sheer activity as signs of progress and higher scores.

- Keep breathing! Weak test takers tend to forget to breathe properly as the test proceeds. They start holding their breath without realizing it, or they breathe erratically or arrhythmically. Improper breathing interferes with clear thinking.

- Some quick isometrics during the test—especially if concentration is wandering or energy is waning—can help. Try this: Put your palms together and press intensely for a few seconds. Concentrate on the tension you feel through your palms, wrists, forearms, and up into your biceps and shoulders. Then, quickly release the pressure. Feel the difference as you let go. Focus on the warm relaxation that floods through the muscles. Now you're ready to return to the task.

- Here's another isometric that will relieve tension in both your neck and eye muscles. Slowly rotate your head from side to side, turning your head and eyes to look as far back over each shoulder as you can. Feel the muscles stretch on one side of your neck as they contract on the other. Repeat five times in each direction.

What Are "Signs of a Winner," Alex?

Here's some advice from a Kaplan instructor who won big on *Jeopardy!*™ In the green room before the show, he noticed that the contestants who were quiet and "within themselves" were the ones who did great on the show. The contestants who did not perform as well were the ones who were fact-cramming, talking a lot, and generally being manic before the show. Lesson: Spend the final hours leading up to the test getting sleep, meditating, and generally relaxing.

SHSAT
Practice Tests
and
Explanations

SHSAT

Practice Test 1

HOW TO TAKE THIS PRACTICE TEST

Before taking this practice test, find a quiet room where you can work uninterrupted for two and a half hours. Make sure you have a comfortable desk and several No. 2 pencils.

Use the answer sheet provided to record your answers. (You can cut it out or photocopy it.)

Once you start this practice test, don't stop until you've finished. Remember that you are in control of how you spend your time on the SHSAT. Inside your test booklet, you will see that 75 minutes is the "suggested time" for each portion of the test. You are allowed a total of 150 minutes for the entire test, and you may divide your time as you see fit. Unlike most standardized tests, the SHSAT *does* allow you to work on whichever part of the test you want to first. You can also go back and forth between sections if you choose to.

You'll find an answer key and answer explanations following each practice test.

Scoring information follows Practice Test 2.

Good luck.

SHSAT Practice Test 1
Answer Sheet

Remove (or photocopy) this answer sheet and use it to complete the practice test.
(See answer key following the test when finished.)

SCRAMBLED PARAGRAPHS

	The first sentence is:	The second sentence is:	The third sentence is:	The fourth sentence is:	The fifth sentence is:
Paragraph 1	Q R S T U	Q R S T U	Q R S T U	Q R S T U	Q R S T U
Paragraph 2	Q R S T U	Q R S T U	Q R S T U	Q R S T U	Q R S T U
Paragraph 3	Q R S T U	Q R S T U	Q R S T U	Q R S T U	Q R S T U
Paragraph 4	Q R S T U	Q R S T U	Q R S T U	Q R S T U	Q R S T U
Paragraph 5	Q R S T U	Q R S T U	Q R S T U	Q R S T U	Q R S T U

LOGICAL REASONING

11 (A) (B) (C) (D) (E)
12 (F) (G) (H) (J) (K)
13 (A) (B) (C) (D) (E)
14 (F) (G) (H) (J) (K)
15 (A) (B) (C) (D) (E)

16 (F) (G) (H) (J) (K)
17 (A) (B) (C) (D) (E)
18 (F) (G) (H) (J) (K)
19 (A) (B) (C) (D) (E)
20 (F) (G) (H) (J) (K)

READING

21 (A) (B) (C) (D) (E)
22 (F) (G) (H) (J) (K)
23 (A) (B) (C) (D) (E)
24 (F) (G) (H) (J) (K)
25 (A) (B) (C) (D) (E)

26 (F) (G) (H) (J) (K)
27 (A) (B) (C) (D) (E)
28 (F) (G) (H) (J) (K)
29 (A) (B) (C) (D) (E)
30 (F) (G) (H) (J) (K)

31 (A) (B) (C) (D) (E)
32 (F) (G) (H) (J) (K)
33 (A) (B) (C) (D) (E)
34 (F) (G) (H) (J) (K)
35 (A) (B) (C) (D) (E)

36 (F) (G) (H) (J) (K)
37 (A) (B) (C) (D) (E)
38 (F) (G) (H) (J) (K)
39 (A) (B) (C) (D) (E)
40 (F) (G) (H) (J) (K)

41 (A) (B) (C) (D) (E)
42 (F) (G) (H) (J) (K)
43 (A) (B) (C) (D) (E)
44 (F) (G) (H) (J) (K)
45 (A) (B) (C) (D) (E)

46 (F) (G) (H) (J) (K)
47 (A) (B) (C) (D) (E)
48 (F) (G) (H) (J) (K)
49 (A) (B) (C) (D) (E)
50 (F) (G) (H) (J) (K)

MATHEMATICS PROBLEMS

51 (A) (B) (C) (D) (E)
52 (F) (G) (H) (J) (K)
53 (A) (B) (C) (D) (E)
54 (F) (G) (H) (J) (K)
55 (A) (B) (C) (D) (E)

56 (F) (G) (H) (J) (K)
57 (A) (B) (C) (D) (E)
58 (F) (G) (H) (J) (K)
59 (A) (B) (C) (D) (E)
60 (F) (G) (H) (J) (K)

61 (A) (B) (C) (D) (E)
62 (F) (G) (H) (J) (K)
63 (A) (B) (C) (D) (E)
64 (F) (G) (H) (J) (K)
65 (A) (B) (C) (D) (E)

66 (F) (G) (H) (J) (K)
67 (A) (B) (C) (D) (E)
68 (F) (G) (H) (J) (K)
69 (A) (B) (C) (D) (E)
70 (F) (G) (H) (J) (K)

71 (A) (B) (C) (D) (E)
72 (F) (G) (H) (J) (K)
73 (A) (B) (C) (D) (E)
74 (F) (G) (H) (J) (K)
75 (A) (B) (C) (D) (E)

76 (F) (G) (H) (J) (K)
77 (A) (B) (C) (D) (E)
78 (F) (G) (H) (J) (K)
79 (A) (B) (C) (D) (E)
80 (F) (G) (H) (J) (K)

81 (A) (B) (C) (D) (E)
82 (F) (G) (H) (J) (K)
83 (A) (B) (C) (D) (E)
84 (F) (G) (H) (J) (K)
85 (A) (B) (C) (D) (E)

86 (F) (G) (H) (J) (K)
87 (A) (B) (C) (D) (E)
88 (F) (G) (H) (J) (K)
89 (A) (B) (C) (D) (E)
90 (F) (G) (H) (J) (K)

91 (A) (B) (C) (D) (E)
92 (F) (G) (H) (J) (K)
93 (A) (B) (C) (D) (E)
94 (F) (G) (H) (J) (K)
95 (A) (B) (C) (D) (E)

96 (F) (G) (H) (J) (K)
97 (A) (B) (C) (D) (E)
98 (F) (G) (H) (J) (K)
99 (A) (B) (C) (D) (E)
100 (F) (G) (H) (J) (K)

DIRECTIONS

Mark your answers on the separate sheet provided. You will receive credit only for answers marked on the answer grid. DO NOT MAKE ANY STRAY MARKS ON THE ANSWER GRID. You can write in the test booklet, or use the paper provided for scratchwork.

Part 1   Questions 1–50   75 minutes

Part 2   Questions 51–100   75 minutes

If you finish part 2 early you may go back to questions in either part. Your score is based on the number of questions answered correctly. There is no penalty for wrong answers. IF YOU DO NOT KNOW THE ANSWER TO A QUESTION, IT IS TO YOUR ADVANTAGE TO GUESS.

PART 1—VERBAL

Recommended Time—75 Minutes
50 Questions

Paragraphs 1–5: Scrambled Paragraphs

DIRECTIONS: Below are six sentences that form a paragraph. The first sentence is given; the remaining five sentences are listed in random order. Choose the order for these five sentences that will create the **best** paragraph, one that is both well organized and gramatically correct. Each correctly ordered paragraph is worth **double** the value of a question in any other section of the test. No credit will be given for responses that are only partially correct.

Paragraph 1

The climate of a major city is often markedly different from the climate of surrounding rural areas.

_____ **Q.** However, the geographic differences do not have to be dramatic to affect climatic differences.

_____ **R.** Other climatic changes are brought about by the construction of artificial structures and surfaces.

_____ **S.** Even between the center of a city and its suburbs, there are often differences in air temperature, humidity, wind speed, and direction.

_____ **T.** Many of these differences are caused by the high concentrations of pollutants over urban centers.

_____ **U.** For example, tall buildings, paved streets, and parking lots affect such patterns as wind flow and precipitation runoff.

Paragraph 2

In the "Gunpowder Plot" of 1605, a group of conspirators planned to blow up the English king and Parliament.

_____ **Q.** A small group of English Catholics, the conspirators objected to the government's policy of religious intolerance and decided to carry out a daring assassination.

_____ **R.** Taking advantage of poor security, they rented a cellar under the Palace of Westminster and hid twenty barrels of gunpowder there.

_____ **S.** The foiled attempt, which avoided a tragedy, is celebrated in the verse "Remember, remember, the fifth of November; Guy Fawkes and the Gunpower Plot."

_____ **T.** However, the conspirators were unable to keep the plot secret, and their infamous plan was foiled.

_____ **U.** Their intent was to explode the gunpowder when the king and Parliament next met.

GO ON TO THE NEXT PAGE ➡

Paragraph 3

In computer design, the effectiveness of a program generally depends on the ability of the programmer.

_____ **Q.** Still, remarkable progress has been made in the development of artificial intelligence.

_____ **R.** Despite this accomplishment, others argue that while computers may imitate the human mind, they will never possess the capacity for true intelligence.

_____ **S.** When a computer defeated Garry Kasparov, considered by many as a virtually unbeatable chess player, it was taken to be a vindication of the claims of the strongest supporters of artificial intelligence.

_____ **T.** Proponents of artificial intelligence believe that human intelligence consists of the very processes that computers can be taught to employ.

_____ **U.** This progress has scientists wondering whether it would be possible to develop a computer capable of intelligent thought.

Paragraph 4

The presence or absence of water can have a dramatic effect on the flora in a given environment.

_____ **Q.** Many desert plants, as a result, can complete an entire life cycle in a matter of months or even weeks.

_____ **R.** Areas in which it rains once a year, for example, are rewarded with a brief, stunning display of color that must be seen to be appreciated.

_____ **S.** Since desert plants are dependent on intermittent rain for survival, they must act quickly to make the most of scant resources.

_____ **T.** Generally, the more barren a desert is, the more rare and astounding these periods of bloom will be.

_____ **U.** The desert, for example, is a biologically complex place where rain is often violent and unpredictable.

Paragraph 5

It is a common belief among aspiring writers that great art is born from experience.

_____ **Q.** Their achievements illustrate that if you have a good imagination, you can write a novel—no matter how unadventurous your life may seem.

_____ **R.** Similarly, Robert Louis Stevenson, the author of classic adventures such as _Treasure Island_ and _Kidnapped_, was an invalid who was imprisoned in his bed for much of his life.

_____ **S.** And yet, just by observing the people around her, she was able to write universally acclaimed comedies about love and marriage.

_____ **T.** However, some of the greatest writers in literary history have been people with a very limited knowledge of the world.

_____ **U.** Nineteenth-century novelist Jane Austen, for example, didn't venture far beyond her circle of family and friends.

GO ON TO THE NEXT PAGE ➡

QUESTIONS 11–20, Logical Reasoning

Questions 13 and 14 refer to the following information.

Sam has seven books in a row on a shelf above his desk. Exactly three of the books are history books. Each history book is separated from the next history book by at least one math book. An English book and a social studies book are directly next to each other on the shelf, and neither one is next to a math book. The seven books are numbered 1 through 7 from left to right.

11. Whenever Kunio rings the bell, Rita plays the trumpet and Omar bangs the drum.

   If Rita is not playing the trumpet, which of the following **must** be true?

   A. Kunio is ringing the bell.
   B. Kunio is not ringing the bell.
   C. Omar is banging the drum.
   D. Omar is not banging the drum.
   E. Either Kunio is ringing the bell or Omar is banging the drum.

13. If Book 1 is a social studies book, which of the following **must** be math books?

   A. books 3 and 4
   B. books 3 and 5
   C. books 4 and 6
   D. books 5 and 6
   E. books 5 and 7

14. Book 3 **must** be on which subject?

   F. history
   G. math
   H. English
   J. social studies
   K. Cannot be determined from the information given.

12. Dan and Sonya are married and have exactly three children—Betty, George, and Tara—and exactly three grandchildren. If George sometimes babysits for Betty's twin daughters, but Tara never babysits for George's child, which of the following **must** be true?

   F. All of Dan's and Sonya's grandchildren are female.
   G. Tara has no children.
   H. Tara sometimes babysits for Betty's children.
   J. Betty has three children.
   K. Sonya has at least one grandson.

15. The plane took off from the runway at 6 P.M. as scheduled. Tom arrived at the airport at five minutes past 6 P.M.

Based only on the information above, which of the following statements is a valid conclusion?

A. Tom expected the plane's departure to be delayed.

B. The airline prides itself on sticking to the schedule.

C. Tom missed his flight by five minutes.

D. If Tom had driven faster, he wouldn't have missed his flight.

E. If Tom did not miss his plane, he was not supposed to be on the 6 P.M. flight.

16. The youngest employee of the financial consulting firm makes twenty-five thousand dollars per year. Matthew only makes nineteen thousand dollars per year.

Based only on the information above, which of the following **must** be true?

F. Matthew does not work for the financial consulting firm.

G. Matthew is not the youngest employee of the financial consulting firm.

H. The size of an employee's income is related to the employee's age.

J. Other employees in the financial consulting firm make more than twenty-five thousand dollars per year.

K. The youngest employee of the financial consulting firm makes less money per year than any other employee.

17. In the code below, each letter represents one syllable. The letters are not necessarily listed in the correct order.

CD = "befit"

FD = "fitful"

FH = "vengeful"

JH = "revenge"

MP = "misuse"

FP = "useful"

What letters are needed to write the code for the word "misfit"?

A. CF

B. CD

C. DP

D. MD

E. CM

18. Tania is an extremely versatile actress. In a recent series of plays, she played a schoolteacher, two divorcées, three best friends, and a stepmother. She played a divorcée throughout the first play, but in subsequent plays she often played more than one part.

If she never plays more than two parts in any one play, what is the **least** number of plays she could have performed in?

F. 3

G. 4

H. 5

J. 6

K. Cannot be determined from the information given.

GO ON TO THE NEXT PAGE ➡

19. Lisa has just caught the flu again. Her friend Jen concludes that she must have forgotten to take her vitamin C tablets.

Which of the following statements **must** be true in order for Jen's conclusion to be valid?

A. Lisa is often susceptible to catching the flu.

B. Lisa has run out of vitamin C tablets.

C. Lisa could only have caught the flu by forgetting to take her vitamin C tablets.

D. Lisa often forgets to take her vitamin C tablets.

E. Lisa is generally conscientious about taking care of her health.

20. When Joe attends orchestra rehearsal, he plays the first violin part. When Joe is not at rehearsal, Carl and Sonya compete for the first violin part.

Based only on the information above, which of the following is a valid conclusion?

F. Joe is considered the best violinist in the orchestra.

G. Carl and Sonya are equally talented as musicians.

H. Joe is frequently unable to attend orchestra rehearsal.

J. If Carl misses a rehearsal, Sonya plays the first violin part.

K. If Joe and Carl both attend rehearsal, Joe plays the first violin part.

QUESTIONS 21–50: Reading Passages

> **DIRECTIONS:** Read each passage and answer the questions that follow it. Choose the **best** answer for each question. Base your answers **only on what you have read in a given passage**. You may reread any passage you wish to.

Many people dream about living on a coral island, but probably few of us would be able to describe one with any accuracy. Popular books and films create a
Line romantic image of these islands, and it is not always
(5) entirely justified if seen from sea level. Beneath the waves, however, the coral island is a fantastic and very beautiful world, depending entirely upon a complex web of interrelationships between plants and animals.

The environment of the coral reef is formed over
(10) thousands of years by the life cycle of vast numbers of coral animals. The main architect of the reef is the stony coral, a relative of the sea anemone that lives in tropical climates and secretes a skeleton of almost pure calcium carbonate. Its partner is the green alga, a
(15) tiny unicellular plant, which lives within the tissues of the coral. The two organisms coexist in a mutually beneficial relationship, with the algae consuming carbon dioxide given off by the corals, and the corals thriving in the abundant oxygen produced
(20) photosynthetically by the algae. When the coral dies, its skeleton is left, and other organisms grow on top of it. Over the years, the sheer mass of coral skeletons, together with those of associated organisms, combines to form the petrified underwater forest that divers find
(25) so fascinating.

Many aspects of coral reefs still puzzle scientists, however. One mystery concerns the transformation of coral reefs into islands. Many of today's coral reefs are attached to much larger land masses. The northeastern
(30) coast of the continent of Australia, for example, is fringed by coral communities which have gradually grown into vast ribbons of barrier reefs. Scientists have proposed a theory to explain the transformation of "fringing reefs" such as these into islands. It's
(35) suggested that many of today's reef islands resulted from a rise in sea level at the end of the last Ice Age. Land masses to which reefs were once attached were gradually submerged by rising ocean levels. Scientists also believe that certain reef islands resulted from

(40) volcanic activity. Reefs which originally surrounded volcanic islands were transformed into atolls, or ring-shaped reef islands, as the volcanoes within gradually eroded and disappeared.

21. Which of the following best tells what this passage is about?

    A. the varieties of unusual animal life that live in coral reefs

    B. how coral reefs manage to survive wave erosion

    C. some biological and geological aspects of coral reefs

    D. the physical beauty of coral reefs

    E. the geological origins of reef islands

22. The skeleton of the stony coral is mostly made up of what?

    F. cartilage

    G. stone

    H. calcium carbonate

    J. carbon dioxide

    K. sediment

23. The relationship between the coral and the algae is best described as

    A. unfriendly.

    B. competitive.

    C. predatory.

    D. cooperative.

    E. mysterious.

GO ON TO THE NEXT PAGE ➡

24. What is the "puzzling" feature of coral reefs discussed in this passage?

    F. their evolution into islands

    G. their ability to support diverse communities of life

    H. the ease with which they withstood the destructive effects of the last Ice Age

    J. their evolution from isolated reefs into great land masses

    K. the frequent appearance of new volcanoes in their vicinity

25. Which of the following is mentioned as resulting from volcanic activity?

    A. barrier reefs

    B. fringing reefs

    C. land masses such as Australia

    D. ring-shaped reef islands

    E. barrier islands

26. What does the passage suggest about the image of coral islands in popular culture?

    F. It is widely held but totally inaccurate.

    G. It is justified except in the case of fringing reefs.

    H. It is the product of divers with rich imaginations.

    J. It is a perception most scientists would like to correct.

    K. It is more accurate from an underwater perspective.

At the end of the nineteenth century, a new wave of immigration caused a massive population explosion in the United States. Between 1880 and 1910, 18
Line   million immigrants flooded into the U.S. from
(5)   southern and eastern Europe, attracted by economic opportunity, religious freedom and political democracy. Few immigrants of this period found life in America easy, however. Many of those who lacked professional skills and did not speak English found
(10)   themselves living in slum conditions in the sprawling cities of the Northeast, exploited by their employers and trapped at poverty level.

Around the turn of the century a number of different organizations made efforts to help these
(15)   newly arrived immigrants adapt to American life. Two groups in particular emerged as leaders in these efforts. These two groups, however, had very dissimilar ideas about how to go about assimilating the immigrants.
(20)   One organization that contributed to assimilation efforts was a conservative group called the Daughters of the American Revolution. This group approached immigrants with the expectation that newcomers should completely adopt American customs and
(25)   culture. Consequently they supported laws that required immigrants to take oaths of loyalty and to pass English language tests. They also tried to discourage the use of languages other than English in the schools.

Another conception of assimilation came from
(30)   the experience of reformers such as Jane Addams. In 1889, Addams founded a volunteer organization in Chicago called Hull House, that attempted to improve conditions in the city's poor immigrant neighborhoods. Hull House served as a model for
(35)   many similar "settlement houses" throughout the country. These institutions sought to ease the immigrants' adjustment to an unfamiliar society by offering whatever social services were not provided by local governments, including medical care, legal
(40)   assistance, and adult education. Fundamental to the settlement house philosophy was a respect for the cultural heritage of the new arrivals. Workers such as Jane Addams who saw at first hand the alienation of first- and second-generation immigrants feared that
(45)   attempts to "Americanize" the immigrants would lead to ethnic self-hatred and deprive the country of a variety of distinct cultural contributions.

27. Which of the following best tells what this passage is about?

  A. the story of immigration to the United States.

  B. the cultural contributions offered by immigrants

  C. how to assimilate immigrants into American life

  D. how immigrants changed life in U.S. cities

  E. two different concepts of assimilating immigrants

28. Which of the following is **not** mentioned as a characteristic of the life that awaited immigrants to the United States between 1890 and 1910?

  F. poor housing

  G. harsh working conditions

  H. religious persecution

  J. lack of opportunity for advancement

  K. pressure to assimilate

29. The conservatives' methods of assimilation are most similar to those of someone who renovates a house

  A. to look more expensive than it really is.

  B. to reveal the structural elements of the house.

  C. to look like all of the other houses on the block.

  D. to make it stand out from the rest of the houses on the block.

  E. to preserve the original style of design.

GO ON TO THE NEXT PAGE ➡

30. The services provided by the settlement houses were intended to

    F. supplement the services provided by local government.

    G. discourage the use of foreign languages in schools.

    H. enable immigrants to open similar settlement houses elsewhere.

    J. instruct immigrants in the beliefs of the reformers.

    K. teach immigrants to conform to rigid standards.

31. Which of the following would most probably have been supported by the reformers?

    A. a language course to help immigrants lose their accents

    B. a law that would require all immigrants to leave the country after five years

    C. a program to relocate immigrant populations out of the cities

    D. a requirement that all immigrants pledge absolute loyalty to their adopted country

    E. a program that would teach other Americans about the culture of the immigrants

32. The phrase "cultural contributions" (line 47) refers to what?

    F. money given to immigrant groups by the reformers

    G. foreign influences that enrich national life

    H. cultural programs offered at the settlement houses

    J. new tax revenues provided by the immigrants

    K. learning provided by adult education programs

Animals that use coloring to safeguard themselves from predators are said to have "protective coloration." One common type of protective coloration

Line is called cryptic resemblance, where an animal
(5) adapts in color, shape, and behavior in order to blend into its environment. The camouflage of the pale green tree frog is a good example of cryptic resemblance. The tree frog blends so perfectly into its surroundings that when it sits motionless it is all but
(10) invisible against a background of leaves. Another type of camouflage, shown by zebras and leopards, is a pattern that diverts the eye from the outline of the animal. The leopard's splotchy markings serve this purpose as it crouches in the mottled light of tree
(15) branches. This type of protective coloration is known as disruptive coloring.

Many animals change their protective pigmentation with the seasons. The caribou sheds its brown coat in winter, replacing it with white fur. The
(20) stoat, a member of the weasel family, is known as the ermine in winter, when its brown fur changes to the white fur prized by royalty. The chameleon, even more versatile than these, changes color in just a few minutes to match whatever surface it happens to be
(25) lying on or clinging to. Some animals use protective coloration not for camouflage but to stand out against their surroundings. The skunk's brilliant white stripe is meant to be seen, as a warning to predators to avoid the animal's stink. Similarly, the hedgehog uses its
(30) "salt and pepper" look to loudly announce its identity, since it depends on its evil stench and unpleasant texture to make it unpalatable to the predators around it.

Protective coloration is not absolute; it changes
(35) and evolves. One example of adaptive coloration concerns the English peppered moth. Originally, the light coloring of these insects disguised them from birds as they rested on tree trunks covered with pale lichens. In the nineteenth century, industrial pollution
(40) began killing the lichens. The moths now stood out against bare tree trunks and smoke-darkened vegetation. Soon, dark-colored peppered moths, which had always existed in small numbers, began to outnumber the light-colored moths. But in the
(45) twentieth century, strong antipollution laws were passed, and light-colored peppered moths made a comeback.

33. Which of the following best tells what the passage is about?
   A. how animals blend into their surroundings
   B. several types of protective coloration
   C. contrasts among the tree frog, the zebra, the caribou, and the skunk
   D. a description of predators in the animal kingdom
   E. the difference between cryptic resemblance and disruptive coloring

34. According to the passage, which of the following is **not** a form of protective coloration?
   F. disruptive coloring
   G. seasonal changes in pigmentation
   H. adaptive coloration
   J. cryptic resemblance
   K. mottled light

35. The author uses the caribou and the stoat as examples of animals that
   A. change their color according to the time of year.
   B. are protected by disruptive coloring.
   C. possess valuable white fur.
   D. have prominent markings to warn predators.
   E. protect themselves by constantly changing their coloring.

36. The feature of the chameleon discussed in this passage is its ability to

   F. camouflage itself despite frequent changes in location.

   G. cling to surfaces that are hidden from attackers.

   H. adapt easily to seasonal changes.

   J. use disruptive coloring to confuse predators.

   K. change the colors of surfaces it is resting on.

37. Dark-colored peppered moths probably began to outnumber light-colored moths because

   A. they were not injured by pollutants in the air.

   B. environmental laws protected them against pollution.

   C. unlike light-colored moths, they did not feed on lichens.

   D. they were now harder for birds to see than light-colored moths.

   E. birds that preyed on moths were killed by pollution.

38. The peppered moth's protective strategy is most similar to that of the

   F. caribou.

   G. skunk.

   H. tree frog.

   J. zebra.

   K. stoat.

GO ON TO THE NEXT PAGE ➡

The four brightest moons of Jupiter were the first objects in the solar system discovered through the use of the telescope. Their proven existence played a

Line central role in Galileo's famous argument in support

(5) of the Copernican model of the solar system, in which the planets are described as revolving around the Sun.

For several hundred years after their discovery by Galileo in 1610, scientific understanding of these moons increased fairly slowly. Observers on Earth

(10) succeeded in measuring their approximate diameters, their relative densities, and eventually some of their light-reflecting characteristics. But it was the spectacular series of photographs sent back by the 1979 Voyager missions that forever changed our

(15) impressions of these bodies.

All four of the moons, named after Jupiter's lovers in Greco-Roman mythology, probably experienced early, heavy asteroid bombardment. The very ancient, relatively unchanged surface of Callisto

(20) remains badly scarred by impact craters. The younger surface of Ganymede shows more variety, featuring distinctive light and dark areas. Ancient craters dot the dark areas, while the light areas are crisscrossed by ridges and grooves that resulted from more recent ice

(25) flows. The impact sites on Europa have almost completely disappeared under vast oceans of ice.

But perhaps the biggest surprise of the Voyager mission was the discovery of intense volcanic or geyser-like activity on Io. Eruptions first recognized as

(30) plumes of dust and gas were immediately noticeable on the Voyager photographs. Further inspection revealed at least seven such events occurring all at once on Io's otherwise frigid surface—massive plumes of material were being ejected from the

(35) surface of the satellite to form clouds 500 kilometers high. At other points, scientists detected three hot spots believed to be ponds of molten lava, sulfur, or sodium overlain by a crust. The largest of these hot lakes was estimated to have a greater surface area than

(40) the state of Hawaii.

39. Which of the following best tells what this passage is about?

   A. Galileo's invention of the telescope

   B. the discovery of the Galilean moons

   C. scientific knowledge about the solar system

   D. the damage caused by asteroid bombardment

   E. Jupiter's four brightest moons

40. This passage suggests that Galileo was one of the first scientists to

   F. attack the Copernican theory of the solar system.

   G. make accurate measurements of the diameters of Jupiter's moons.

   H. engage in studies of stars.

   J. compare the various densities of the four Galilean moons.

   K. make important use of the telescope.

41. Galileo's relationship to the ideas of Copernicus is similar to

   A. a patron's support of an artist.

   B. a boy's love for his dog.

   C. a landlord's distrust of a tenant.

   D. a patient's admiration of her nurse.

   E. a scholar's defense of an educator.

GO ON TO THE NEXT PAGE ➡

42. The geologic features found in the light areas of Ganymede were probably formed

    F. after the features found in Ganymede's dark areas.

    G. in an earlier period than those in the dark areas.

    H. at about the same time as the features in the dark areas.

    J. mainly by ancient bombardment.

    K. by the moon's volcanic activity.

43. Which of the following is not mentioned in the passage as being a feature of Jupiter's moons?

    A. ancient impact craters

    B. current volcanic activity

    C. recent asteroid bombardment

    D. ponds of molten sulfur

    E. atmospheric clouds

44. What was the most unexpected fact to emerge from the Voyager photographs?

    F. the size of Io's molten lakes

    G. the disappearance of impact sites on Europa

    H. the discovery of volcanic activity on Io

    J. the evidence of asteroid bombardment on all four moons

    K. the accuracy of Galileo's original observations

GO ON TO THE NEXT PAGE ➡

For thousands of years, smallpox was one of the world's most dreaded diseases. An acutely infectious disease spread by a virus, smallpox was the scourge of
Line   medieval Europe, where it was known by its
(5)   symptoms of extreme fever and disfiguring rash as "the invisible fire." In many outbreaks, mortality rates were higher than 25 percent. Ancient Chinese medical texts show that the disease was known as long ago as 1122 BCE. But as recently as 1967, more than 2
(10)   million people died of smallpox in one year.

The first method developed to combat smallpox was an attempt to immunize healthy patients. In a procedure called variolation, known since the ninth century CE, a healthy patient's skin was deliberately
(15)   scratched with infectious material from a person with a mild case of smallpox. If the treatment was successful, the patient suffered a mild smallpox infection and then became immune to the disease. By the 18th century, when smallpox epidemics were
(20)   regular occurrences, variolation was a common practice among the wealthy and aristocratic. Unfortunately, variolation sometimes led to severe, even fatal, infections. Moreover, even if it was successful, the patient could spread smallpox to
(25)   others.

A safer method of conferring immunity was discovered in 1796 by an English doctor named Edward Jenner. Jenner, who had himself undergone the variolation process as a child, was fascinated by
(30)   the fact that people who caught cowpox, a harmless disease spread by cattle, became immune to smallpox. To test whether this immunity could be replicated, Jenner inoculated a young boy with infectious matter taken from a child who had cowpox. The boy
(35)   developed a slight infection. Later, Jenner inoculated the boy with smallpox matter and discovered that no disease developed. Jenner wrote a paper describing his results, but the Royal Society of Physicians, who were skeptical about his unconventional approach, rejected
(40)   it. Jenner published his findings independently, and his paper became a bestseller. Within a matter of years, the new procedure known as vaccination was in general use throughout Europe and the United States, and the fight against smallpox was underway.
(45)   It was not until 1966, however, that the World Health Organization was able to find the resources to launch a worldwide campaign to wipe out the disease altogether. In an immense project involving thousands of health workers, WHO teams moved from country to
(50)   country, locating every case of active smallpox and vaccinating all potential contacts. In 1977, the last active case of smallpox was found and eliminated.

Since there are no animal carriers of smallpox, the WHO was able to declare in 1980 that the dreaded
(55)   killer had been conquered. For the first time in the history of medicine, a disease had been completely destroyed.

45. Which of the following best tells what this passage is about?

A. how to treat viral diseases

B. the dangers of variolation

C. how Edward Jenner discovered vaccination

D. the history of the fight against smallpox

E. early efforts at controlling infectious diseases

46. When was a method of immunizing against smallpox first developed?

F. 1122 BCE

G. the ninth century CE

H. 1796

J. 1966

K. 1980

47. As discussed in this passage, one disadvantage of variolation was that

A. the inoculated patient could still spread smallpox.

B. variolation did not give immunity to cowpox.

C. immunity wore off after a time.

D. variolation was hard to carry out.

E. many doctors refused to use the procedure.

GO ON TO THE NEXT PAGE ➡

48. The passage implies that Jenner began to experiment with vaccination because he

   F. was suffering from a mild case of smallpox himself.

   G. had noticed a relationship between two diseases.

   H. wanted to be accepted into the Royal Society of Physicians.

   J. had attempted variolation without success.

   K. preferred unconventional approaches to scientific problems.

49. When did vaccination against smallpox become widespread?

   A. as soon as Jenner wrote a report of his findings

   B. several years after Jenner's discovery

   C. only in countries where variolation was not practiced

   D. early in the twentieth century

   E. when adopted by the World Health Organization in 1966

50. The passage implies that smallpox was not eliminated before 1966 because

   F. vaccination did not prevent all forms of the disease.

   G. not enough was known about immunity to disease.

   H. there was no effective protection against animal carriers.

   J. there had never been a coordinated worldwide vaccination campaign.

   K. the disease would lie dormant for many years and then reappear.

GO ON TO THE NEXT PAGE ➡

PART 2—MATHEMATICS

Recommended Time—75 Minutes
50 Questions
NOTES:

- Reduce all fractions to lowest terms.

- Diagrams are **not** necessarily drawn to scale.

- Do your figuring in the test booklet or on paper distributed by the proctor.

QUESTIONS 51–100, Mathematics Problems

DIRECTIONS: Solve each problem. Find your answer among the answer choices given. Mark the letter of your answer on the answer sheet.

51. $5(8 - 7) - 7(5 - 8) =$

- A. −21
- B. −16
- C. 16
- D. 21
- E. 26

52. John gets paid $6 for each of the first 40 toy cars he makes in a week. For any additional toy cars beyond 40, his pay increases by 50%. How much does John get paid in a week in which he makes 48 toy cars?

- F. $288
- G. $300
- H. $312
- J. $321
- K. $324

53. If $b = 2$ and $c = 3$, what is the value of a in the equation $a = 2b + 3c - 8$?

- A. 2
- B. 3
- C. 4
- D. 5
- E. 6

54. Two large sodas contain the same amount as three medium sodas. Two medium sodas contain the same amount as three small sodas. How many small sodas contain the same amount as eight large sodas?

- F. 12
- G. 16
- H. 18
- J. 24
- K. 32

55. $-2[(-18) \div 6] - 5[8 \div (-4)] =$

- A. −16
- B. −4
- C. 4
- D. 12
- E. 16

56. Henry has 4 chocolate ice cream bars, 3 vanilla ice cream bars, and 12 strawberry ice cream bars in his refrigerator freezer. If he picks one ice cream bar at random, what is the probability that it is vanilla?

    F. $\frac{3}{19}$

    G. $\frac{4}{19}$

    H. $\frac{3}{7}$

    J. $\frac{12}{19}$

    K. $\frac{16}{19}$

57. The area of a rectangle is 48, and its length is 8. What is the perimeter of this rectangle?

    A. 14
    B. 28
    C. 42
    D. 49
    E. 64

58. The president of France delivered a $3\frac{1}{2}$-hour speech beginning at 5 P.M. in Paris. The speech was broadcast live to New York. The time in Paris is 6 hours ahead of New York time. What was the time in New York when the speech ended?

    F. 8:30 A.M.
    G. 11:30 A.M.
    H. 2:30 P.M.
    J. 5:30 P.M.
    K. 7:30 P.M.

59. If each digit 5 is replaced with the digit 7, by how much will 258,546 be increased?

    A. 1,100
    B. 10,100
    C. 20,100
    D. 20,200
    E. 22,000

$$z\overline{)275} \quad 55$$

60. In the division problem above, there was no remainder. What is the remainder when 24 is divided by z?

    F. 1
    G. 4
    H. 5
    J. 6
    K. 12

The following question refers to the graph below.

Wind Speed mph	Temperature °F				
	30°	20°	10°	0°	−10°
10	15	0	−10	−20	−35
20	5	−10	−25	−40	−50
30	0	−20	−35	−50	−65

WIND CHILL FACTOR CHART

61. The chart above gives wind chill factors for certain temperature-wind combinations. For example, a temperature of 10°F and a wind speed of 20 mph have a wind chill factor of −25. If the temperature is −10°F and the wind chill factor is −50, what is the wind speed?

    A. 30 mph
    B. 20 mph
    C. 10 mph
    D. 0 mph
    E. −10 mph

GO ON TO THE NEXT PAGE ➡

62. What number is halfway between $\frac{5}{12}$ and $\frac{1}{2}$?

F. $\frac{3}{14}$

G. $\frac{3}{7}$

H. $\frac{11}{24}$

J. $\frac{13}{24}$

K. $\frac{22}{24}$

63. If x and y are negative integers, which of the following expressions **must** be negative?

A. xy

B. $x + y$

C. $x - y$

D. $x^2 + y^2$

E. $x^2 - y^2$

64. The value of $800,000 + 75,000 + 400 + 3$ is

F. 800,403

G. 807,503

H. 807,903

J. 875,403

K. 8,075,403

65. The average of five consecutive multiples of 5 is 20. What is the **largest** of these numbers?

A. 20

B. 25

C. 30

D. 35

E. 50

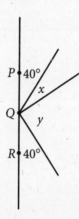

66. In the figure above, points P, Q, and R lie on a straight line. What is the value of $x + y$?

F. 50

G. 90

H. 100

J. 111

K. 120

67. A grocer sells eggs only in boxes of 8. If he starts with 175 eggs and fills as many boxes as he can with eggs, how many eggs will he have left over?

  A. 1
  B. 3
  C. 4
  D. 5
  E. 7

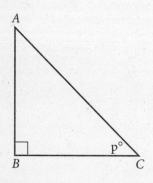

68. In the figure above, $AB = BC$. What is the value of p?

  F. 30
  G. 45
  H. 60
  J. 90
  K. 135

69. Which of the following is closest to the product $\frac{41}{70} \times \frac{7}{6}$?

  A. $\frac{1}{4}$

  B. $\frac{1}{3}$

  C. $\frac{1}{2}$

  D. $\frac{2}{3}$

  E. $\frac{4}{5}$

Here are two different ways to add:

Method 1: First add the numbers, then round to the nearest 10.

Method 2: First round the numbers to the nearest 10, then add.

70. For which of the following expressions will the result be the same with either method?

  F. $16 + 26$
  G. $14 + 34$
  H. $17 + 47$
  J. $24 + 57$
  K. $37 + 86$

71. What is the value of $\frac{5}{12} \times \frac{3}{2} \times \frac{3}{5}$?

  A. $\frac{5}{24}$

  B. $\frac{1}{4}$

  C. $\frac{3}{10}$

  D. $\frac{3}{8}$

  E. $\frac{1}{2}$

GO ON TO THE NEXT PAGE ➡

72. If 25% of x is 120, what is the value of x?

    F.   30

    G. 120

    H. 145

    J. 240

    K. 480

73. Reduce $\dfrac{432}{656}$ to lowest terms.

    A. $\dfrac{2}{3}$

    B. $\dfrac{7}{10}$

    C. $\dfrac{27}{41}$

    D. $\dfrac{107}{164}$

    E. $\dfrac{216}{328}$

74. Express 0.02718 in scientific notation.

    F. 2718×10^{-1}

    G. 2.718×10^{-2}

    H. 0.2718×10

    J. 0.02718×10^{2}

    K. 2.718×10^{2}

75. If $x = -3$ and $y = 2$, what is the value of $(5y - xy)^2$?

    A.   16

    B.   64

    C.   81

    D. 136

    E. 256

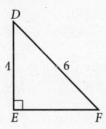

76. In the figure above, what is the value of EF?

    F. 2

    G. $2\sqrt{3}$

    H. 4

    J. $2\sqrt{5}$

    K. 5

    $> x > = 3x$ if x is even.

    $> x > = 4x$ if x is odd.

    For example, $> 1 > = 4$ and $> 4 > = 12$.

77. What is the value of $> -2 >$?

    A. −8

    B. −6

    C.   3

    D   6

    E.   8

78. What is the value of $(-ab)(a)$ when $a = -2$ and $b = 3$?

    F. −12

    G. −6

    H.   6

    J. 12

    K. 18

79. If the circumference of a circle is 10π, what is its area?

    A. 5π

    B. 10π

    C. 25π

    D. 50π

    E. 100π

80. What is the value of $7 + |3y| + 7 + |-2y|$ when $y = 4$?

    F. −6

    G. −1

    H. 16

    J. 28

    K. 34

81. Each square in the grid above has a side length of 4. What is the area of the shaded triangle?

    A. 12

    B. 24

    C. 48

    D. 64

    E. 96

82. If $x = \frac{1}{2}$, what is the value of y when $\frac{x}{3} = \frac{4}{y}$?

    F.   2

    G.   4

    H.   6

    J. 12

    K. 24

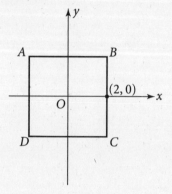

83. The center of square $ABCD$ is located at the origin, and its sides are parallel to the coordinate axes. What is the area of square $ABCD$?

    A. 4

    B. 8

    C. 16

    D 36

    E. Cannot be determined from the information given.

84. Michael bought $2\frac{1}{4}$ pounds of lumber at \$4 per pound. If a 7% sales tax was added, how much did Michael pay?

    F. \$9.63

    G. \$9.98

    H. \$10.63

    J. \$11.77

    K. \$12.84

GO ON TO THE NEXT PAGE ➡

85. If $z = 9$, what is the value of $\dfrac{9(3 + z)}{5z}$?

    A. $\dfrac{9}{5}$

    B. $\dfrac{12}{5}$

    C. $\dfrac{81}{25}$

    D. $\dfrac{18}{5}$

    E. $\dfrac{108}{25}$

86. A rectangle with a length of 9 inches and a width of 8 inches is divided into squares with sides of length 1 inch. One-third of these squares are painted red, $\dfrac{1}{8}$ of the remaining squares are painted green, and the others are left unpainted. How many squares are left unpainted?

    F. 24
    G. 33
    H. 36
    J. 42
    K. 48

87. Which of the following is a prime factor of 726?

    A. 6
    B. 7
    C. 9
    D. 11
    E. 13

88. If N is an odd integer, which of the following **must** be even?

    F. $2N - 1$
    G. $3N + 2$
    H. $4N$
    J. $N^2 + 2N$
    K. $2N^2 + 1$

89. Frank has x stamps, and Chris has 8 more than 7 times the number of stamps Frank has. How many stamps do Frank and Chris have in total?

    A. $8x$
    B. $7x + 8$
    C. $8x + 7$
    D. $8x + 8$
    E. $56x + 7$

90. Five less than 4 times the number n is 2 more than 3 times the number m. Which of the following expresses this relationship?

    F. $5 + 4n = 2 - 3m$
    G. $5 - 4n = 2 + 3m$
    H. $4n - 5 = 3m + 2$
    J. $4(n - 5) = 3(m + 2)$
    K. $4(n + 5) = 3m - 2$

GO ON TO THE NEXT PAGE ➡

91. $\sqrt{100} - \sqrt{64} =$

A. 1

B. 2

C. 4

D. 6

E. 8

$$y = x^2$$

92. The only possible values of x in the above equation are those in the set $\{-2, 0, 2\}$. Which set is the set of all possible values y can have?

F. $\{0, 2\}$

G. $\{0, 4\}$

H. $\{-2, 0\}$

J. $\{-4, 0\}$

K. $\{-4, 0, 4\}$

Color of chip	Number of chips
red	4
orange	2
yellow	3
green	1
blue	6

93. The table above shows the number of chips of each color in an urn. Which color has a probability of 1 in 8 of being chosen if 1 chip is chosen at random from the urn?

A. red

B. orange

C. yellow

D. green

E. blue

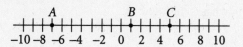

94. What is the distance from the midpoint of $\overline{AB}$ to point C?

F. 4

G. 6

H. 7

J. 8

K. 9

95. Which of the following fractions is closest to $\frac{1}{4}$?

A. $\frac{107}{200}$

B. $\frac{65}{365}$

C. $\frac{27}{1,000}$

D. $\frac{101}{499}$

E. $\frac{41}{160}$

96. A cat is fed $\frac{3}{8}$ of a pound of cat food every day. For how many days will 60 pounds of this cat food feed the cat?

F. 160

G. 180

H. 240

J. 360

K. 480

GO ON TO THE NEXT PAGE ➡

97. If $3 = \frac{9b}{a}$, what is $\frac{a}{b}$ equal to?

   A. 3

   B. $3a$

   C. $3ab$

   D 27

   E. $27b$

2, 5, 10, 17, 26, 37, 50, 65, d, 101

98. What value of d fits the intended pattern of the sequence above?

   F. 80

   G. 82

   H. 83

   J. 89

   K. 90

99. What is the value of $2(5b - 7)$ in terms of y if $b = 3y$?

   A. $15y - 7$

   B. $30y$

   C. $30y + 7$

   D. $30y - 7$

   E. $30y - 14$

The following question refers to the graph below.

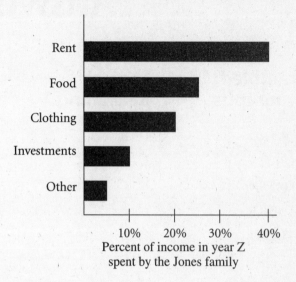

Percent of income in year Z spent by the Jones family

100. Approximately what percent of the Jones family income was spent on food and clothing in year Z?

   F. 45%

   G. 50%

   H. 55%

   J. 60%

   K. 65%

THIS IS THE END OF THE TEST. IF TIME REMAINS, YOU MAY CHECK YOUR ANSWERS TO PART 2 AND PART 1. BE SURE THAT THERE ARE NO STRAY MARKS, PARTIALLY FILLED ANSWER CIRCLES, OR INCOMPLETE ERASURES ON YOUR ANSWER SHEET.

DO NOT TURN TO THE NEXT PAGE. EXPLANATIONS FOLLOW.

STOP

Practice Test 1
Answer Key

Scrambled Paragraphs

1. QSTRU
2. QRUTS
3. QUTSR
4. USQRT
5. TUSRQ

Logical Reasoning

11. B
12. G
13. C
14. F
15. E
16. G
17. D
18. G
19. C
20. K

Reading Comprehension

21. C
22. H
23. D
24. F
25. D
26. K
27. E
28. H
29. C
30. F
31. E
32. G
33. B
34. K
35. A
36. F
37. D
38. H
39. E
40. K
41. E
42. F
43. C
44. H
45. D
46. G
47. A
48. G
49. B
50. J

Mathematics Problems

51. E
52. H
53. D
54. H
55. E
56. F
57. B
58. H
59. D
60. G
61. B
62. H
63. B
64. J
65. C
66. H
67. E
68. G
69. D
70. J
71. D
72. K
73. C
74. G
75. E

76. J
77. B
78. F
79. C
80. K
81. C
82. K
83. C
84. F
85. B
86. J
87. D
88. H
89. D
90. H
91. B
92. G
93. B
94. J
95. E
96. F
97. A
98. G
99. E
100. F

Practice Test 1 Answers and Explanations

SCRAMBLED PARAGRAPHS

1. **QSTRU.** Although S could possibly follow the Topic Sentence, Q is the better choice because it bridges the gap between urban and rural areas in the Topic Sentence and urban and suburban areas in S. S then follows, as it explains why climatic differences occur. T follows up with the linking phrase "these differences" and identifies cause number one—high concentrations of pollutants. R identifies cause number two—construction of artificial structures. Finally, U concludes by providing examples of how "artificial structures" lead to climactic changes.

2. **QRUTS.** Q best follows the Topic Sentence, as it provides details about the conspirators mentioned in the Topic Sentence. R, U, and T provide details in chronological order. "They" in R refers to "conspirators" in Q. "The gunpowder" in U refers to the "twenty barrels" in R. T wraps up the details, and S summarizes the whole incident.

3. **QUTSR.** The keyword "generally" in the Topic Sentence indicates that an exception is coming next, and Q provides that: The author is saying that *in spite of* the fact that computers are generally only as good as their programmers, progress has been made in artificial intelligence (i.e., in developing computers that can "think" for themselves). The linking phrase "this progress" indicates that U must come next. T follows by noting what "proponents...believe," S provides a specific example, and R wraps with a counterargument.

4. **USQRT.** U provides an example of a place (the desert) with sporadic rain. S points out that "making the most of scant resources" is required. What would you predict next? Some description of *how* desert plants "make the most of" meager rainfall, right? Q connects with this theme—plants maximize resources by having short life cycles. R illustrates one effect of this short rainfall (short periods of bloom). T concludes the paragraph by expanding on this point, explaining that the more barren the desert, the more spectacular these periods of bloom are.

5. **TUSRQ.** The phrase "it is a common belief" in the Topic Sentence indicates that a contrast will follow. T provides the goods by stating the opposite (i.e., that great art can not always be born from experience if many great writers had limited knowledge of the world). What would you provide next? An example or two, right? U provides an example of a writer who fits this category—Jane Austen. S describes her accomplishment. R provides a second example—Robert Louis Stevenson. Q wraps up by drawing a lesson from these authors' achievements.

LOGICAL REASONING

11. **B** This is an if/then statement—whenever Kunio rings the bell, both Rita and Omar start playing their instruments. The golden rule with if/then questions is that the only deduction that **must** be true is the "contrapositive": If Kunio's bell ringing always results in Rita and Omar joining in, you can be sure that if Rita and Omar *aren't* both playing, then Kunio *isn't* ringing his bell. This makes (B) the correct answer.

12. **G** In Dan and Sonya's family, there are exactly three children—Betty, George, and Tara—and three grandchildren. George babysits for Betty's twin daughters, so you already know that Betty has two out of the three grandchildren. Tara *doesn't* babysit for George's child, but this tells us that George has the one remaining grandchild and Tara has none—choice (G).

Just to check the wrong answers: (F) and (K) are out because we don't know whether George's child is male or female; (H) is out because Tara may or may not babysit for Betty's kids. (J) is wrong on numerical grounds—Betty has two of the grandchildren, and George has the other.

13. **C**   This is the first of two sequence problems about Sam's overloaded bookshelf. Let's sort through the evidence and use some diagrams to help reconstruct the situation. We're told that Sam has seven books total, three of which are history books. *At least one* math book separates each history book. Since there are three history books, you can conclude that there must be *at least* two math books to fulfill this function. Without even considering the other books, you should picture the shelf looking something like this: HMHMH. We're also told that an English book and a social studies book are positioned next to each other, *neither* of them touching a math book. In order to fulfill this rule, the English and social studies books must be positioned on either end of the row. If the social studies book was first, the row would look like this: (SE)HMHMH. This would make the math books numbers 4 and 6 in the sequence—choice (**C**).

14. **F**   Given the setup, there are four possible combinations on Sam's shelf: (SE)HMHMH, (ES)HMHMH, HMHMH(SE), and HMHMH(ES). Since a history book is book 3 in each case, (F) is the correct answer.

15. **E**   Always be on your guard with Logical Reasoning questions. It's almost automatic to assume here that Tom was supposed to be on that 6 P.M. plane, which leads to the conclusion that he missed his flight (C). But how

do you know for sure? Tom could just be coming to the airport to pick someone up, for all you know (which rules out (A) and (D) as well as (C). All that can be said for sure is that if he didn't miss his plane, then he was not supposed to be on the flight. (E) is correct.

16. **G**   The assumption to avoid is that the younger an employee is, the less money he or she is going to make. There could be older employees of the firm making less money than the youngest employee, and Matthew could be one of them. It could even be the case that the youngest employee makes the most money, as far as you know. This eliminates every choice but (G). Since Matthew and the youngest employee of the firm don't make the same salary, they can't be the same person.

17. **D**   The words "befit" and "fitful" have the syllable "fit" in common, and their codes have the letter D in common, so D must represent "fit." This eliminates choices (A) and (E). "Mis" only appears in "misuse," which is MP. You can tell that the P must stand for "use" because "misuse" and "useful" have only the syllable "use" and the letter P in common. Therefore, M represents "mis." "Misfit" would be MD or DM (the order doesn't matter).

18. **G**   This one calls for a diagram. You don't have to worry about the different types of parts Tanya had; the important pieces of information are that she had seven parts total, one part in the first play and at most two in each succeeding play.

Play: 1 2   3   4

             P PP PP PP

As you can see, if she did have the maximum of two parts per play after play 1, she could have had all seven parts in as few as four plays, choice (G).

19. **C**   There are quite a few reasons that someone could be especially susceptible to the flu, but Jen concludes that Lisa must have forgotten to take her vitamin C. In order for Jen to be so sure, she would have to know that there is no other way Lisa could have caught the flu. This makes (C) correct. (D) is tempting but wrong. If all that Jen knows is that Lisa has caught the flu and that she often forgets to take her vitamin C, the most Jen could conclude is that Lisa **may** have forgotten to take her vitamin C and **may** have caught the flu for this reason. This isn't good enough for the conclusion in the question stem to be valid.

20. **K**   Let's go through the answer choices. (F) is tempting but wrong. You cannot be absolutely sure that the person playing the first violin part is considered the best violinist in the orchestra; maybe someone even better on the violin always plays another instrument when playing with the orchestra. There's no reason to think that Carl and Sonya are "equally talented," so (G) is incorrect. (H) is out because you don't know how often Joe misses rehearsal. (J) doesn't make sense because Joe may be there to play the first part when Carl misses the rehearsal. (K) is the correct choice: Joe always plays the first part when he attends rehearsal, regardless of who else is there.

READING COMPREHENSION

Passage I is a science passage about coral reefs. Paragraph 1 introduces the main idea, which is a focus on "the complex web of interrelationships between plants and animals." Paragraph 2 describes how reefs are formed out of the skeletons of the reefs' two main inhabitants, the stony coral and the green alga. Paragraph 3 describes several theories about how coral reefs are transformed into islands.

21. **C**   Which choice describes the whole passage? Skim the paragraph topics—paragraph 2 is about the animals involved in reef formation. And paragraph 3 describes how reefs become islands. Choice (C) summarizes the passage best—since both biological and geological issues are discussed. The wrong choices are too narrow—animal life (A) is only discussed in paragraph 2; physical beauty (D) only crops up in paragraph 1; and wave erosion (B) and geological origins (E) only appear in paragraph 3.

22. **H**   Paragraph 2 is the only place where the stony coral is discussed. Lines 13–14 indicate that the stony coral's skeleton is composed of "almost pure calcium carbonate."

23. **D**   Paragraph 2 outlines the relationship between the coral and the algae. The animals are described as "partners" that "coexist in a mutually beneficial relationship" (lines 16–17). "Cooperative" (D) is the choice that best summarizes this subsea partnership.

24. **F**   Paragraph 3 discusses the issue that scientists find "puzzling." Lines 26–27 indicate that scientists find the "transformation of coral reefs into islands" a mystery. Choice (F) summarizes the issue. Wrong choice (J) is a distortion—the passage talks about islands, not "great land masses."

25. **D** Where is volcanic activity mentioned? The last few lines of the passage discuss volcanic activity as one possible way in which reefs are transformed into islands. Specifically, we're told that reefs are transformed into "atolls, or ring-shaped reef islands" (lines 41–42), making (D) the correct answer.

26. **K** The passage states that the popular perception of coral islands "is not always entirely justified . . . from sea level"—that is, on the surface. "Beneath the waves," however, coral islands are "fantastic and very beautiful" (lines 6–7). (F)'s "totally inaccurate" is too sweeping. Nothing in paragraph 3 suggests that (G)'s "fringing reefs" are aesthetically displeasing. (H) distorts the last sentence of paragraph 2; the author never suggests that divers are waging a disinformation campaign about coral islands. As for (J), nothing here suggests that scientists are trying to dispel the romantic image of coral islands.

Passage II is a social sciences passage about immigration into the United States. Paragraph 1 introduces the topic, focusing on a period of massive immigration between 1880 and 1910. Paragraph 2 tells us that there were two main aid organizations helping these immigrants assimilate to the United States. Paragraph 3 describes the approach of the Daughters of the American Revolution—encouraging immigrants to adapt to mainstream U.S. culture. Paragraph 4 portrays the contrasting approach of "settlement houses"—providing vital services and promoting a respect for the immigrants' original cultures.

27. **E** The passage starts off talking about immigration around the turn of the century. But in paragraphs 2, 3, and 4, the author gets even more specific, highlighting the contrasting efforts of two immigrant aid organizations. Choice (E) fits the focus best. Choices (A) and (D) are too broad—the passage isn't just about immigration in general—it's about a specific period and two specific ideas about assimilating immigrants. (B) only relates to paragraph 4. (C) is wrong because the passage doesn't recommend one way of assimilating immigrants—it just describes two concepts that occurred in the past.

28. **H** Paragraph 1 states that "few immigrants of this period found life in America easy," because they "lived in slum conditions" (F), were "exploited by their employers" (G), and "trapped at poverty level" (J). And paragraph 3 implies that groups like the DAR pressured immigrants to assimilate, (K). So these choices *are* mentioned as characteristic of the life that awaited immigrants of this period. However, the passage does not state that immigrants suffered religious persecution in America (H). Rather, it strongly implies (line 6) that they had faced religious persecution in their native countries.

29. **C** This question asks about the conservatives' approach, described in paragraph 3. Basically the conservative philosophy was that all immigrants should adopt American customs and culture (lines 24–25). Choice (C)—making a house look like all the other ones on the block—is the best analogy here. Choices (D) and (E) are wrong because they suggest preserving the nationality of immigrants.

30. **F** Paragraph 4 describes the services offered by settlement houses. We're told in lines 37–39 that settlement houses aimed to offer "whatever social services were not provided by local governments."

31. **E** This question asks you to identify a program consistent with the ideas of the reformers (paragraph 4). Well, what's the gist of paragraph 4? Reformers such as Jane Addams set out to provide social services and promote respect for immigrants' cultures. Choices (A) through (D) all sound too harsh for the reformers. But choice (E) fits the idea of encouraging a "respect for the cultural heritage of the new arrivals" (lines 41–42).

32. **G** This question requires you to read between the lines. Whose "cultural contributions" is the author talking about? He's talking about the immigrants' contributions: If immigrants were Americanized too quickly, the settlement house workers thought, this would lead to "ethnic self-hatred" (line 46) and immigrants would not give anything culturally to their new country of residence. Choice (G) reflects this idea; the author is talking about the immigrants' foreign influences enriching life in the United States.

Passage III is a science passage about the camouflage animals use to protect themselves from predators, called "protective coloration." Paragraph 1 describes a couple of different types of protective coloration—cryptic resemblance and disruptive coloring. Paragraph 2 describes cases in which animals change their coloration or use coloration to make themselves noticed. Paragraph 3 discusses the peppered moth, an example of an animal whose coloration can evolve in response to environmental changes.

33. **B** The first sentence indicates that the overall topic of the passage is protective coloration. But the author's focus is a bit more specific than this; the author is talking about *different types* of protective coloration—coloration that changes, coloration that stands out, coloration that evolves, and so on. So (B) is the correct answer. Choice (A) is wrong because the passage also talks about animals that stand out from their surroundings. (C) is wrong because the author is not contrasting the animals, just their coloration. Predators (D) are only mentioned in passing; each of the animals described is trying to *avoid* predators. And cryptic resemblance and disruptive coloration (E) are discussed only in paragraph 1.

34. **K** Protective coloration is defined in paragraph 1 as an animal's adaptation to its environment. So the only choice that isn't a protective coloration is mottled light (K), described in lines 13–15 as the background against which the leopard disguises itself. Cryptic resemblance (J) and disruptive coloration (F) are both types of protective coloration described in paragraph 1. Seasonal changes in pigmentation (G) are mentioned in paragraph 2, and adaptive coloration (H) is the topic of paragraph 3.

35. **A** The caribou and the stoat crop up at the beginning of paragraph 2. Lines 17–18 indicate that they are animals that "change their protective pigmentation with the seasons"—choice (A). Constant changes of color (choice E) are discussed later in paragraph 2 as a safeguard of the chameleon—but this isn't a seasonal change.

36. **F** The chameleon's special talent is described in lines 23–24—it changes color to match the surface it rests on. Choice (F) summarizes this idea.

Just clinging to surfaces (G) wouldn't make the chameleon noteworthy or protect it from attackers. (K) distorts the passage—the chameleon doesn't change the color of the surfaces it comes into contact with.

37. D This question asks you to make an inference based on the last paragraph. Why did dark-peppered moths begin to outnumber their light-colored counterparts? Lines 40–42 tell us that light-colored moths began to stand out against their environment because of all the pollution. You can infer from this that dark-colored moths flourished because their predators, the birds, couldn't see them anymore—choice (D).

38. H Paragraph 3 states that light-colored peppered moths hide from birds by blending in with lichens on tree trunks and that, after pollution killed off the lichens, dark-colored moths blended in against the bare tree trunks. Both shades of peppered moth are examples of "cryptic resemblance, where an animal adapts in color . . . to blend into its environment" (lines 4–6). The author goes on in paragraph 1 to state that the tree frog is a "good example of cryptic resemblance," so (H) is correct. The caribou (F) and the stoat (K) are examples of seasonal change in pigmentation. The skunk (G) protects itself by standing out from its surroundings. And the zebra (J) is an example of disruptive coloring.

Passage IV is a science passage about four of Jupiter's moons. Paragraph 1 relates their discovery and role in debates about the solar system. Paragraph 2 introduces the main idea—scientists didn't know much about these moons until the 1979 Voyager missions "changed our impressions of these bodies." Paragraphs 3 and 4 describe what the scientists learned about each of the four moons.

39. E Remember that the main idea of the passage is the choice that covers the whole passage. Here, it's the simplest choice that describes the passage best: Since the passage covers both how Jupiter's moons were discovered, and what scientists learned about them from the Voyager mission, the passage is basically about Jupiter's four brightest moons (E). Choices (A) and (B) are wrong because they're only discussed in paragraphs 1 and 2. Choice (C) is too broad; this passage isn't about the whole solar system. And (D) is mentioned only in paragraph 3.

40. K Paragraph 1 contains the answer to this question. Lines 1–3 tell us that the Galilean moons were the "first objects in the solar system discovered through the use of the telescope." Lines 3–6 go on to say that Galileo's discovery played a central role in a famous debate about the solar system. You can infer from this that Galileo was one of the first to "make important use of the telescope"—choice (K). (F) is wrong because Galileo supported Copernicus. (G) and (J) are wrong because accurate measurements of the moons didn't come until centuries later. (H) is out because there's no evidence that Galileo was one of the first astronomers ever.

41. E Lines 4–6 indicate that Galileo supported Copernicus's famous model of the solar system. This loyalty to an abstract theory is analogous to a scholar's defense of an educator (E).

42. F This question asks about Ganymede's light areas—discussed in lines 20–23. How were they formed? We're told that "*ancient* craters dot the dark areas, while the light areas are crisscrossed by ridges and grooves that resulted from *more recent* ice flows." You can infer from this that the light areas were formed *later* than the

Practice Test 1—Explanations

PRACTICE TESTS AND EXPLANATIONS

dark areas—choice (F). (J) refers to Callisto, and (K) refers to Io.

43. **C** Paragraph 4 states that current volcanic activity (B) has been observed on Io, as have ponds of molten sulfur (D) and atmospheric clouds (E). Paragraph 3 says that all four of the moons "probably experienced early, heavy asteroid bombardment," choice (A), but no mention is made there or elsewhere of recent asteroid bombardment, so (C) is correct.

44. **H** What's another way of saying "the most unexpected fact?" "Biggest surprise" would be another possible description—leading to the first sentence of paragraph 4, where the author expresses big surprise at "the discovery of intense volcanic or geyser-like activity on Io" (lines 28–29).

Passage V is a social studies passage about smallpox, "one of the world's most dreaded diseases." Paragraph 1 gives us some historical background on the disease. Paragraph 2 describes one of the first attempts to protect people against the disease, a process called variolation. Paragraph 3 details Edward Jenner's discovery of a superior method—the process of vaccination. Paragraph 4 tells the story of the WHO's successful effort to wipe out the disease altogether.

45. **D** Skimming paragraphs 2, 3, and 4 should indicate that the focus of the passage is on the fight against smallpox, from the ninth century until the 1970s (D). Choices (A) and (E) are too broad—the passage isn't about *all* infectious or viral diseases. Choices (B) and (C) relate only to paragraphs 2 and 3 respectively.

46. **G** Lines 13–16 indicate that variolation, the first known immunization process, was known since the ninth century CE. Wrong choice (F) describes the earliest recorded instances of the

disease. (H) dates Jenner's discovery of vaccination—but variolation came before this. (J) dates the first *worldwide immunization campaign*—not the first ever immunization process.

47. **A** What were the problems associated with variolation? According to lines 22–23, variolation patients were sometimes fatally infected, and they could spread the disease to others even when successfully inoculated. Choice (A) summarizes this second disadvantage. Cowpox (B) was an aspect of Jenner's treatment (paragraph 3). No description of variolation wearing off (C), being difficult to carry out (D), or controversial among doctors (E) is given.

48. **G** Lines 29–31 indicate that Jenner became "fascinated" by the fact that having had cowpox somehow immunized people to smallpox and tried to see "whether this immunity could be replicated." Thus, he had noticed a relationship between cowpox and smallpox, and (G) is correct. (F) is never stated. Though we can infer that Jenner wanted his vaccination work to be recognized by the Royal Society of Physicians, there's no evidence that his motivation was to be accepted into the society (H). Jenner underwent variolation as a boy, but it's never implied that he worked with variolation himself (J). And (K) goes too far: Jenner tried vaccination not because he preferred unconventional approaches in general but because variolation was unsafe and only partially successful.

49. **B** When did Jenner's vaccination process become widespread? It wasn't immediately (A) because Jenner's findings were initially rejected. (B) is the answer— Jenner's process became widespread "within a matter of years" after he published them (lines 41–42).

50.   J   Paragraph 4 describes the massive effort involved in wiping out small-pox altogether—every active case of the disease had to be found and isolated worldwide. You can infer from this that it was the difficulty of coordinating such an effort that had prevented the elimination of the disease (J), not any problem with the inoculation process.

PART 2—MATH

51.   E   Follow the order of operations. Operations inside parentheses must be done first, so $5(8 - 7)$ becomes 5×1, and $7(5 - 8)$ becomes $7 \times (-3)$. So the expression now reads $(5 \times 1) - [7 \times (-3)]$, or $5 - (-21)$, which is 26, choice (E).

52.   H   First, you must see that there are two rates by which John gets paid: one for the first 40 cars ($6 per car) and a different rate for all other cars after those first 40 ($6 per hour plus 50% of $6, which is $6 + $3, or $9 per car). Since he makes 48 cars, he gets paid $6 × 40 cars ($240) plus 8 extra cars at $9 per car ($72) which totals $312.

53.   D   Plug in the values given for b and c into the equation $a = 2b + 3c - 8$. Then $a = (2 \times 2) + (3 \times 3) - 8$, or $a = 4 + 9 - 8$, so $a = 5$.

54.   H   This problem sets up relationships among large, medium, and small sodas—2 large (L) sodas are equal to 3 medium (M), and 2 medium are equal to 3 small (S): $2L = 3M$ and $2M = 3S$. The goal is to find what $8L$ is equivalent to. Therefore, multiply both sides of the first equation by 4, getting $8L = 12M$, and then multiply the second equation by 6, resulting in $12M = 18S$.

55.   E   Remember PEMDAS? Operations inside parentheses come first, so $-2[(-18) \div 6]$ becomes $-2(-3)$, and $5[8 \div (-4)]$

becomes $5(-2)$. The full expression now reads $-2(-3) - [5 \times (-2)]$, or $6 - (-10)$, which is $6 + 10$, or 16.

56.   F   First you must determine how many ice cream bars there are in total by adding all the numbers ($4 + 3 + 12 = 19$). Since there are only 3 vanilla bars, the probability of Henry getting one is 3 out of 19, or $\frac{3}{19}$.

57.   B   If the area is 48, the length is 8, and Area = Length × Width, then $48 = 8 \times w$ and w is 6. The perimeter is $2 \times \ell + 2 \times w$ which is $2 \times 8 + 2 \times 6$, or $16 + 12 = 28$.

58.   H   If Paris is 6 hours ahead of NYC and the speech begins at 5 P.M. in Paris, then it begins at 11 A.M. in NYC. The speech ends 3.5 hours later, which is 2:30 P.M. in NYC.

59.   D   The number 258,546 becomes 278,746. The difference is found by subtracting the two numbers: 278,746 − 258,546 leaves you with 20,200.

60.   G   Since there is no remainder, $z \times 55 = 275$. Thus, $z = 5$, and when 24 is divided by 5, the remainder is 4.

61.   B   Look down the −10° column to the −50 (two boxes down), then look left to find the wind speed of 20.

62.   H   The key here is to express $\frac{5}{12}$ and $\frac{1}{2}$ with a common denominator that results in numerators that differ by 2 or more so that a halfway point will be easy to find. Just re-expressing $\frac{1}{2}$ as $\frac{6}{12}$ doesn't make it easy enough, as the halfway point between $\frac{5}{12}$ and $\frac{6}{12}$ is not an integer multiple of $\frac{1}{12}$; 5 and 6 differ by only 1. However, converting

both numbers to 24ths results in $\frac{5}{12} = \frac{10}{24}$ and $\frac{1}{2} = \frac{12}{24}$. The number halfway between is $\frac{11}{24}$.

63. **B** Choice (A) is incorrect because the product of any two negative numbers is positive. Choice (B) is correct because the sum of any two negative numbers must be negative. You could also solve this question by picking numbers like $x = -2$ and $y = -3$ and plugging them into each answer choice. If you pick numbers, all four incorrect answer choices must be eliminated. In this question, choices (C) and (E) **could** be true; however, only choice (B) **must** be true.

64. **J** Just be careful to line up each number in the right column.

65. **C** The formula for average is
$$\text{Average} = \frac{\text{Sum of the terms}}{\text{Number of terms}}.$$
So if the average is 20 and the number of terms is 5, their sum is 20×5, or 100. The average must be the middle term of the 5 consecutive terms, so the series looks like $a, b, 4 \times 5, d, e$. If they are consecutive multiples of 5, the largest number must be 6×5, or 30. Checking that the terms add up to the sum confirms that this is correct: $10 + 15 + 20 + 25 + 30 = 100$.

66. **H** Since the degree measure of a line is 180 degrees, all four angles must add up to 180. Your equation should read $180 = 40 + x + y + 40$. Subtract 80 from both sides to get rid of each 40 next to $x + y$, and you are left with $100 = x + y$.

67. **E** This is just a division problem: How many times will 8 (eggs) go into 175 (the total number of eggs to be sold)? We calculate 175 divided by 8 is 21 with a remainder of 7. There will be 7 eggs left over.

68. **G** Because $AB = BC$, this must be an isosceles triangle. Therefore angle A must also be $p°$. Adding the three angles results in $90 + p + p = 180$, or $2p = 90$, or $p = 45$.

69. **D** When you multiply the two fractions, you get $\frac{41}{60}$, which is very close to $\frac{40}{60}$, which reduces to $\frac{2}{3}$.

70. **J** You could add each answer choice in both ways to get (J) by process of elimination, **or** you can see the pattern: (J) is the only choice that has one number with a units digit that is less than 5 and one number with a units digit that is at least 5.

71. **D** Canceling terms quickly brings us to our answer. Cancel the 5 in the numerator of the first fraction and the 5 in the denominator of the third fraction. Then cancel a 3 in the numerator of one of the last two fractions with the factor 3 of $3 \times 4 = 12$ in the denominator of the first fraction. We are left with $\frac{3}{4 \times 2} = \frac{3}{8}$.

72. **K** Remember, *of* means multiply and *is* means equals. Hence, we have $\frac{25}{100}x = 120$. Reduce $\frac{25}{100}$ to $\frac{1}{4}$. Now our equation is $\frac{1}{4}x = 120$, so you can multiply both sides of the equation by 4, leaving $x = 120(4) = 480$.

73. **C** We can begin by noticing the numerator and denominator are even and thus both are divisible by 2, leaving us with $\frac{216}{328}$. Use the division by 2 again: $\frac{108}{164}$; and again: $\frac{54}{82}$; and one more time: $\frac{27}{41}$. Then 41 is a prime number, so the fraction $\frac{27}{41}$ can no longer be reduced.

74. **G**   Moving the decimal 2 places to the right yields 2.718, and because we moved the decimal 2 places to the right, we multiply by 10^{-2}.

75. **E**   Simply substitute the values given for x and y: $[5(2) - (-3)(2)]^2$. PEMDAS (order of operations) tells us Parentheses must be done first and Multiplication must come before Subtraction: $[5(2) - (-3)(2)]^2 = [10 - (-6)]^2 = (10 + 6)^2 = 16^2$. Now that the parentheses are gone, multiply 16 by itself. $16 \times 16 = 256$.

76. **J**   Use the Pythagorean theorem, which says that in a right triangle, the square of the hypotenuse is equal to the sum of the squares of the legs. If the hypotenuse has length c and the legs have lengths a and b, then $c^2 = a^2 + b^2$. Let leg EF be called b. Substitute 6 for c and 4 for a and solve for b. Then $6^2 = 4^2 + b^2$. So $36 = 16 + b^2$. Subtract 16 from both sides, and you get $20 = b^2$.

Finally, $b = \sqrt{20} = \sqrt{4 \times 5} = \sqrt{4} \times \sqrt{5} = 2\sqrt{5}$. Thus, $EF = 2\sqrt{5}$.

77. **B**   Be sure to read the definition of $> x >$. Because -2 is an even number, the value of $> -2 >$ equals $3x = 3(-2) = -6$.

78. **F**   Substitute the values given for a and b into the expression: $[-(-2)(3)] \times (-2) = (2)(3)(-2) = -12$.

79. **C**   Use the formula for circumference of a circle: $C = 2\pi r$. Here $10\pi = 2\pi r$. Divide both sides by π and you have $10 = 2r$. Hence $r = 5$. Next, use the formula for the area of a circle, which is $A = \pi r^2$. Here $A = \pi(5^2) = \pi(25) = 25\pi$.

80. **K**   Substitute the value of 4 for y in the expression and evaluate: $7 + |3(4)| + 7 + |-2(4)| = 7 + |12| + 7 + |-8| = 7 + 12 + 7 + 8 = 34$. Remember that any values within absolute value symbols, whether positive or negative, become positive when the symbols are removed.

81. **C**   This triangle has a height of 8 (each box counts as 4) and a base of 12. The area of a triangle is $\frac{1}{2}$ (base)(height) $= \frac{1}{2}(12)(8) = 48$.

82. **K**   In order to avoid a messy denominator, begin by cross multiplying the equation given: $xy = 12$. Next substitute $\frac{1}{2}$ for x: $\frac{1}{2}y = 12$. Solve for y by multiplying both sides by 2. We are left with $y = 24$, choice (K).

83. **C**   The figure given is a square. All the points on segment BC have an x-coordinate of 2, so $DC = AB = 4$, and because it is a square, all 4 sides must have a length of 4. Thus, the area is $4^2 = 4 \times 4 = 16$.

84. **F**   You must calculate the total cost first: $2\frac{1}{4} \times \$4 = \$9$. Then 7% of \$9 is $\frac{7}{100} \times \$9$, or \$0.63, so the total is \$9.63.

85. **B**   Plug in the number 9 for each z in the problem, which will yield 9×12 in the numerator and 5×9 in the denominator. The 9s cancel, leaving you with $\frac{12}{5}$.

86. **J**   The total area is $8 \times 9 = 72$. One-third of that is red ($\frac{1}{3} \times 72 = 24$ RED). Then $\frac{1}{8}$ of the remaining squares (48) are GREEN, so there are 6 GREEN squares. That leaves 42 uncolored squares.

87. **D** A prime factor means that the number you want must be a factor *as well as* a prime number. (So, you should determine which answer choices are prime numbers and choose from among them to find which one is also a factor of 726. What you're left with is a prime factor.) The numbers 6 and 9 are automatically wrong since they are not prime numbers. The number 11 is a prime factor of 726. (The prime numbers 7 and 13 are not factors of 726).

88. **H** This is a perfect problem for picking numbers. Pick a simple number for *N*; let's use 3. Then plug it into the answer choices and see which one is correct.

    F. $2(3) + 1 = 6 - 1 = 5$ wrong

    G. $3(3) + 2 = 9 + 2 = 11$ wrong

    H. $4(3) = 12$ correct

    J. $(3)^2 + 2(3) = 9 + 6 = 15$ wrong

    K. $2(3)^2 + 1 = 2(9) + 1 = 19$ wrong

    Only answer (H) works.

89. **D** $F = x$ and $C = 7x + 8$, so to find what $F + C$ represents, just plug in x for F and $(7x + 8)$ for C. You should now have $x + 7x + 8$ or $8x + 8$.

90. **H** This is a direct translation problem. Just make sure that when you translate, you write out your equation in the same order as the sentence.

91. **B** $10 - 8 = 2$. (Look at the rules for radicals: You can't subtract 64 from 100 first and then find the square root. You must first find $\sqrt{100}$ and $\sqrt{64}$, then subtract.)

92. **G** When you plug in the values for x, you get 4, 0, and 4 as values for y.

93. **B** The temptation is to answer (D), but you must first find the total number of chips by adding them all together (giving you 16). Let x be the number of chips with the color that has a probability of $\frac{1}{8}$ of being chosen.

    Then $\frac{x}{16} = \frac{1}{8}$. Cross-multiplying and solving for x gives you $x = 2$, so the color is orange.

94. **J** The first step is to find the midpoint between A (−7) and B (1), which is $\frac{(-7) + 1}{2}$ or −3. Once you've found this point, you find the distance from −3 to 5, which is 8.

95. **E** Estimate which ones are close to $\frac{1}{4}$. (A) is greater than $\frac{1}{2}$ so that's out. (B) is close to $\frac{1}{6}$, which is too small, so that's out. (C) is close to $\frac{1}{40}$, so that's too small. (D) is close to $\frac{1}{5}$, which leaves you with (E).

96. **F** This is just another disguised division problem. Divide 60 by $\frac{3}{8}$, and you get 160.

97. **A** Multiply both sides of $3 = \frac{9b}{a}$ by a to get $3a = 9b$. Divide both sides by 3 to get $a = 3b$, and divide both sides by b to get $\frac{a}{b} = 3$.

98.   G   The trick is to find the pattern of the sequence. The difference between the first two terms is 3. The difference between the second and third terms is 5. The difference between the third and fourth terms is 7. In this sequence, the difference between terms increases by 2 each time. The difference between 50 and 65 is 15, so the difference between 65 and d should be 17. $65 + 17 = 82$.

99.   E   You can begin by getting rid of the parentheses in $2(5b - 7)$: $2(5b - 7) = 2(5b) - 2(7) = 10b - 14$. When you substitute $3y$ in for b, you get $10(3y) - 14 = 30y - 14$.

100.   F   We know that 20% was spent on clothing and 25% was spent on food. So the total expenditure on food and clothing was $20 + 25 = 45\%$, choice (F).

SHSAT

Practice Test 2

HOW TO TAKE THIS PRACTICE TEST

Before taking this practice test, find a quiet room where you can work uninterrupted for two and a half hours. Make sure you have a comfortable desk, your calculator, and several No. 2 pencils.

Use the answer sheet provided to record your answers. (You can cut it out or photocopy it.)

Once you start this practice test, don't stop until you've finished. Remember that you are in control of how you spend your time on the SHSAT. Inside your test booklet, you will see that 75 minutes is the "suggested time" for each portion of the test. You are allowed a total of 150 minutes for the entire test, and you may divide your time as you see fit. Unlike most standardized tests, the SHSAT *does* allow you to work on whichever part of the test you want to first. You can also go back and forth between sections if you choose to.

You'll find an answer key, score conversion charts, and explanations following the test.

Good luck.

SHSAT Practice Test 2
Answer Sheet

Remove (or photocopy) this answer sheet and use it to complete the practice test.
(See answer key following the test when finished.)

SCRAMBLED PARAGRAPHS

	The first sentence is:	The second sentence is:	The third sentence is:	The fourth sentence is:	The fifth sentence is:
Paragraph 1	Q R S T U	Q R S T U	Q R S T U	Q R S T U	Q R S T U
Paragraph 2	Q R S T U	Q R S T U	Q R S T U	Q R S T U	Q R S T U
Paragraph 3	Q R S T U	Q R S T U	Q R S T U	Q R S T U	Q R S T U
Paragraph 4	Q R S T U	Q R S T U	Q R S T U	Q R S T U	Q R S T U
Paragraph 5	Q R S T U	Q R S T U	Q R S T U	Q R S T U	Q R S T U

LOGICAL REASONING

11 A B C D E
12 F G H J K
13 A B C D E
14 F G H J K
15 A B C D E

16 F G H J K
17 A B C D E
18 F G H J K
19 A B C D E
20 F G H J K

READING

21 A B C D E
22 F G H J K
23 A B C D E
24 F G H J K
25 A B C D E

26 F G H J K
27 A B C D E
28 F G H J K
29 A B C D E
30 F G H J K

31 A B C D E
32 F G H J K
33 A B C D E
34 F G H J K
35 A B C D E

36 F G H J K
37 A B C D E
38 F G H J K
39 A B C D E
40 F G H J K

41 A B C D E
42 F G H J K
43 A B C D E
44 F G H J K
45 A B C D E

46 F G H J K
47 A B C D E
48 F G H J K
49 A B C D E
50 F G H J K

MATHEMATICS PROBLEMS

51 A B C D E
52 F G H J K
53 A B C D E
54 F G H J K
55 A B C D E

56 F G H J K
57 A B C D E
58 F G H J K
59 A B C D E
60 F G H J K

61 A B C D E
62 F G H J K
63 A B C D E
64 F G H J K
65 A B C D E

66 F G H J K
67 A B C D E
68 F G H J K
69 A B C D E
70 F G H J K

71 A B C D E
72 F G H J K
73 A B C D E
74 F G H J K
75 A B C D E

76 F G H J K
77 A B C D E
78 F G H J K
79 A B C D E
80 F G H J K

81 A B C D E
82 F G H J K
83 A B C D E
84 F G H J K
85 A B C D E

86 F G H J K
87 A B C D E
88 F G H J K
89 A B C D E
90 F G H J K

91 A B C D E
92 F G H J K
93 A B C D E
94 F G H J K
95 A B C D E

96 F G H J K
97 A B C D E
98 F G H J K
99 A B C D E
100 F G H J K

DIRECTIONS

Mark your answers on the separate sheet provided. You will receive credit only for answers marked on the answer grid. DO NOT MAKE ANY STRAY MARKS ON THE ANSWER GRID. You can write in the test booklet, or use the paper provided for scratchwork.

Part 1   Questions 1–50   75 minutes

Part 2   Questions 51–100   75 minutes

If you finish part 2 early you may go back to questions in either part. Your score is based on the number of questions answered correctly. There is no penalty for wrong answers. IF YOU DO NOT KNOW THE ANSWER TO A QUESTION, IT IS TO YOUR ADVANTAGE TO GUESS.

PART 1—VERBAL

Recommended Time—75 Minutes

50 Questions

Paragraphs 1–5: Scrambled Paragraphs

> DIRECTIONS: Below are six sentences that form a paragraph. The first sentence is given; the remaining five sentences are listed in random order. Choose the order for these five sentences that will create the **best** paragraph, one that is both well organized and gramatically correct. Each correctly ordered paragraph is worth **double** the value of a question in any other section of the test. No credit will be given for responses that are only partially correct.

Paragraph 1

The wimple was a type of headdress originally worn by women in medieval Europe.

_____ **Q.** Europeans adopted this design in the 12th century when crusaders returned with Muslim veils from the Near East.

_____ **R.** More elaborate than the modern hat, the wimple draped down from the top of the wearer's head to cover her neck and wrap around her chin.

_____ **S.** The wimple eventually fell out of fashion in the 14th century, but descendants of the hat are still worn by members of certain religious orders.

_____ **T.** While the Muslim veils were often colorful, the European wimple was generally made of white linen or silk.

_____ **U.** Like many developments in dress, this design was not an indigenous evolution but the direct influence of an alien group.

Paragraph 2

Although Columbus is usually credited with the discovery of America in 1492, he may not have been the first European to visit the New World.

_____ **Q.** After a long and arduous journey, Eriksson and his men landed on an unexplored continent with particularly lush vegetation.

_____ **R.** He named this new country "Vinland," because he believed that excellent wines could be grown there.

_____ **S.** According to Scandinavian historians, Leif Eriksson landed in a wooded part of North America in the year 1000 CE.

_____ **T.** This was the age when the Vikings had already established themselves as a seafaring nation and periodically raided neighboring countries such as England.

_____ **U.** Eriksson reputedly set sail with a crew of 35 men to find a mysterious island sighted in the Atlantic Ocean by earlier explorers.

GO ON TO THE NEXT PAGE ➡

Paragraph 3

The special effects used in today's movies would have been unimaginable as recently as ten years ago.

_____ **Q.** In addition, when music was added to movies in the late 1920s, it added an exciting element to the movie-making process.

_____ **R.** Nonetheless, even back in the era of the silent film, movie makers had at their disposal a complex mixture of musical and dramatic effects.

_____ **S.** Thus, even during the era of the "silent" movies, filmmakers wrestled with how to incorporate new technological advances into their work.

_____ **T.** This innovation presented an enormous challenge to movie makers because they needed to consider how to combine music with visual effects.

_____ **U.** Of course, the presence of music meant that "silent" movies were not actually silent.

Paragraph 4

One irony of war is that this greatest of human tragedies often leads to breakthroughs in science.

_____ **Q.** In World War I, the sheer number of casualties led to advances in the treatment of bleeding and shock.

_____ **R.** However, medicine is not the only science that has advanced in the wake of war, as illustrated by the development of rockets by German scientists during World War II.

_____ **S.** Medics adjusted to this problem by developing techniques to quickly staunch bleeding.

_____ **T.** In the field of medicine, for example, war has often accelerated scientific understanding of disease and injury.

_____ **U.** Field surgeons found that most fatalities occurred not from the direct physical damage of bullet wounds but from a loss of blood.

Paragraph 5

It is not uncommon for music aficionados to fail to realize that seemingly recent innovations have ancient origins.

_____ **Q.** Nevertheless, chromaticism in music dates back to ancient Greece.

_____ **R.** In ancient Greek music, chromatic intervals would be used to introduce color or texture to a piece of music.

_____ **S.** For example, fans of classical music often regard chromaticism as a recent development in music.

_____ **T.** They associate it with twentieth-century composer Arnold Schoenberg, the most famous recent exponent of chromaticism.

_____ **U.** Thus, Schoenberg's revolutionary-sounding music is actually quite ancient in origin.

GO ON TO THE NEXT PAGE ➡

QUESTIONS 11–20, Logical Reasoning

DIRECTIONS: Read the information given for each question and choose the **best** answer. Base your answer **only on the information given**.

Questions 11 and 12 refer to the following information.

In the code below, (1) each letter represents the same word in each of the four sentences; (2) each word is represented by one letter only; and (3) in any given sentence, letters may or may not appear in the same order as the words they represent.

D	X	E	Z	R	means
"Miguel	plays	tennis	with	Betsy."	

G	B	X	C	Y	means
"Janice	plays	guitar	at	night."	

E	B	Z	Y	X	means
"Betsy	plays	guitar	with	Janice."	

Z	R	X	F	H	means
"Rasheen	plays	tennis	with	friends."	

11. Which letter represents "guitar"?

A. X
B. B
C. Z
D. Y
E. Cannot be determined from the information given.

12. Which word is represented by D?

F. Betsy
G. tennis
H. Miguel
J. with
K. Cannot be determined from the information given.

13. The actor who played the Tin Man in the movie *The Wizard of Oz* was not the first choice to play that role. Another actor was cast for the role but had to be replaced because he was allergic to the makeup for the role.

According to the given information, which statement **must** be true?

A. The originally cast actor was generally considered a better actor than his replacement.
B. Actors can be allergic to the makeup used in films.
C. It is very unusual for actors to be allergic to makeup.
D. The originally cast actor had to give up his acting career because of his unusual illness.
E. The actor originally cast as the Tin Man would be rich and famous now if he had played that role.

14. Carla gave three different sports cars a test drive.

1) Car A was faster and sleeker than Car B.
2) Car C was cheaper than Car A but not as fast.
3) Car B was cheaper than Car C but not as sleek.

Based only on the information above, which of the following **must** be true?

F. Car C was the slowest car.
G. Car A was the most expensive car.
H. Car B was more expensive than Car C.
J. Car C was the sleekest car.
K. Car B was faster than car C.

GO ON TO THE NEXT PAGE ➡

15. Dr. Gray sees seven patients on a particular day: two infants, two teenagers, and three senior citizens. The two teenagers have back-to-back appointments, as do the infants. If Dr. Gray's second appointment is a senior citizen, which other appointment must be a senior citizen?

    A. the first

    B. the third

    C. the fourth

    D. the seventh

    E. Cannot be determined from the information given.

16. A traveling salesperson plans to visit ten companies on her trip to Hawaii. On the first day, she visits three companies. But over the rest of her trip, she is only able to visit a maximum of two companies per day.

    What is the **least** number of days her trip will take?

    F. 3

    G. 4

    H. 5

    J. 6

    K. Cannot be determined from the information given.

17. Since Fred was accepted to Harvard Law School, he must have studied very hard.

    Which of the following most clearly leads to the above conclusion?

    A. Few of Fred's friends expected him to be accepted to Harvard Law School.

    B. Harvard Law School is among the most difficult law schools to be accepted to.

    C. Fred lacks the ability to pass his law school entrance exams without studying.

    D. Only people who study very hard are accepted to Harvard Law School.

    E. Fred could also have been accepted at many other less competitive law schools.

GO ON TO THE NEXT PAGE ➡

18. Scientists are able to predict the occurrence of earthquakes with a reasonable degree of accuracy using a device called a seismograph. In 1990, scientists used a seismograph to predict that city X would experience a major earthquake in 1994. But no major earthquake actually occurred.

Based only on the information above, which of the following statements is a valid conclusion?

F. City X will probably experience a major earthquake in the next few years.

G. Natural disasters are impossible for scientists to predict.

H. Scientists are currently researching other ways of predicting earthquakes.

J. Seismographic predictions are not always reliable.

K. City X actually experienced a minor earthquake in 1994.

Questions 19 and 20 refer to the following information.

Six card players are sitting in a circle around a table. Each sits across from his or her partner in the game.

1) Ron and Liz are partners.
2) Sean and Tracy are partners.
3) Karen and Jim are partners.
4) Tracy sits next to Ron.
5) Liz sits next to Jim, on his right.

19. Who sits on Sean's left?

A. Tracy

B. Liz

C. Karen

D. Jim

E. Cannot be determined from the information given.

20. Who sits on Karen's right?

F. Ron

G. Liz

H. Tracy

J. Jim

K. Cannot be determined from the information given.

GO ON TO THE NEXT PAGE ➡

QUESTIONS 21–50: Reading Passages

DIRECTIONS: Read each passage and answer the questions that follow it. Choose the **best** answer for each question. Base your answers **only on what you have read in a given passage**. You may reread any passage you wish to.

Desert plants have evolved very special adaptations for living in extremely dry conditions. Most have small, thick leaves, an adaptation that limits
Line water loss by reducing surface area relative to volume.
(5) During the driest months, some desert plants shed their leaves. Others, such as cacti, subsist on water the plant stores in its fleshy stems during the rainy season. Some send out long, deep taproots in order to reach underlying water. Others have developed shallow,
(10) widespread root systems, which allow them to take advantage of very occasional but heavy rainfalls. Some plants have ways of actively protecting their water supplies. The creosote bush, for instance, produces a powerful poison that discourages the
(15) growth of competing root systems.

In addition, desert plants must survive similar, water-related difficulties imposed on them by their food-making process, photosynthesis. In order to produce food, plants must use carbon dioxide from the
(20) air around them. When absorbing carbon dioxide, however, plants lose significant amounts of water, because the same tiny openings on the plant surfaces serve both purposes. Desert plants solve this problem in various ways. The food-producing periods of many
(25) plants are extremely short; some of these plants survive long, dry periods in the form of seeds, while many others simply drop their leaves and are bare for much of the year. Still other plants have solved the problem by developing cell mechanisms that
(30) control the opening and closing of the stomates, the tiny openings on the plant surfaces. These guard cells keep the stomates closed during hot, dry daylight hours and allow the stomates to open and function at night. Certain other plants have mechanisms that
(35) cause stomates to remain closed for much longer periods of time—for days and weeks, even months at a time—until environmental conditions become more favorable.

21. Which of the following best tells what the passage is about?

  A. the discovery of stomates

  B. the process of photosynthesis

  C. how desert plants adapt to survive

  D. competition between plants in the desert

  E. the shortage of water in the desert

22. The passage suggests that most successful desert plants must be able to

  F. reach deep sources of groundwater.

  G. survive in loose, sandy soil.

  H. adapt to very low levels of rainfall.

  J. withstand frigid nighttime temperatures.

  K. destroy potential competitors.

23. In comparison to the root systems of desert plants, the root systems of tropical rain forest plants will probably be

  A. similar, because tropical rain forests are also hot.

  B. more widespread, in order to absorb the excess moisture in the soil.

  C. smaller, because large root systems are less necessary in wet rain forest soil.

  D. larger, because little sunlight reaches the forest floor.

  E. more complex, because the rain forest is a more complex environment than the desert.

GO ON TO THE NEXT PAGE ➡

24. What is the function of stomates in desert plants?

- **F.** to allow carbon dioxide to enter and water to leave the plants
- **G.** to allow water to enter and carbon dioxide to leave the plants
- **H.** to allow oxygen to enter and carbon dioxide to leave the plants
- **J.** to allow sunlight to enter the plants
- **K.** to allow food to be absorbed

25. Which of the following best describes what is suggested by the statement that the tiny surface openings of desert plants "serve both purposes" (line 23)?

- **A.** They cause the plant to shed its leaves or close them up.
- **B.** They enable the plant survive hot days and cool nights.
- **C.** They take in water and also secrete poison.
- **D.** They aid in photosynthesis but let out moisture.
- **E.** They secrete carbon dioxide and manufacture seeds.

26. Which of the following weather conditions would most benefit plants with wide, shallow root systems?

- **F.** a prolonged drought
- **G.** a windstorm
- **H.** a light spring rain
- **J.** a winter snowfall
- **K.** a flash flood

GO ON TO THE NEXT PAGE ➡

Alchemy is the name given to the attempt to change lead, copper, and other metals into silver or gold. Today, alchemy is regarded as a pseudoscience.

Line (5) Its associations with astrology and the occult suggest primitive superstition to the modern mind, and the alchemist is generally portrayed as a charlatan obsessed by dreams of impossible wealth. For many centuries, however, alchemy was a highly respected art. In the search for the elusive secret to making gold,

(10) alchemists helped to develop many of the apparatuses and procedures that are used in laboratories today. Moreover, the results of their experiments laid the basic conceptual framework of the modern science of chemistry.

(15) The philosophy underlying the practice of alchemy emerged in similar forms in ancient China, India, and Greece. The alchemists believed that all matter consisted of various combinations of five elements—air, water, earth, fire, and space—and that

(20) there were correspondences among the elements, the planets, and metals. They regarded gold as the "purest" and "noblest" of all metals and believed that "base" metals such as copper and lead were only imperfectly developed forms of gold. The base metals were said to

(25) contain impurities that "weighed down" their perfect qualities. Under certain astrological conditions, the alchemists believed that these metals could be purified through long heating or other treatments. Since they believed in the interrelationship between the natural

(30) world and the human world, this "purification" process had a profound significance for the alchemists. With purification, the alchemists believed that base metals attained a state of perfection, just as human souls attained a perfect state in heaven.

(35) In the twelfth century, translations of Arabic works on alchemy started to become available in Europe, generating a new wave of European interest in the art. In this period, alchemists made many important chemical discoveries, such as the mineral

(40) acids and alcohol. As late as the seventeenth century, that supreme genius of rationalism, Sir Isaac Newton, devoted thirty years to the study of alchemy. Ultimately, the possibility of making gold was conclusively disproved in the nineteenth century. But

(45) this belief provided the basis for some of the most fascinating chapters in the history of science.

27. Which of the following best tells what the passage is about?

   A. the history of alchemy

   B. how the alchemists manufactured gold

   C. the chemicals discovered by the alchemists

   D. how modern chemistry evolved from alchemy

   E. the pioneering research of Isaac Newton

28. Why are the alchemists not favorably regarded today?

   F. Their secret techniques have mostly been forgotten.

   G. The results of all their experiments were disproved.

   H. The Europeans were not interested in an Eastern art form.

   J. Their use of astrology seems superstitious to scientists.

   K. Many of their apparatuses and procedures are out-of-date.

29. What did the alchemists believe about metals such as copper and lead?

   A. They were imperfect forms of gold.

   B. They were the noblest of all metals.

   C. They consisted primarily of air and water.

   D. They were heavier than other metals.

   E. They originated in China, India, and Greece.

GO ON TO THE NEXT PAGE ➡

30. What does the passage imply about the process of "purifying" metals?

   F. It was perfected by Isaac Newton.

   G. It was distorted in translations of Arabic works.

   H. The alchemists believed it had a spiritual parallel.

   J. It was discovered in the twelfth century.

   K. Few people realized its commercial value.

31. Which of the following questions is **not** answered in the passage?

   A. What constituted favorable astrological conditions for purifying base metals?

   B. Did alchemists make theoretical contributions to modern chemistry?

   C. When was alchemy finally discredited as a science?

   D. What did alchemists believe about the relationship between humanity and the natural world?

   E. What was responsible for the European wave of interest in alchemy?

32. With which of the following statements about alchemy would the author most likely agree?

   F. Belief in alchemy delayed scientific progress for centuries.

   G. Some of the principles of alchemy are still valid today.

   H. Modern chemistry owes nothing to the achievements of the alchemists.

   J. Though not a science, alchemy is an important part of scientific history.

   K. Most alchemists wanted to produce gold only for their own financial benefit.

Most life is fundamentally dependent on photosynthetic organisms that store radiant energy from the sun. In almost all the world's ecosystems and food chains, photosynthetic organisms such as plants and algae are eaten by other organisms, which are then consumed by still others. The existence of organisms that are not dependent on the sun's light has long been established, but until recently they were regarded as anomalies. Over the last twenty years, however, research in deep sea areas has revealed the existence of entire ecosystems in which the primary producers are bacteria that are dependent on energy from within the earth itself. Indeed, growing evidence suggests that these subsea ecosystems model the way in which life first came about on this planet.

The first of these unique chemosynthetic ecosystems was discovered in 1977 by a small research submarine investigating the Galapagos Rift, a volcanically active area 7,000 feet below the surface of the eastern Pacific Ocean. At a boundary between adjacent plates in the earth, scientists found a surprisingly congenial environment for life. They discovered that water was seeping down through cracks in the ocean floor, being heated by the volcanic rocks, and rising again to create an oasis of warmth in the near-freezing waters. Moreover, under conditions of extreme heat and pressure, chemical reactions were taking place that supplied sufficient energy for "chemosynthetic" bacteria to develop. In this ecosystem and others discovered since, bacteria become the primary producers in the ecosystem by transforming chemicals into compounds that can serve as nourishment for more complex forms of life.

What do these underwater worlds look like? More than a dozen of these warm-water oases have been discovered in the Pacific so far, and the specific life forms that arise in them vary according to whichever species of larva first colonize the site. But the inhabitants of these deep-sea communities can include clams, mussels, crabs, and octopods. The environment often produces sights that are spectacular to behold—clams measuring some 20 centimeters can cover the ocean floor. One oasis, ironically known as the Garden of Eden, is populated by huge tube worms that lack mouths and digestive tracts and obtain their energy instead from bacteria living in their tissues.

Line (5)

(10)

(15)

(20)

(25)

(30)

(35)

(40)

(45)

33. Which of the following best tells what the passage is about?

   A. the origin of life on earth

   B. the importance of photosynthesis for animal life

   C. the spectacular sights of deep sea exploration

   D. the evolution of chemosynthetic ecosystems

   E. the ecology of the eastern Pacific Ocean

34. This passage suggests that most life is ultimately dependent on what?

   F. deep-sea hot springs

   G. the world's oceans

   H. bacterial microorganisms

   J. light from the sun

   K. chemosynthesis

35. Why is the ecosystem described in this passage called "unique" (line 16)?

   A. It has no need for an environmental source of energy.

   B. It thrives in the absence of sunlight.

   C. It exists in airless, waterless surroundings.

   D. It is infested by dangerous octopods.

   E. It is the only ecosystem found in deep ocean water.

GO ON TO THE NEXT PAGE ➡

36. Which of the following best describes why the Galapagos Rift is called "a surprisingly congenial environment for life" (line 22)?

    F. Chemosynthetic bacteria do not generally provide life-sustaining nourishment.

    G. Previous searches of the Galapagos Rift had not revealed the presence of any ecosystems.

    H. Tube worms found there are larger than any known to exist on dry land.

    J. The water temperature at depths of 7,000 feet is too low to sustain life.

    K. Scientists had not expected to find life in volcanically active underwater areas.

37. What does the term "primary producers" (line 31) refer to?

    A. producers of new and exciting scientific discoveries

    B. organisms that serve as the first link in an ecosystem's food chain

    C. organisms that consume other organisms in a food chain

    D. simple chemicals that can be transformed into more complex compounds

    E. geologic formations, such as deep-sea vents, that support an independent ecosystem

38. Which of the following conclusions about photosynthetic and chemosynthetic organisms is supported by this passage?

    F. Both perform similar functions in different food chains.

    G. Both are known to support communities of higher organisms at great ocean depths.

    H. Sunlight is a basic source of energy for both.

    J. Chemosynthetic organisms are less nourishing than photosynthetic organisms.

    K. Chemosynthetic organisms always thrive in environments that cannot support photosynthetic organisms.

GO ON TO THE NEXT PAGE ➡

The dancer and choreographer Martha Graham is regarded as one of the outstanding innovators in the history of dance. In a career that lasted over 50 years,
Line Graham created more than 170 works ranging from
(5) solos to large-scale pieces and danced in most of them herself. Trained in a variety of different international styles of dance, she set out in the mid-1920s to break away from the rigid traditions of classical ballet. She wanted to create new dance forms and movements that
(10) would reflect the changed atmosphere of the postwar period.

Her early dances reflect this spirit. She rejected the extravagant stylization of classical ballet, using the natural breath pulse as the basis for movement instead
(15) of formalized classical motions. She avoided decorative sets and costumes and used an all-female dance troupe. Moreover, her productions used music purely as an accompaniment to dance rather than as an elaborate showpiece in itself. In fact, Graham's early
(20) work was so stark and severe that it was described by one critic as "uncompromisingly ugly."

For the most part, the critics and the public understood little of Graham's break with tradition. Although her work addressed universal feelings and
(25) ideas, many people could not perceive this; they reacted only to the unfamiliar and original dance movements with which these feelings and ideas were expressed. Graham denied that she was experimenting merely for the sake of being different. Her new style,
(30) she said, "was not done perversely to dramatize ugliness, or to strike at sacred tradition. The point was that the old forms could not give voice to the fully awakened man."

As the decades passed, Graham's work found
(35) wider acceptance. By the 1940s, it had already become the tradition against which a new avant-garde was rebelling; this is a fate common to all artistic revolutions. But Graham continued to explore the essence of human conflicts and emotions through her
(40) dances, and success did not cause her to give up experimenting. She continued to revise her ideas throughout her career, incorporating men into her company and broadening her subject matter to include sources from Greek mythology and the Old
(45) Testament.

39. Which of the following best tells what this passage is about?

A. changes in the art world during the 1920s

B. the revolution in classical ballet

C. Graham's role and purpose as an innovator

D. the critical reception of Graham's early works

E. the experience of seeing Graham's dances performed

40. Martha Graham introduced new dance techniques in order to

F. attract attention to her all-female troupe.

G. visually dramatize the ugliness of life.

H. express the changed mood of her time.

J. strike a blow at the traditions of classical ballet.

K. emphasize the rigidity of conventional dance movement.

41. What can be inferred from the passage about the "formalized classical motions" (line 15) of ballet dancers prior to the 1920s?

A. They were originally developed to reflect the spirit of the times.

B. They expressed universal ideas and feelings.

C. They depicted characters from Greek mythology.

D. They were not based on natural breathing rhythms.

E. They were easier than the motions used by Graham's dancers.

GO ON TO THE NEXT PAGE ➡

42. It can be inferred that classical ballet of the early twentieth century generally

F. was loose and formless.

G. was disliked by critics and the public.

H. sought to dramatize ugliness.

J. reflected the changing times.

K. employed elaborate sets and costumes.

43. Critics and the public did not understand the universality of Graham's early work because they

A. rejected the appropriateness of an all-female troupe.

B. failed to appreciate the spirit of the postwar era.

C. were distracted by the novelty of the dance movements.

D. tried to fit her work into the traditions of classical ballet.

E. demanded that her work concern itself only with personal feelings and ideas.

44. The "fate common to all artistic revolutions" (lines 37–38) is best illustrated by which of the following?

F. a revolutionary method of painting that is eventually accepted, but later rejected by innovative artists

G. a style of musical composition that ignores the rules of harmony and emphasizes dissonance and ugly sounds

H. a movement in fiction that focuses on the gritty aspects of everyday life rather than its beautiful aspects

J. a new trend in theatrical performance that becomes immensely popular but is soon forgotten

K. a technical innovation in cinematography that makes moviemaking much less expensive

GO ON TO THE NEXT PAGE ➡

All telescopes use curved lenses to focus the light from distant objects, such as stars. Generally, the larger a telescope is, the greater its magnifying power.
Line Two different kinds of lenses can be used. Some
(5) telescopes use a transparent lens that focuses light rays as they pass through it. These telescopes are called refractors. Other telescopes, called reflectors, use a curved mirror shaped like a dish. The mirror focuses light on a viewing lens placed between the opening of
(10) the telescope and the mirror. Because the viewing lens is small, it does not interfere with the image.

The first telescopes, made during the sixteenth century, were refractors. Their perfectly round lenses, however, did not focus light sharply. Lenses made of a
(15) single piece of glass also bent light of different colors differently, producing color distortions. Opticians eventually overcame these problems by changing the curvature of the lens and constructing lenses out of layers of different kinds of glass.
(20) Meanwhile, the problems of refractors led some telescope makers to experiment with reflectors. They used mirrors that were not perfectly round, so that light was sharply focused. Moreover, mirrors did not produce color distortions. But these early reflectors
(25) had other problems. They were made of polished metal, which did not reflect light well. Also, metal mirrors often cracked as they cooled after being cast.

For two hundred years opticians worked to perfect both kinds of telescopes. Finally, in 1851, two
(30) Englishmen, Varnish and Mellish, found a way to cover glass with a very thin sheet of silver. This made it possible to build reflecting telescopes using a large curved mirror made of silver-covered glass. These telescopes reflected much more light than earlier
(35) reflectors and did not crack so easily. Today, nearly all large optical telescopes are built on this basic design.

45. Which of the following best tells what this passage is about?

A. the design of modern telescopes

B. how the telescope was developed

C. the problems of early telescopes

D. the experiments of Varnish and Mellish

E. how lenses are made

46. The passage suggests that there is usually a relationship between the size of a telescope and its

F. ability to reflect light.

G. magnifying power.

H. resistance to cracking.

J. accuracy in focusing light.

K. ability to bend light of different colors equally.

47. Which of the following was a problem of early refracting telescopes?

A. They did not transmit colored light.

B. They produced blurred images.

C. Their glass lenses cracked frequently.

D. They could not be used to view the stars.

E. They were made of colored glass.

GO ON TO THE NEXT PAGE ➡

48. Some early telescope makers experimented with reflecting telescopes because

    F. refractors had not yet been invented.

    G. they did not need telescopes with great magnifying power.

    H. opticians had stopped working to build better refractors.

    J. early refractors produced distorted images.

    K. opticians had found a way to coat glass with silver.

49. Opticians began using lenses made of several layers of glass in order to

    A. gather more incoming light.

    B. increase the size of their telescopes.

    C. construct stronger lenses that would not crack.

    D. avoid color distortion.

    E. focus light more sharply.

50. Telescope makers probably want to construct larger telescopes in order to

    F. avoid the blurred images produced by small telescopes.

    G. be able to view a wider range of colors.

    H. enlarge the focused image for easier viewing.

    J. create a more polished metal surface.

    K. see farther into the universe.

GO ON TO THE NEXT PAGE ➡

PART 2—MATH

Recommended Time—75 Minutes
50 Questions
NOTES:

- Reduce all fractions to lowest terms.

- Diagrams are **not** necessarily drawn to scale.

- Do your figuring in the test booklet or on paper distributed by the proctor.

QUESTIONS 51–100, Mathematics Problems

> **DIRECTIONS:** Solve each problem. Find your answer among the answer choices given. Mark the letter of your answer on the answer sheet.

51. What is the value of c in the equation $2a + 3b + 5 = c$ if $a = 3$ and $b = -3$?

    A.   −7

    B.   −5

    C.   1

    D.   2

    E.   8

52. Leontyne sings for $1,000 an hour. Her rate increases by 50% after midnight. If she sings one night from 8:30 P.M. until 1:00 A.M., how much should she be paid?

    F. $4,500

    G. $5,000

    H. $5,500

    J. $6,000

    K. $7,500

53. $6(4 - 6) + 3(1 - 2) =$

    A.   −9

    B.   −12

    C.   −15

    D.   −16

    E.   −18

54. Three apples cost as much as 4 pears. Three pears cost as much as 2 oranges. How many apples cost as much as 72 oranges?

    F.   36

    G.   48

    H.   64

    J.   81

    K.   108

55. $2[8 \div (-4)] + [(-12) \div (-3)] =$

    A.   −8

    B.   −4

    C.   −2

    D.   0

    E.   8

GO ON TO THE NEXT PAGE ➡

56. Fran has a drawer containing 4 black T-shirts, 3 orange T-shirts, and 5 blue T-shirts. If these are the only T-shirts in the drawer and she picks one at random, what are the chances it will **not** be orange?

F. $\frac{1}{4}$

G. $\frac{1}{3}$

H. $\frac{5}{12}$

J. $\frac{2}{3}$

K. $\frac{3}{4}$

57. What number is midway between $\frac{1}{7}$ and $\frac{1}{5}$?

A. $\frac{1}{12}$

B. $\frac{6}{70}$

C. $\frac{1}{6}$

D. $\frac{6}{35}$

E. $\frac{12}{35}$

58. What value does the digit 7 represent in the number 263,471,589?

F. 7,000

G. 10,000

H. 70,000

J. 100,000

K. 700,000

59. After a 5-hour flight from Newark, Harry arrived in Denver at 2:30 P.M. If the time in Newark is 2 hours later than the time in Denver, what was the time in Newark when Harry began the flight?

A. 10:30 A.M.

B. 11:30 A.M.

C. 12:30 P.M.

D. 3:30 P.M.

E. 5:30 P.M.

60. If q and r are integers, in which of the following equations **must** q be positive?

F. $q + r = 1$

G. $q - r = 1$

H. $qr = 1$

J. $q^2r = 1$

K. $qr^2 = 1$

$$25\overline{)\begin{array}{c} R9 \\ 8 \\ \overline{D} \end{array}}$$

61. In the division problem above, what is the remainder when D is divided by 8?

A. 1

B. 3

C. 6

D. 7

E. 9

Practice Test 2—Part 2

The following question refers to the graph below.

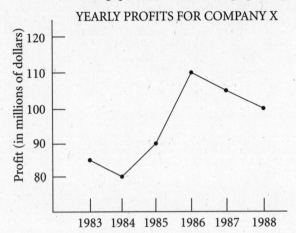

YEARLY PROFITS FOR COMPANY X

62. According to the graph, how much greater was the profit in the most profitable year than in the least profitable year?

- F. $15,000,000
- G. $20,000,000
- H. $25,000,000
- J. $30,000,000
- K. $110,000,000

63. A wall is 12 feet high. If its area is 132 sq ft, what is its perimeter?

- A. 44 feet
- B. 46 feet
- C. 48 feet
- D. 88 feet
- E. 96 feet

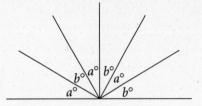

64. In the figure above, $a + b =$

- F. 45
- G. 60
- H. 75
- J. 90
- K. 120

65. What is the value of $400,000 + 1,000 + 300 + 20$?

- A. 4,132
- B. 41,320
- C. 401,302
- D. 401,320
- E. 410,320

66. A full box of chocolates contains 24 pieces of chocolate. If Doris starts out with 200 pieces of chocolate, how many pieces will she have left over if she fills as many boxes as she can?

- F. 0
- G. 4
- H. 8
- J. 10
- K. 16

GO ON TO THE NEXT PAGE ➡

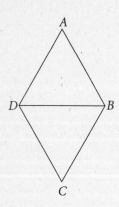

67. All the line segments in the figure above are equal. What is the measure of angle *ABC*?

A. 75°

B. 90°

C. 120°

D. 135°

E. 150°

68. Which of the following is equal to 483 × 0.0793?

F. 48.3 × 7.93

G. 4.83 × 793

H. 0.0483 × 7930

J. 48.3 × 79.3

K. 4.83 × 7.93

69. Which of the following fractions is closest to the product $\frac{39}{186} \times \frac{31}{10}$?

A. $\frac{1}{6}$

B. $\frac{1}{3}$

C. $\frac{1}{2}$

D. $\frac{2}{3}$

E. $\frac{3}{4}$

The following question refers to the chart below.

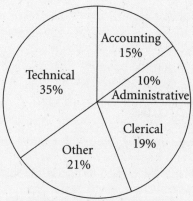

DISTRIBUTION OF EMPLOYEES
AT COMPANY X

70. What percent of the employees at company X are either clerical or technical?

F. 40%

G. 50%

H. 54%

J. 56%

K. 64%

GO ON TO THE NEXT PAGE ➡

71. $\dfrac{7 \cdot 3 \cdot 2}{9 \cdot 14 \cdot 3} =$

    A. $\dfrac{2}{63}$

    B. $\dfrac{1}{9}$

    C. $\dfrac{2}{9}$

    D. $\dfrac{1}{2}$

    E. $\dfrac{4}{7}$

    Here are two ways to add numbers:

    Abe's method: Round the numbers to the nearest integer and add.

    Ben's method: Add the numbers, then round the result to the nearest integer.

72. What is the difference between Abe's method and Ben's method when adding 6.4 and 3.3?

    F. 0
    G. 0.7
    H. 1.0
    J. 1.7
    K. 2.0

73. If 65% of x is 130, what is the value of x?

    A. 84.5
    B. 130
    C. 165
    D. 200
    E. 260

74. What is the value of x if $4(6x - x) = -10$?

    F. -2

    G. $-\dfrac{1}{2}$

    H. 0

    J. $\dfrac{1}{2}$

    K. 2

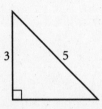

75. What is the area of the triangle above?

    A. 6
    B. 7.5
    C. 12
    D. 15
    E. Cannot be determined from the information given.

GO ON TO THE NEXT PAGE ➡

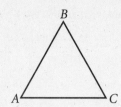

76. Triangle *ABC* is an equilateral triangle. If its perimeter is 24, what is the length of *AC*?

F. 3

G. 4

H. 6

J. 8

K. 12

77. Circle *O* above has a diameter of 6, an area of *b* square units, and a circumference of *c* units. What is the value of *b + c*?

A. 9π

B. 15π

C. 18π

D. 36π

E. 48π

78. If $x = \frac{1}{8}$, what is the value of *y* when $\frac{2}{x} = \frac{y}{4}$?

F. $\frac{1}{4}$

G. 1

H. 4

J. 16

K. 64

79. In the figure above, square *ABCD* is made up of 4 smaller, equal squares. If the perimeter of *ABCD* is 16, what is the sum of the perimeters of squares I, II, III, and IV?

A. 16

B. 24

C. 32

D. 48

E. 64

80. Assume that the notation ➤(*a, b, c*) means "Subtract the sum of *a, b,* and *c* from the product of *a, b,* and *c*." What is the value of ➤(4, 5, 6) + ➤(3, 2, 1)?

F. −111

G. −105

H. 0

J. 105

K. 111

GO ON TO THE NEXT PAGE ➡

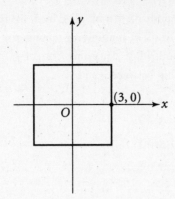

(3, 0)

81. In the figure above, O is the center of the square with sides parallel to the coordinates axes. What is the perimeter of the square?

   A.   9
   B.   12
   C.   24
   D.   36
   E.   48

82. If $x = -3$, what is the value of $\frac{1}{2}|2x - 2|$?

   F.   −4
   G.   −2
   H.   2
   J.   3
   K.   4

83. What is the length of a side of a square with a perimeter of 36?

   A.   4
   B.   6
   C.   9
   D.   12
   E.   18

84. A delivery service charges $25 per pound for making a delivery. If there is an additional 8% sales tax, what is the cost of delivering an item that weighs $\frac{4}{5}$ of a pound?

   F. $20.00
   G. $21.60
   H. $22.60
   J. $24.00
   K. $27.00

85. John must type 70 pages. He wants to type $\frac{1}{5}$ of the number of pages tomorrow morning, $\frac{1}{7}$ of the number of remaining pages tomorrow afternoon, and the remaining pages tomorrow evening. How many pages does John intend to type tomorrow evening?

   A.   8
   B.   28
   C.   40
   D.   46
   E.   48

86. What is the value of $\dfrac{8(y+5)}{3(3y+7)}$ if $y = 3$?

    F. $\dfrac{1}{3}$

    G. $\dfrac{4}{3}$

    H. $\dfrac{3}{2}$

    J. $\dfrac{5}{3}$

    K. $\dfrac{8}{3}$

87. Which of the following is **not** a prime factor of 210?

    A. 2
    B. 3
    C. 5
    D. 7
    E. 11

88. If n is an integer, which of the following **must** be odd?

    F. $n + 1$
    G. $2n + 1$
    H. $3n + 2$
    J. n^2
    K. $n^2 + 2$

89. When a number x is multiplied by 5, the result is 8 less than the result of multiplying a number y by 3. Which of the following equations correctly expresses the relationship between x and y?

    A. $5x = 24y$
    B. $5x - 8 = 3y$
    C. $5x + 8 = 3y$
    D. $5x + 3y = 8$
    E. $5x = 3(y - 8)$

90. If Tony bought z stamps and John bought 3 more than 5 times the number of stamps Tony bought, what is the total number of stamps they both bought?

    F. $4z$
    G. $5z$
    H. $5z + 3$
    J. $6z + 3$
    K. $7z + 3$

GO ON TO THE NEXT PAGE ➡

$$2x = 3y$$

91. All the possible values of x in the equation above are those in the set $\{3, 6, 12\}$. Which of the following sets is the set of all possible values of y?

    A. $\{1, 4, 6\}$

    B. $\{2, 3, 8\}$

    C. $\{2, 4, 6\}$

    D. $\{2, 4, 8\}$

    E. $\{4, 6, 8\}$

92. $\sqrt{64} + \sqrt{36} =$

    F.   2

    G. 10

    H. 14

    J.   50

    K. 100

93. A square with a side of length 4 inches is divided into squares having sides of length 1 inch. Three of the small squares are labeled A, 5 are labeled B, 4 are labeled C, 2 are labeled D, and the remainder are labeled E. If one small square is then chosen at random, what is the chance it's labeled E?

    A. 1 in 16

    B. 1 in 8

    C. 3 in 16

    D. 1 in 4

    E. 1 in 2

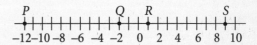

94. What is the distance from the midpoint of $\overline{PQ}$ to the midpoint of $\overline{RS}$?

    F. 12

    G. 14

    H. 16

    J. 18

    K. 21

GO ON TO THE NEXT PAGE ➡

95. Four consecutive even numbers have a sum of 28. What is the **largest** of these numbers?

    A. 10

    B. 12

    C. 14

    D. 18

    E. 24

96. What is the value of $\frac{x}{y}$ if $\frac{28}{x^2} = 2\frac{7}{xy}$?

    F. 4

    G. $4x^2$

    H. $4xy$

    J. $28y$

    K. 196

97. What is the value of $10(c + 3) + 6(c - 5)$ in terms of d if $c = 2d$?

    A. $4d$

    B. $8d$

    C. $16d$

    D. $32d$

    E. $16d + 30$

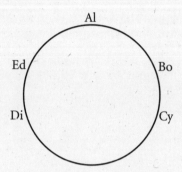

98. Five people are seated at a round table as shown above. If 52 cards are dealt to the five people beginning with Al and continuing clockwise (alphabetically), who gets the last card?

    F. Al

    G. Bo

    H. Cy

    J. Di

    K. Ed

GO ON TO THE NEXT PAGE ➡

99. Which of the following fractions is closest to $\frac{1}{8}$?

    A. $\frac{19}{160}$

    B. $\frac{197}{801}$

    C. $\frac{64}{321}$

    D. $\frac{151}{400}$

    E. $\frac{167}{1,000}$

100. A cake recipe requires $\frac{3}{5}$ of an ounce of vanilla extract. How many cakes can be made using a package containing 60 ounces of vanilla extract?

    F. 36

    G. 48

    H. 80

    J. 96

    K. 100

THIS IS THE END OF THE TEST. IF TIME REMAINS, YOU MAY CHECK YOUR ANSWERS TO PART 2 AND PART 1. BE SURE THAT THERE ARE NO STRAY MARKS, PARTIALLY FILLED ANSWER CIRCLES, OR INCOMPLETE ERASURES ON YOUR ANSWER SHEET.

DO NOT TURN TO THE NEXT PAGE. EXPLANATIONS FOLLOW.

STOP

Practice Test 2
Answer Key

Scrambled Paragraphs	Logical Reasoning	Reading Comprehension	Mathematics Problems	
1. RUQTS	11. E	21. C	51. D	81. C
2. STUQR	12. H	22. H	52. G	82. K
3. RUQTS	13. B	23. C	53. C	83. C
4. TQUSR	14. G	24. F	54. J	84. G
5. STQRU	15. A	25. D	55. D	85. E
	16. H	26. K	56. K	86. G
	17. D	27. A	57. D	87. E
	18. J	28. J	58. H	88. G
	19. B	29. A	59. B	89. C
	20. F	30. H	60. K	90. J
		31. A	61. A	91. D
		32. J	62. J	92. H
		33. D	63. B	93. B
		34. J	64. G	94. F
		35. B	65. D	95. A
		36. K	66. H	96. F
		37. B	67. C	97. D
		38. F	68. K	98. G
		39. C	69. D	99. A
		40. H	70. H	100. K
		41. D	71. B	
		42. K	72. H	
		43. C	73. D	
		44. F	74. G	
		45. B	75. A	
		46. G	76. J	
		47. B	77. B	
		48. J	78. K	
		49. D	79. C	
		50. H	80. J	

Practice Test 2 Answers and Explanations

SCRAMBLED PARAGRAPHS

1. **RUQTS.** The Topic Sentence tells us that the paragraph is about the wimple. You'd expect more detail describing the wimple next, and sentence R provides this. This linking phrase "this design" in U provides the transition to the introduction of the wimple into European fashion. Q then specifically describes how this happened. T expands on this topic by contrasting European and Muslim types of headdress. Finally, sentence S wraps up by describing the wimple's demise in the 14th century.

2. **STUQR.** Erikkson's reputed discovery of America is the topic of this paragraph. S must follow the Topic Sentence because it is the only time that Leif Erikkson's full name is used. "...the age" in T refers to "1000 CE" in S and, therefore, must follow S. Then just follow the sequence from voyage to landing to naming the continent—UQR wraps up the paragraph.

3. **RUQTS.** R follows the Topic Sentence. The clue "nonetheless" expresses the unexpected connection between movies made "as recently as ten years ago" and those made "in the era of the silent film." U comes next, adding quotation marks to the word "silent" to indicate that the term was not entirely accurate. Q is next, with the clue "in addition" leading into a second statement about old movies. The "exciting element" in Q is referred to as "This innovation" in T; therefore, T must follow Q. S is the final sentence, with the word "thus" leading to a conclusive statement.

4. **TQUSR.** T provides an example of a "breakthrough in science"—a revolution in the field of medicine. Q provides an example of a specific war in which this occurred—World War I. U and S describe the nature of the medical advance, and R wraps up with a reminder that other scientific advances have resulted from other wars.

5. **STQRU.** The linking phrase "for example" connects S to the Topic Sentence. "They" in T refers back to "fans" in S. "Nevertheless" in Q provides contrast and introduces ancient Greece, which then leads us to R and more information about chromaticism in ancient Greek music. U wraps up with a conclusion.

LOGICAL REASONING

11. **E** It would be great if there were two sentences that differed only in whether or not they included "guitar," like "Janice plays guitar at night" and "Janice plays tennis at night." That way, the codes would differ by only one letter, and you'd know which letter was "guitar" for sure. No such luck here, though. Compare sentence 2 to sentence 3: They have "Janice," "plays," and "guitar" in common, and their codes both have B, X, and Y. Of these words and letters, only "plays" and the letter X appear in other sentences and their codes, so X must represent "plays." But since "Janice" and "guitar" and B and Y are found only in sentences 2 and 3, there's no way to tell which letter goes with which number.

12. **H** The letter D is found only in the code for the first sentence. "Miguel" appears only in the first sentence, while all of the other words can be found in other sentences. You can conclude, then, that the letter D represents "Miguel."

13. **B** Let's review the facts. The original Tin Man couldn't play the part because he was allergic to makeup, so he was replaced by another actor. The only conclusion you can draw from this is that it is possible for an actor to be allergic to the makeup used in films

(B). We don't know which actor was better, how unusual this allergy is, what subsequently happened to the original actor, or what would have happened had he played the role, so none of the other choices have to be true.

14.   **G**   Set up the diagrams for the three pieces of information you're given.

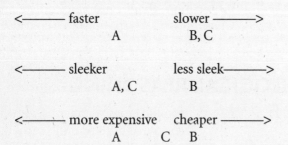

Note that you can't tell whether B or C is faster or how sleek A is compared to C. This rules out choices (F), (J), and (K). You do know, however, the order of the cars in terms of value, which allows you to see that (H) is wrong and (G) is correct.

15.   **A**   Here's Dr. Gray's appointment schedule with a senior citizen holding the second appointment:

$$1 \quad 2 \quad 3 \quad 4 \quad 5 \quad 6 \quad 7$$
$$\quad S$$

The thing to realize right off the bat is that you can't put a teenager or an infant in the first slot because both the teenagers and the infants have to have back-to-back appointments, and the senior citizen in slot 2 blocks the possibility of a 1-2 back-to-back for either. Therefore, a senior citizen must have the first appointment.

16.   **H**   Let's take a look at a diagram of the salesperson's schedule, keeping in mind that she can visit 3 companies the first day and at most 2 every day thereafter:

Day: 1 2 3 4 5 6
       3 2 2 2 1

After four days she'll still have one company to visit, so it will take her five days total to visit all ten companies (H).

17.   **D**   Several of these choices might seem reasonable to you, but the correct choice is going to be the assumption underlying the statement that since Fred was accepted to Harvard Law, he must have studied very hard. No other information is given about Fred, so the only way you could conclude that he must have studied very hard is to assume that **everyone** who gets into Harvard Law must have studied hard (in other words, only people who study hard are accepted—choice (D)).

You're given no info about Fred's friends or his ability to pass entrance exams, so (A) and (C) are out. (B) is wrong because the fact that Harvard Law School is hard to get into doesn't necessarily force us to the conclusion that Fred must have studied hard to get in; he may be naturally brilliant or have an inside connection with the admissions office. (E) is a conclusion most people would draw after hearing of Fred's success, but it too does not help us to the conclusion that Fred must have studied hard.

18.   **J**   There isn't much that you can conclude from the information in the question stem except that the earthquake that was predicted by seismograph didn't occur, which shows that seismographs aren't always correct in their predictions. This makes (J) the correct answer. There is no reason to think, at least as far as you know, that the earthquake is still coming (F) or that there was a minor earthquake instead of the predicted major one (K), although both are of course possible. (G) is far too harsh an

indictment of scientists based on the failure of one prediction, and there is no evidence to support (H).

19.　**B**　Draw a circle to represent the table and seat the players according to the given information. It's easiest to start with Liz and Jim, since you know exactly where they are in relation to each other. Since Karen is Jim's partner, she has to be directly across from him; Ron has to sit across from Liz. You can see as you work on the diagram that Karen sits to Ron's left, which means that Tracy must be sitting next to Ron on his right. Finally, Sean goes across from Tracy, between Karen and Liz.

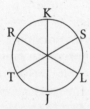

From the completed diagram, you see that Liz sits on Sean's left, choice (B).

20.　**F**　This question is easy once you have the diagram. Ron sits on Karen's right (F).

READING COMPREHENSION

Passage I is a science passage about desert plants and how they adapt to their environment. Paragraph 1 describes a variety of different ways in which plants adapt to the shortage of water in the desert. Paragraph 2 gets into the ways in which plants regulate their food-making process, photosynthesis, without losing "significant amounts of water" (line 21).

21.　**C**　The first sentence of the passage indicates what it's about—the "special adaptations" that desert plants have made for "living in extremely dry conditions." Wrong choice (A) is just a detail mentioned towards the end of paragraph 2. (B) is too broad—photosynthesis is discussed in paragraph 2, but the whole passage isn't about photosynthesis. Competition (D) is only one aspect of how plants survive. And shortage of water in the desert (E) is only discussed in reference to desert plants.

22.　**H**　What do most successful desert plants have to do? The passage goes into a lot of detail about how specific plants deal with their environment. Most of these adaptations relate to how plants deal with the lack of water around them—they're desert plants, right? Choices (F) and (K) are mentioned as ways in which specific plants cope with the water shortage. Choices (G) and (J) are aspects of desert life that aren't mentioned in the passage.

23.　**C**　Lines 9–11 tell us that some desert plants have shallow, widespread root systems to help them soak up "very occasional but heavy rainfalls." What kind of root systems would plants in tropical rain forests need? Well, rain forests have a plentiful supply of water, so you can infer that rain forest plants wouldn't need such widespread root systems, making (C) the correct answer.

24.　F　Lines 22–23 indicate that the stomates are tiny openings on the surface of plants that open and close as part of the process of photosynthesis. The function of these openings is described earlier in lines 19–20; the plants absorb carbon dioxide through them, and lose water through them.

25.　D　Lines 16–21 state that plants make their food by the process of photosynthesis, which involves absorbing carbon dioxide through tiny openings on the plant surfaces. "When absorbing carbon dioxide, however, plants lose significant amounts of water...." Therefore, (D) is correct. The mechanism by which plants shed their leaves or close them up (A) is not described in the passage. The tiny openings, or stomates, do enable the plant to survive both day and nighttime temperatures (B), but this is not either of the twin purposes being discussed in line 21. The ability to secrete poison (C) is mentioned only in reference to the creosote bush in paragraph 1. And plants absorb carbon dioxide; they don't secrete it as (E) suggests.

26.　K　Once again, we're told that wide, shallow root systems help plants adjust to "occasional, but heavy rainfalls" (lines 10–11). Choice (K), a flash flood, fits this description best.

Passage II is a social studies passage about alchemy, the ancient science of trying to turn various different metals into gold. Paragraph 1 emphasizes the historical importance of alchemy—even though it seems ridiculous to the modern mind, we're told, alchemy helped lay the basic framework for the science of chemistry. Paragraph 2 describes the philosophy behind alchemy—the idea was that "base" metals such as copper and lead were just "imperfect" and could somehow be "purified" and turned into gold. Paragraph 3 gives us some more history—Europeans were interested in alchemy from the twelfth century until

the seventeenth, and even Sir Isaac Newton dabbled in it.

27.　A　This passage covers a lot of ground. There's some discussion of how important alchemy was historically, there's a paragraph describing the theory behind alchemy, and there's a paragraph on alchemy in Europe from the twelfth century onwards. So really the passage can only be about the history of alchemy—choice (A). (B) is wrong because the alchemists never actually managed to make gold, despite centuries of trying. Choices (C), (D), and (E) are all details that are part of the history of alchemy.

28.　J　Lines 3–7 describe the reputation of alchemists today—we're told that alchemy's associations with astrology suggest "primitive superstition" to the modern mind. (F) goes against the gist of the passage, which suggests overall that historians know a lot about alchemy. (G) is a detail from paragraph 3, where we're told that the alchemists' idea of making gold was disproved. But that just stopped people from trying to make gold—it wasn't responsible for the unfavorable reputation of alchemists today. (H) is contradicted in paragraph 3. And (K) distorts paragraph 1, where it's stated that alchemists helped develop modern "apparatuses and procedures."

29.　A　Copper and lead are discussed in paragraph 2. Lines 23–24 indicate that the alchemists believed they were "only imperfectly developed forms of gold."

30.　H　The "purification" process is described in paragraph 2; towards the end of the paragraph, we're told that the process had a "profound significance for the alchemists"—metals attained a state of perfection just as souls attained perfection in heaven. You can infer from this that the alchemists regarded the process as being parallel to a spiritual experience—choice (H). Sir Isaac Newton (F) is not mentioned in connection with purification. No distortion of Arabic works (G) is stated or implied. The twelfth century (J) is described as the time when alchemy became widespread in Europe, so presumably the purification process was first attempted earlier. (K) is a big distortion—alchemists were clearly aware that they were trying to make gold, the most valuable of metals.

31.   **A**   Lines 26–27 state that alchemists believed base metals could be purified "under certain astrological conditions," but we never learn what these conditions are. All the other questions **are** answered: (B) in the final sentence of paragraph 1; (C) in lines 41–42; (D) in lines 28–29; and (E) in the first sentence of paragraph 3.

32.   **J**   The author sums up his point of view on alchemy at the end of the passage—though not practiced today, alchemy "provided the basis for some of the most fascinating chapters in the history of science." (F) and (H) are wrong because the passage argues that alchemy did contribute to the development of science. (K) is a point of view that the author contradicts in paragraph 1. And (G) distorts lines 8–11; sure, the alchemists left us some valuable apparatuses and procedures. But their basic principles have been disproved.

Passage III is a science passage about underwater ecosystems. Paragraph 1 explains that most ecosystems on our planet depend upon the light of the sun. Through the process of photosynthesis, the sun provides energy for plants and algae, which in turn provide energy for animals higher up the food chain. Towards the end of the paragraph, however, we're told that a new type of ecosystem has been discov-

ered in deep-sea areas, where the first link in the food chain is provided by bacteria that are dependent on energy from within the earth itself. Paragraph 2 describes how these "chemosynthetic" bacteria develop. Paragraph 3 tells us a bit about the sea life that inhabits these deep sea oases.

33.   **D**   The passage is about the newly discovered "chemosynthetic" ecosystems described in paragraphs 2 and 3. Wrong choice (A) is way too broad. The origins of life on earth are mentioned at the end of paragraph 1, but the passage doesn't really address this difficult topic. (B) is wrong because it's chemosynthesis, not photosynthesis, that the author is most interested in. (C) describes paragraph 3, but it doesn't cover the passage as a whole. (E), like (A), is too broad—the author's not writing about the whole eastern Pacific.

34.   **J**   Lines 1–3 provide the answer here; we're told that "most life is fundamentally dependent on photosynthetic organisms that store radiant energy from the sun." So it's light from the sun (J), not bacterial microorganisms (H), that powers most life on earth.

35.   **B**   Paragraph 1 describes the contrast that makes the chemosynthetic ecosystems "unique"—most life on earth depends on the sun's energy, but chemosynthetic ecosystems depend on energy provided from within the earth itself. Choice (B) expresses this idea best. (A) distorts the passage—it's not that chemosynthetic ecosystems have no need for a source of energy. (C) is illogical—these deep-sea ecosystems are plainly not airless and waterless. (D) is not mentioned as a feature that makes chemosynthetic ecosystems unique, and we're not told if these are the only ecosystems found at these depths (E).

36. **K** The keyword here is "surprisingly." Scientists in a submarine found something they weren't looking for in 1977—namely, a unique, previously unknown ecosystem 7,000 feet underwater in a volcanically active area. Thus, (K) is best. (F) is contradicted by the final sentence of paragraph 2. (G), (H), and (J) are not substantiated in the passage: We're not told that there were "previous searches" of the Rift (G), that tube worms even exist on dry land (H), or what water temperature is necessary to sustain life (J).

37. **B** The phrase "primary producers" crops up at the end of paragraph 2. Lines 31–33 describe chemosynthetic bacteria as primary producers because they "[transform] chemicals into compounds that can serve as nourishment for more complex forms of life." So the bacteria's role is basically to provide food for other animals, choice (B). (D) is wrong because the bacteria is described as "transforming chemicals into compounds"—so the bacteria isn't the simple chemical in this process. (C) is the opposite of how the bacteria in line 30 are described. (A) isn't justified at all by the passage. (B) doesn't relate to the bacteria described in the cited lines.

38. **F** Photosynthetic organisms such as plants and algae convert the sun's energy into energy for other animals in their food chain (lines 1–6). Chemosynthetic bacteria do the same sort of thing in converting the earth's energy into energy for the deep-sea animals that consume them (lines 27–30). So the answer here is (F)—both types of organisms perform similar functions in different food chains. (G) only applies to chemosynthetic organisms, as far as we know. (H) only applies to their photosynthetic cousins. (J) is not indicated anywhere in the passage. And (K) is not necessarily true—we're not

told that chemosynthetic organisms will thrive everywhere that photosynthetic organisms don't.

Passage IV is a humanities passage about the great American dancer Martha Graham. Paragraph 1 gives us some background on Graham's approach—we're told she wanted to break away from the conventions of classical ballet and create new dance forms for the postwar period. Paragraph 2 describes her characteristic style—stark and severe to some, "uncompromisingly ugly" to others. Paragraph 3 explains why Graham was misunderstood by the critics. Paragraph 4 details her late work.

39. **C** The passage covers most of Graham's career and goes into some detail on her revolutionary style and reputation with the critics. So it's about her role and purpose as an innovator—choice (C). Choices (A) and (B) are too broad. (D) describes paragraph 3 only, and (E) describes paragraph 2 only.

40. **H** Paragraph 1 puts Graham's approach in context—we're told that she wanted to create "new dance forms and movements that would reflect the changed atmosphere of the postwar period." (H) fits the bill here. (F) and (G) touch on minor elements of Graham's style. Choices (J) and (K) exaggerate Graham's reaction against classical ballet; Graham was fed up with classical ballet, so she decided to invent a new dance form that she felt was more appropriate for the period. But she didn't set out to destroy the ballet tradition (J) or just parody it (K).

41. **D** Lines 13–15 provide the answer: Graham used "the natural breath pulse as the basis for movement," instead of ballet's "formalized classical motions." So we can infer that ballet's motions were not based on this natural breath pulse, and (D) is correct. (A) and (B) are things attributed to

Graham's early dances; (C) mentions the subject matter of some of her later work. (E) is not inferable; the passage never discusses the relative difficulty of these two forms of dance.

42. **K** Paragraph 2 contrasts classical ballet with Graham's new style of dance. We're told that Graham "rejected the extravagant stylization of classical ballet, using the natural breath pulse instead of formalized classical notions" (lines 12–15). Other innovations included avoiding "decorative sets and costumes" and using an "all-female dance troupe." You can infer from this that classical ballet of the time did use elaborate sets and costumes. Choices (F) through (J) all describe Graham's style and how it was received.

43. **C** Why was Graham misunderstood? Paragraph 3 says that while her work "addressed universal feelings and ideas," critics "reacted only to the unfamiliar and original dance movements" in which they were expressed. Choice (C) rephrases this key idea. There's no evidence for (A), (B), or (D). (E) distorts the passage—it was universal feelings and ideas, not personal ones, that people didn't understand.

44. **F** Read the lines surrounding the quote. "A tradition against which the avant-garde was rebelling" is the fate the author is referring to. In other words, while Graham's work was revolutionary in the 1920s, it had become quite acceptable by the 1940s, with the result that younger dancers and choreographers were rebelling against it. Choice (F) describes this chain of events.

Passage V is a science passage about telescopes. Paragraph 1 describes how telescopes work and tells us about the two main types of lenses used—reflectors and refractors. Paragraph 2 tells us about the first refractor telescopes and

the problems scientists had in producing a focused image. Paragraph 3 describes the first reflectors developed and details their problems. Paragraph 4 talks about how the basic telescope design used today was finally developed.

45. **B** The passage describes several stages in the development of the modern telescope. So really the passage is about how the telescope was developed—choice (B). (A) and (D) describe paragraph 4 only. (C) describes paragraphs 2 and 3 only. How lenses are made, (E), isn't really discussed anywhere in the passage.

46. **G** The second sentence of the passage states that "Generally, the larger a telescope is, the greater its magnifying power." Lines 25–27 suggest that both a telescope's ability to reflect light (F) and its resistance to cracking (H) are related to the quality of its mirror, not the mirror's size. Lines 20–23 show that accuracy in focusing light (J) was achieved, regardless of the telescope's size, by "using mirrors that were not perfectly round." And paragraph 2 states that color distortions—bending different colors of light differently—were avoided by changing the curvature of the lens or making layered lenses, not by changing the size of the lens.

47. **B** Paragraph 2 describes the problems of refractors—they didn't "focus light sharply," and they produced "color distortions." Choice (B) hits on the first problem. (A) is an exaggeration—the passage doesn't say that the refractors didn't transmit colored light at all. (C) describes a reflector problem. There's no evidence for (D), and (E) is not presented in the passage as a problem.

48. **J** Lines 20–21 describe why scientists moved on to experimenting with reflectors—there were too

many problems with refractors. Refractors produced distorted images (a major problem in a telescope), as correct choice (J) suggests. (F) is wrong because refractors had been invented—it's just that they didn't work. Lack of magnifying power (G) is not mentioned as a problem. (H) is nonsense, and silver-coating (K) wasn't invented until later in 1851.

49. D The practice of constructing lenses from layers of different kinds of glass is described at the end of paragraph 2. Scientists investigated this option in order to overcome the problem discussed earlier—color distortion. The focusing problem (E) was remedied by changing the curvature of lenses (lines 16–19). Cracking (C) was a problem associated with refractors (paragraph 3).

50. H Lines 2–3 indicate the advantages of building large telescopes; "generally, the larger a telescope is, the greater its magnifying power." You can infer from this that larger telescopes are produced in order to enlarge the focused image for easier viewing—choice (H).

MATH PROBLEMS

51. D Plug in the values you have for a and b. Since $a = 3$ and $b = -3$, our equation reads $2(3) + 3(-3) + 5 = c$. After doing the multiplication, we have $6 + (-9) + 5 = c$. And after doing this addition, we get $2 = c$, choice (D).

52. G Let's break this question down into pieces. Before midnight, Leontyne gets paid $1,000 an hour. If she starts singing at 8:30 P.M., then she sings for $3\frac{1}{2}$ hours before midnight. Her earnings for that time are $3\frac{1}{2}$ times $1,000, or $3,500. Now let's find out how

much she earns after midnight. Her rate increases 50% after midnight, so her hourly rate after midnight is $1,000 + 50% of $1,000. Then 50% of $1,000 is $500, so her rate per hour after midnight is $1,000 + $500 = $1,500. So she earns $1,500 for the hour she sings after midnight. For the last step, we add that to the amount she earns before midnight, so her total pay is $3,500 + $1,500 = $5,000, choice (G).

53. C Remember the order of operations here, PEMDAS (Parentheses, Exponents, Multiplication, Division, Addition and Subtraction). So first we do the operations inside the parentheses: $4 - 6 = -2$ and $1 - 2 = -1$. Now our expression reads $6(-2) + 3(-1)$. The next operation to do is the multiplication: $6 \times (-2) = -12$, and $3 \times (-1) = -3$. So now our expression becomes $(-12) + (-3)$, which is -15, choice (C).

54. J The key to this problem is to start at the end. Because 3 pears cost the same as 2 oranges, set up the proportion $\frac{3p}{2o} = \frac{xp}{72o}$, where x is the number of pears that cost as much as 72 oranges, p is the price of 1 pear, and o is the price of 1 orange. Cross multiply and solve for x: $(2o)(xp) = (3p)(72o)$, so $2x = 216$ and $x = 108$. Now you can set up another proportion from the other relationship described in the question: $\frac{3a}{4p} = \frac{ya}{108p}$, where y is the number of apples that cost as much as 108 pears and a is the price of 1 apple. Cross multiply and solve for y: $(3a)(108p) = (4p)(ya)$, so $4y = 324$ and $y = 81$. Therefore, 81 apples cost the same as 72 oranges. Note that this problem

could also be solved by picking a number for the cost of an orange, solving for the cost of a pear, and then solving for the cost of an apple.

55.　　D　　Another order of operations question: First we have to do the operations inside the parentheses. So $8 ÷ (−4)$ is $−2$, and $−12 ÷ (−3)$ is 4. Now our expression reads $2(−2) + 4$. Next we do multiplication: $2 × (−2) = −4$. Now we can do the addition: $−4 + 4 = 0$, choice (D).

56.　　K　　The probability of an event occurring is a fraction—the number of possible outcomes in which the event can occur divided by the total number of possible outcomes. Fran is going to pick one shirt, and we want to figure out the probability that it will not be orange. In other words, what is the probability of picking a non-orange shirt? Aside from the orange shirts, there are 4 black shirts and 5 blue shirts, so altogether there are 9 non-orange shirts. So there are 9 possible successful outcomes. The total number of shirts to choose from, including the orange shirts, is 12, so there are 12 possible outcomes. So the probability of Fran picking a non-orange shirt is $\frac{9}{12}$, which can be reduced to $\frac{3}{4}$, answer choice (K).

57.　　D　　You might be tempted to say that $\frac{1}{6}$ is midway between $\frac{1}{7}$ and $\frac{1}{5}$, but that's not the answer. Even if you don't know what to do, you can eliminate choice (A) because $\frac{1}{12}$ is less than $\frac{1}{7}$ so it can't be between $\frac{1}{7}$ and $\frac{1}{5}$. You can solve this problem by picturing

$\frac{1}{7}$ and $\frac{1}{5}$ on a number line. The fraction we're looking for is the midpoint between $\frac{1}{7}$ and $\frac{1}{5}$. To find this midpoint, first we will add the two fractions together, and then we will divide the sum by 2. In order to add the fractions together, we have to give them the same denominator. The least common denominator is 35. Then $\frac{1}{7}$ is equal to $\frac{5}{35}$, and $\frac{1}{5}$ is equal to $\frac{7}{35}$; $\frac{5}{35} + \frac{7}{35} = \frac{12}{35}$ and $\frac{12}{35} ÷ 2 = \frac{6}{35}$, answer choice (D).

58.　　H　　The digit 7 is in the ten-thousands place, so the 7 represents $7 × 10,000$, or $70,000$, choice (H).

59.　　B　　Draw a chart or table to help organize the information. Newark is two hours later than Denver, so if the time in Denver when Harry arrives is 2:30 P.M., then the time in Newark when he arrives in Denver is 4:30 P.M. The flight takes 5 hours, so the time he began in Newark is 5 hours earlier than 4:30 P.M., or 11:30 A.M., choice (B).

60.　　K　　Let's answer this question by trying each answer choice and trying to show that the statement can be true with a negative q. In choice (F), can $q + r = 1$ if q is negative? Yes. Let's say $q = −2$. Then the equation would read $−2 + r = 1$, which would mean that $r = 3$, an integer. What about (G)? If q is $−2$, then the equation reads $−2 − r = 1$. Solving for r we find that $r = −3$, which is also an integer. In choice (H), if q is $−1$, then the equation reads $−1r = 1$. Solving for r, we find that $r = −1$, so we can discard (H). In choice (J), if q is $−1$, the equation reads $(−1)^2 × r = 1$, so $r = 1$. This leaves only choice (K). In choice (K), if $q = −1$, then the equation reads $(−1) × r^2 = 1$. This means that r^2 must equal $−1$. But any nonzero number squared becomes positive, so r^2 can't be −1. The same problem would occur with any negative value of q, so q must be positive, making (K) the correct answer. You can also prove that q must be positive if $qr^2 = 1$ because $qr^2 = 1$, $q \neq 0$, and $r \neq 0$. The square of any nonzero number is positive, so r^2 is positive. Since $qr^2 = 1$, q must be positive.

61. **A** First we have to find out what D is. We are given that $D \div 25 = 8$ with a remainder of 9. So $D = (25 \times 8) + 9$, or $200 + 9$, or 209; $209 \div 8 = 26$ remainder 1, so the answer is choice (A).

62. **J** To find company X's profit for a given year, first find the year on the horizontal scale of the graph and then draw a line straight up until you reach the dot directly above the year. Then draw a line straight to the left from the dot until you reach the vertical scale on the left side of the graph. The number on the left is the profit for that year. The most profitable year was 1986, when the profit was $110 million. The least profitable year was 1984, when the profit was $80 million. So all we have to do is subtract: 110 million − 80 million = $30 million, choice (J).

63. **B** We can assume that the wall is rectangular, so the area of the wall is base times height. We are given that the height is 12 feet and the area is 132 square feet, so we can express this in an equation: $132 = 12 \times$ base. If we divide both sides by 12, we find that the base is equal to $132 \div 12$, or 11 feet. The perimeter of a rectangle is the sum of the lengths of the four sides, so the perimeter of this wall is $11 + 12 + 11 + 12$, or 46 feet, choice (B).

64. **G** We don't have enough information to figure out what a or b is individually, but we can figure out what the sum of a and b is. Altogether, the three angles

marked a and the three angles marked b add up to make a straight line, or a 180° angle. So we can say that $3a + 3b = 180$. Then we can divide both sides by 3 and find that $a + b = 180 \div 3$, or 60, choice (G).

65. **D** You can just add these numbers up. But you can also eliminate choices (A) and (B) because they are too small. Since several numbers are being added to 400,000, we know that the answer will have to be greater than 400,000. The correct answer is (D).

66. **H** How many times does 24 go into 200? Calculate $200 \div 24 = 8$ with a remainder of 8, so Doris can fill 8 boxes of chocolates.

67. **C** This figure is made up of two triangles put together. Since all of the line segments are the same length, these triangles are equilateral. In an equilateral triangle, each angle is 60°. Angle ABC is made up of angle ABD and angle CBD, which each measure 60°, so the measure of angle $ABC = 60° + 60° = 120°$, choice (C).

68. **K** To solve this problem, we will try to make the expression in the question look like each of the answer choices until we find one that works. To turn 483 into 48.3, we would have to multiply it by 0.1. To keep the expression balanced, we would then have to multiply 0.0793 by 10, which is 0.793, so our expression would read 48.3 × 0.793. There are two answer choices that include 48.3—choices (F) and (J)—and neither of them includes 0.793, so we can eliminate these two choices. To make 483 look like 4.83, we would have to multiply it by 0.01. To keep the expression balanced, we would have to multiply 0.0793 by 100. So our expression would read 4.83 × 7.93. This is choice (K).

69. **D** Since this question doesn't ask for an exact answer, we can round off the numbers involved. Let's change $\frac{39}{186}$ to $\frac{40}{180}$ and change $\frac{31}{10}$ to $\frac{30}{10}$. So now we have $\frac{40}{180} \times \frac{30}{10}$, and we can do some canceling. Then 10 goes into 40 four times, so we can replace 10 with a 1 and 40 with a 4. And 30 goes into 180 six times, so we can replace 30 with a 1 and 180 with a 6. Now we have $\frac{4}{6} \times \frac{1}{1}$ or $\frac{2}{3}$, choice (D).

Be very careful when rounding. Notice in this problem that the first fraction was rounded to a larger value and the second was rounded to a smaller one. This will result in a similar product to that of the original numbers. However, when dividing rounded numbers, try to round them in the same direction (either both larger or both smaller) to get a similar dividend to that of the original numbers.

70. **H** We know that 35% of employees are technical and 19% are clerical, so to find the percent of employees who are either technical or clerical, we just have to add the two percentages together: 35% + 19% = 54%, choice (H).

71. **B** Begin by cancelling terms: The 3s cancel as well as the 7 and 2 with the 14 in the denominator. We are left with $\frac{1}{9}$, choice (B).

72. **H** Abe's method yields 6 + 3 = 9, and Ben's method yields 6.4 + 3.3 = 9.7, rounded = 10. Hence, the difference is 1.

73. **D** Remember: *Of* means multiply, and *is* means equals. Here, we needed to set up the following equation: $\frac{65}{100}x = 130$. Multiply both sides by $\frac{100}{65}$ and we get $x = (130)\left(\frac{100}{65}\right) = 200$.

74. **G** Solve for x according to PEMDAS: $4(5x) = -10$, thus $20x = -10$. Dividing both sides by 20, we get $x = -\frac{1}{2}$.

75. **A** Time is saved here if you recognize the given triangle is a 3-4-5 triangle. Thus, the height = 3 and the base = 4. Recall that area of a triangle equals one-half times the base times the height. Here Area = $\frac{1}{2}$ (4)(3) = 6.

76. **J** The problem tells us this is an equilateral triangle; hence, all sides are equal. Thus, dividing the perimeter by 3 will give the length of each side: $\frac{24}{3} = 8$.

77. **B** Given a diameter of 6, the radius must equal 3. Next, the circumference = $2\pi r$ = $2\pi(3) = 6\pi$. The area formula gives you $\pi r^2 = \pi(3)^2 = 9\pi$. Adding these two values together results in $6\pi + 9\pi = 15\pi$.

78. **K** In order to avoid a fraction in the denominator, begin by cross multiplying: $8 = xy$. Next, substitute $\frac{1}{8}$ for x. Then $8 = \frac{1}{8}y$. Multiply both sides of this equation by 8, and we have $64 = y$, choice (K).

79. **C** With a perimeter of 16, each side of square *ABCD* has a length of $\frac{16}{4} = 4$, and thus each small square has a side length of 2. Each small square has a perimeter of 8, and the 4 small squares have a total perimeter of (4)(8) = 32, choice (C).

80. **J** Here, pay special attention to the definition of the foreign symbol. The sum of 4, 5, and 6 is 4 + 5 + 6 = 15 and the product of 4, 5, and 6 is $4 \times 5 \times 6$ = 120. So (4, 5, 6) = 120 − 15 = 105.

Now $(1, 2, 3) = 1 \times 2 \times 3 - (1 + 2 + 3)$ $= 6 - 6 = 0$. So $(4, 5, 6) - (1, 2, 3) =$ $105 - 0 = 105$.

81. **C** If the distance from O to the edge of the square is 3, then the length of each side must be $2 \times 3 = 6$. The perimeter (the distance around the square) = $4 \times$ the length of one side = $4 \times 6 = 24$.

82. **K** Substitute the value of -3 for x in the given expression: $\frac{1}{2}|(2(-3) - 2)| = \frac{1}{2}$ $|-6 - 2| = \frac{1}{2}|-8| = \frac{1}{2}(8) = 4$. Recall that when working with absolute value, the result of the expression within the bars must become nonnegative when the bars are removed.

83. **C** The perimeter of a square is the distance around it. Hence, because all four sides are equal, the length of one side is simply the perimeter divided by 4: $\frac{36}{4} = 9$.

84. **G** The charge for delivering one pound is $25, so the charge for delivering $\frac{4}{5}$ of a pound is $\frac{4}{5}$ of $25, or $20. The tax is 8% of $20, or 0.08 of $20, or $1.60. The total cost of delivering the item is $20 + $1.60, or $21.60, choice (G).

85. **E** There are several ways to solve this problem. One way is to figure out how many pages John plans to type in the morning and afternoon. In the morning, he plans to type $\frac{1}{5}$ of the pages. Then $\frac{1}{5}$ of 70 is 14, so John plans to type 14 pages in the morning, leaving $70 - 14 = 56$ pages left to type. He plans to type $\frac{1}{7}$ of the remaining pages in the afternoon. Since $\frac{1}{7}$ of 56 is 8, John plans to type 8 pages in the

afternoon, leaving $56 - 8 = 48$ pages for him to type in the evening, choice (E).

86. **G** Plug in the number 3 for each y in this expression. The numerator of the fraction becomes $8(3 + 5)$, and the denominator becomes $3[(3 \times 3) + 7]$. Now we follow the order of operations (PEMDAS). In the numerator, $3 + 5$ is 8, and 8×8 is 64, so our numerator is 64. In the denominator, 3×3 is 9, $9 + 7$ is 16, and 3×16 is 48, making our denominator 48. So the fraction is $\frac{64}{48}$, which can be reduced to $\frac{4}{3}$, choice (G).

87. **E** Since all of the five answer choices are prime numbers, the easiest way to approach this problem is to try each answer choice and see which one does not divide evenly into 210. Because 210 is even, 2 must be a factor; 210 is divisible by 3, because 210 is $10 \times$ 21, and 21 is divisible by 3; 210 ends with a zero, so it is divisible by 5; 210 is divisible by 7 ($210 \div 7 = 30$). So the only choice left is 11, choice (E).

88. **G** To solve this problem, we will pick even and odd numbers to plug in for n and try them in each answer choice. First we'll try choice (F). If $n = 2$, an even number, then $n + 1 = 2 + 1$, or 3, an odd number. If $n = 3$, an odd number, then $n + 1 = 3 + 1$, or 4, an even number. As you can see, $n + 1$ is not always odd, so (F) is not the correct answer. Now we'll try choice (G). If $n = 2$, then $2n + 1 = 2(2) + 1$, or $4 + 1$, or 5, an odd number. If $n = 3$, then $2n + 1 = 2(3) + 1 = 7$, an odd number. This time we got an odd answer whether we started with an odd number or an even number, so $2n + 1$ must be odd, and choice (G) is the correct answer.

89. **C** This is a translation problem. "A number x is multiplied by 5," can be represented as $5x$. "The result is" is represented by an equal sign. And "8 less than the result of multiplying a number y by 3" means $3y - 8$. So the whole sentence can be written as $5x = 3y - 8$. This does not match any of the answer choices, but if we add 8 to both sides, we get $5x + 8 = 3y$, which is (C).

90. **J** Since Tony bought z stamps, 5 times the number of stamps Tony bought is $5z$ stamps. The amount that John bought is 3 more than this—$5z + 3$. The total that both bought is $5z + 3 + z = 6z + 3$, choice (J).

91. **D** To find all possible values of y, plug in each possible value of x and then find the corresponding value of y. If x is 3, then our equation reads $2(3) = 3y$. After multiplying 2 and 3, we have $6 = 3y$. Now we can divide both sides by 3 and find that $y = 2$. This rules out choices (A) and (E), which do not include 2. If $x = 6$, then our equation becomes $2(6) = 3y$, or $12 = 3y$. Dividing both sides by 3, we find that $y = 4$. This rules out choice (B). If $x = 12$, then $2(12) = 3y$, or $24 = 3y$ and $y = 8$. So our three values of y are 2, 4, and 8, choice (D).

92. **H** The positive square roots of 64 and 36 are 8 and 6 respectively, so adding them together makes $8 + 6$, or 14, choice (H).

93. **B** Draw a diagram here. You will find that there are 16 squares—3 are labeled A, 5 are labeled B, 4 are labeled C, and 2 are labeled D. This accounts for 14 of the 16 squares. This leaves 2 squares to be labeled E. The probability of an event occurring is a

fraction—here the probability is $\frac{2}{16}$, which can be reduced to $\frac{1}{8}$, or 1 in 8, as in choice (B).

94. **F** To find the midpoint of a segment on the number line, you add the coordinates of the two endpoints and then divide the sum by 2. So, the midpoint of PQ is $\frac{(-12) + (-2)}{2} = \frac{-14}{2} = -7$. The midpoint of RS is $\frac{1 + 9}{2} = \frac{10}{2} = 5$. The distance between the two points is the positive difference between their coordinates, or $5 - (-7) = 12$, choice (F).

95. **A** Let's call the first number x. Then the second consecutive even number is $x + 2$, the third consecutive even number is $x + 4$, and the fourth consecutive even number is $x + 6$. We can represent the sum of these numbers as $x + x + 2 + x + 4 + x + 6$. If we combine like terms, we have $4x + 12$. When we set this equal to 28, we get $4x + 12 = 28$. The next step is to solve for x. First we subtract 12 from both sides, so we have $4x = 28 - 12$, or $4x = 16$. Now we can divide both sides by 4 and find that $x = 16 \div 4$, or 4. Since $x = 4$ and the largest number is $x + 6$, the largest number must be $4 + 6$, or 10, choice (A).

96. **F** Since we have two fractions equal to each other, we can cross multiply: $(28)(xy) = (x^2)(7)$, or $28xy = 7x^2$. Next we will divide both sides by 7, so we have $4xy = x^2$. Then we can divide both sides by xy, and the result is $4 = \frac{x}{y}$, choice (F).

97. **D** Plug $2d$ in for c. The expression becomes $10(2d + 3) + 6(2d - 5)$. We can't add $2d$ and 3, or subtract 5 from

$2d$, so the next step is to multiply using the distributive property, so we have $(10 \times 2d) + (10 \times 3) + (6 \times 2d) + [6 \times (-5)]$. This can be simplified to $20d + 30 + 12d + (-30)$. Then $30 + (-30) = 0$, so we end up with $20d + 12d$, or $32d$, choice (D).

98. G   Five people are being dealt 52 cards, so we will divide 52 by 5: $52 \div 5 = 10$ remainder 2. Since we are starting with Al, after dealing 5 cards we will be ready to start with Al again. So after 50 cards, we will be ready to start with Al again. Al gets the 51st card, and Bo gets the 52nd card, choice (G).

99. A   Since this question doesn't ask for an exact answer, we can round off the answer choices. Thus, $\frac{19}{160}$ can be rounded off to $\frac{20}{160}$, which equals $\frac{1}{8}$, or choice (A). Rounding off the other choices confirms that (A) is closest.

100. K   To answer this question, we just have to figure out how many times $\frac{3}{5}$ goes into 60. We know that it will be more than 60, so right away we can eliminate (F) and (G). Our equation is $60 \div \frac{3}{5} = \frac{60}{1} \times \frac{5}{3}$. This is easier to multiply if we do some canceling. Because 3 goes into 60 twenty times, we can replace the 3 with a 1 and replace the 60 with a 20. So now we have $\frac{20}{1} \times \frac{5}{1}$, which equals 20×5, or 100, choice (K).

Information on Scoring Your Practice Tests

SHSAT scoring is detailed in Section 1: The Basics. However, here's a quick recap.

There are 50 questions in the Math Section and 45 questions in the Verbal Section. Each section is worth 50 raw points (Scrambled Paragraphs are worth 2 raw points each) to give you a raw score on a 100-point scale. Your raw score is converted into a scaled score out of 800 points. It is not possible to look at your raw score and know what your scaled score will be. The scaled scores are adjusted to fit the normal curve. Kaplan cannot provide a scaled score for you here because your scaled score depends on how well other students do on the test.

The point of this practice is to give you a chance to work through a realistic SHSAT, not to identify whether or not your results on this test would get you into one of the specialized high schools. That will depend not only on how well you do but also on how many applicants take the test and how well they do.

A Few Points to Keep in Mind

As more people take the test, it becomes more competitive, and the scores needed for admission go up. Most likely, next year's cutoff scores will be higher than this year's cutoff scores.

In recent years, cutoff scores have been in the 500–600 range. Although raw scores are not directly proportional to scaled scores, the fact that the cutoff scaled scores are mostly in the 500s tells you that test takers who are getting lots of questions wrong are getting into the specialized high schools. It's a difficult test and you need to do well to get into one of the schools, but you are **expected** to get questions wrong. Therefore, as you practice, don't be demoralized just because you don't know how to answer all the questions. Just do your best and learn from your mistakes.

How to Get the Most from SHSAT Practice Tests

Make sure that you check your answers and **read through the explanations**! Do not simply check to see if you got the question correct. It's crucial that you understand why you are getting answers right or wrong. Figure out if wrong answers were careless mistakes. In other words, learn as much as you can from your performance on this test and then go back and review sections of this book as needed.

SHSAT

100 Essential Math Concepts

NUMBER PROPERTIES

1. Number Categories

Integers are **whole numbers**; they include negative whole numbers and zero.

A **rational number** is a number that can be expressed as a **ratio of two integers**. **Irrational numbers** are real numbers—they have locations on the number line—but they can't be expressed precisely as a fraction or decimal. On the SHSAT, the most important irrational numbers are $\sqrt{2}$, $\sqrt{3}$, and π.

2. Adding/Subtracting Signed Numbers

To **add a positive and a negative number,** first ignore the signs and find the positive difference between the number parts. Then attach the sign of the original number with the larger number part. For example, to add 23 and −34, first ignore the minus sign and find the positive difference between 23 and 34—that's 11. Then attach the sign of the number with the larger number part—in this case it's the minus sign from the −34. So, $23 + (−34) = −11$.

Make **subtraction** situations simpler by turning them into addition. For example, you can think of $−17 − (−21)$ as $−17 + (+21)$ or $−17 −21$ as $− 17 + (−21)$.

To **add or subtract a string of positives and negatives,** first turn everything into addition. Then combine the positives and negatives so that the string is reduced to the sum of a single positive number and a single negative number.

3. Multiplying/Dividing Signed Numbers

To multiply and/or divide positives and negatives, treat the number parts as usual and **attach a minus sign if there were originally an odd number of negatives.** For example, to multiply −2, −3, and −5, first multiply the number parts: $2 \times 3 \times 5 = 30$. Then go back and note that there were *three*—an *odd* number—negatives, so the product is negative: $(−2) \times (−3) \times (−5) = −30$.

4. PEMDAS

When performing multiple operations, remember to perform them in the right order.

PEMDAS, which means **Parentheses** first, then **Exponents**, then **Multiplication** and **Division** (left to right), and lastly **Addition** and **Subtraction** (left to right). In the expression $9 - 2 \times (5 - 3)^2 + 6 \div 3$, begin with the parentheses: $(5 - 3) = 2$. Then do the exponent: $2^2 = 4$. Now the expression is $9 - 2 \times 4 + 6 \div 3$. Next do the multiplication and division to get $9 - 8 + 2$, which equals 3. If you have difficulty remembering PEMDAS, use this sentence to recall it: Please Excuse My Dear Aunt Sally.

5. Counting Consecutive Integers

To count consecutive integers, **subtract the smallest from the largest and add 1**. To count the number of integers from 13 through 31, subtract: $31 - 13 = 18$. Then add 1: $18 + 1 = 19$.

NUMBER OPERATIONS AND CONCEPTS

6. Exponential Growth

If r is the ratio between consecutive terms, a_1 is the first term, a_n is the nth term, and S_n is the sum of the first n terms, then $a_n = a_1 r^{n-1}$ and $S_n = \dfrac{a_1 - a_1 r^n}{1 - r}$.

7. Union and Intersection of Sets

The things in a set are called elements or members. The **union** of Set A and Set B, sometimes expressed as $A \cup B$, is the set of elements that are in either or both of Set A and Set B. If Set $A = \{1, 2, 3\}$ and Set $B = \{3, 4, 5\}$, then $A \cup B = \{1, 2, 3, 4, 5\}$. The **intersection** of Set A and Set B, sometimes expressed as $A \cap B$, is the set of elements common to both Set A and Set B. If Set $A = \{1, 2, 3\}$ and Set $B = \{3, 4, 5\}$, then $A \cap B = \{3\}$.

DIVISIBILITY

8. Factor/Multiple

The **factors** of integer n are the positive integers that divide into n with no remainder. The **multiples** of n are the integers that n divides into with no remainder. For example, 6 is a factor of 12, and 24 is a multiple of 12. Note that 12, like all numbers, is both a factor and a multiple of itself, since $12 \times 1 = 12$ and $12 \div 1 = 12$.

9. Prime Factorization

To find the prime factorization of an integer, continue factoring until **all the factors are prime**. For example, factor 36: $36 = 9 \times 4 = 3 \times 3 \times 2 \times 2$.

10. Relative Primes

Relative primes are integers that have no common factor other than 1. To determine whether two integers are relative primes, break them both down to their prime factorizations. For example, $35 = 5 \times 7$, and $54 = 2 \times 3 \times 3 \times 3$. They have **no prime factors in common**, so 35 and 54 are relative primes.

11. Common Multiple

A common multiple is a number that is a multiple of two or more integers. You can always get a common multiple of two integers by **multiplying** them, but unless the two numbers are relative primes, the product will not be the *least* common multiple. For example, to find a common multiple for 12 and 15, you could just multiply: $12 \times 15 = 180$.

To find the **least common multiple (LCM)**, check out the **multiples of the larger integer** until you find one that's **also a multiple of the smaller**. To find the LCM of 12 and 15, begin by taking the multiples of 15: 15 is not divisible by 12; 30 is not; nor is 45. But the next multiple of 15, 60, *is* divisible by 12, so it's the LCM.

The LCM can also be found by using the prime factorization of the numbers. Note that 15 factors into 5×3, and 12 factors into $2^2 \times 3$. Taking the largest power of each prime factor results in $2^2 \times 3 \times 5 = 4 \times 3 \times 5 = 60$.

12. Greatest Common Factor (GCF)

To find the greatest common factor, break down the integers into their prime factorizations and multiply **all the prime factors they have in common**. For example, $36 = 2 \times 2 \times 3 \times 3$, and $48 = 2 \times 2 \times 2 \times 2 \times 3$. These integers have a 2×2 and a 3 in common, so the GCF is $2 \times 2 \times 3 = 12$.

13. Even/Odd

To predict whether a sum, difference, or product will be even or odd, just **take simple numbers like 1 and 2 and see what happens**. There are rules—"odd times even is even," for example—but there's no need to memorize them. What happens with one set of numbers generally happens with all similar sets.

14. Multiples of 2 and 4

An integer is divisible by 2 (even) if the **last digit** is even. An integer is divisible by 4 if the **last two digits form a multiple of 4**. The last digit of 562 is 2, which is even, so 562 is a multiple of 2. The last two digits form 62, which is *not* divisible by 4, so 562 is not a multiple of 4. The integer 512, however is divisible by 4 because the last two digits form 12, which is a multiple of 4.

15. Multiples of 3 and 9

An integer is divisible by 3 if the **sum of its digits is divisible by 3**. An integer is divisible by 9 if the **sum of its digits is divisible by 9**. The sum of the digits in 957 is 21, which is divisible by 3 but not by 9, so 957 is divisible by 3 but not by 9.

16. Multiples of 5 and 10

An integer is divisible by 5 if the **last digit is 5 or 0**. An integer is divisible by 10 if the **last digit is 0**. The last digit of 665 is 5, so 665 is a multiple of 5 but *not* a multiple of 10.

17. Remainders

The remainder is the **whole number left over after division**. Because 487 is 2 more than 485, which is a multiple of 5, when 487 is divided by 5, the remainder is 2.

FRACTIONS AND DECIMALS

18. Reducing Fractions

To reduce a fraction to lowest terms, **factor out and cancel** all factors the numerator and denominator have in common.

$$\frac{28}{36} = \frac{4 \times 7}{4 \times 9} = \frac{7}{9}$$

19. Adding/Subtracting Fractions

To add or subtract fractions, first find a **common denominator**, then add or subtract the numerators.

$$\frac{2}{15} + \frac{3}{10} = \frac{4}{30} + \frac{9}{30} = \frac{4+9}{30} = \frac{13}{30}$$

20. Multiplying Fractions

To multiply fractions, **multiply** the numerators and **multiply** the denominators.

$$\frac{5}{7} \times \frac{3}{4} = \frac{5 \times 3}{7 \times 4} = \frac{15}{28}$$

21. Dividing Fractions

To divide fractions, **invert** the second one and **multiply**.

$$\frac{1}{2} \div \frac{3}{5} = \frac{1}{2} \times \frac{5}{3} = \frac{1 \times 5}{2 \times 3} = \frac{5}{6}$$

22. Mixed Numbers and Improper Fractions

To convert a mixed number to an improper fraction, **multiply** the whole number part by the denominator, then **add** the numerator. The result is the new numerator (over the same denominator). To convert $7\frac{1}{3}$, first multiply 7 by 3, then add 1, to get the new numerator of 22. Put that over the same denominator, 3, to get $\frac{22}{3}$.

To convert an improper fraction to a mixed number, divide the denominator into the numerator to get a **whole number quotient with a remainder**. The quotient becomes the whole number part of the mixed number, and the remainder becomes the new numerator—with the same denominator. For example, to convert $\frac{108}{5}$, first divide 5 into 108, which yields 21 with a remainder of 3. Therefore, $\frac{108}{5} = 21\frac{3}{5}$.

23. Reciprocal

To find the reciprocal of a fraction, **switch the numerator and the denominator**. The reciprocal of $\frac{3}{7}$ is $\frac{7}{3}$. The reciprocal of 5 is $\frac{1}{5}$. The product of reciprocals is 1.

24. Comparing Fractions

One way to compare fractions is to **re-express them with a common denominator**. For example, $\frac{3}{4} = \frac{21}{28}$ and $\frac{5}{7} = \frac{20}{28}$. Because $\frac{21}{28}$ is greater than $\frac{20}{28}$, $\frac{3}{4}$ is greater than $\frac{5}{7}$. Another method is to **convert them both to decimals**. For example, $\frac{3}{4}$ converts to 0.75, and $\frac{5}{7}$ converts to approximately 0.714.

25. Converting Fractions and Decimals

To convert a fraction to a decimal, **divide the bottom into the top**. To convert $\frac{5}{8}$, divide 8 into 5, yielding 0.625.

To convert a decimal to a fraction, set the decimal over 1 and **multiply the numerator and denominator by 10 raised to the number of digits that are to the right of the decimal point**.

To convert 0.625 to a fraction, you would multiply $\frac{0.625}{1}$ by $\frac{10^3}{10^3}$ or $\frac{1,000}{1,000}$.

Then simplify: $\frac{625}{1,000} = \frac{5 \times 125}{8 \times 125} = \frac{5}{8}$.

26. Repeating Decimal

To find a particular digit in a repeating decimal, note the **number of digits in the cluster that repeats**. If there are 2 digits in that cluster, then every second digit is the same. If there are 3 digits in that cluster, then every third digit is the same. And so on. For example, the decimal equivalent of $\frac{1}{27}$ is 0.037037037…, which is best written $0.\overline{037}$. There are 3 digits in the repeating cluster, so every third digit is the same: 7. To find the 50th digit, look for the multiple of 3 just less than 50—that's 48. The 48th digit is 7, and with the 49th digit the pattern repeats with 0. The 50th digit is 3.

27. Identifying the Parts and the Whole

The key to solving most fraction and percent word problems is to identify the **part** and the **whole**. Usually you'll find the **part** associated with the verb *is/are* and the **whole** associated with the word *of*. In the sentence, "Half of the boys are blonds," the whole is the boys ("*of* the boys"), and the part is the blonds ("*are* blonds").

PERCENTS

28. Percent Formula

Whether you need to find the part, the whole, or the percent, use the same formula:

Part = Percent × Whole

Example:	What is 12 percent of 25?
Setup:	Part = 0.12 × 25
Example:	15 is 3 percent of what number?
Setup:	15 = 0.03 × Whole
Example:	45 is what percent of 9?
Setup:	45 = Percent × 9

29. Percent Increase and Decrease

To increase a number by a percent, **add the percent to 100 percent**, convert to a decimal, and multiply. To increase 40 by 25 percent, add 25 percent to 100 percent, convert 125 percent to 1.25, and multiply by 40: $1.25 \times 40 = 50$.

30. Finding the Original Whole

To find the **original whole before a percent increase or decrease,** set up an equation. Think of the result of a 15 percent increase over x as $1.15x$.

Example: After a 5 percent increase, the population was 59,346. What was the population before the increase?

Setup: $1.05x = 59,346$

31. Combined Percent Increase and Decrease

To determine the combined effect of multiple percent increases and/or decreases, **start with 100 and see what happens.**

Example: A price went up 10 percent one year, and the new price went up 20 percent the next year. What was the combined percent increase?

Setup: First year: $100 + (10 \text{ percent of } 100) = 110$. Second year: $110 + (20 \text{ percent of } 110) = 132$. That's a combined 32 percent increase.

RATIOS, PROPORTIONS, AND RATES

32. Setting up a Ratio

To find a ratio, put the number associated with the word **of on top** and the quantity associated with the word **to on the bottom** and reduce. The ratio of 20 oranges to 12 apples is $\frac{20}{12}$, which reduces to $\frac{5}{3}$.

33. Part-to-Part Ratios and Part-to-Whole Ratios

If the parts add up to the whole, a part-to-part ratio can be turned into two part-to-whole ratios by putting **each number in the original ratio over the sum of the numbers.** If the ratio of males to females is 1 to 2, then the males-to-people ratio is $\frac{1}{1+2} = \frac{1}{3}$ and the females-to-people ratio is $\frac{2}{1+2} = \frac{2}{3}$. In other words, $\frac{2}{3}$ of all the people are female.

34. Solving a Proportion

To solve a proportion, cross multiply:

$$\frac{x}{5} = \frac{3}{4}$$
$$4x = 3 \times 5$$
$$x = \frac{15}{4} = 3.75$$

35. Rate

To solve a rate problem, **use the units** to keep things straight.

Example: If snow is falling at the rate of one foot every four hours, how many inches of snow will fall in seven hours?

$$\frac{1 \text{ foot}}{4 \text{ hours}} = \frac{x \text{ inches}}{7 \text{ hours}}$$

Setup: $\frac{12 \text{ inches}}{4 \text{ hours}} = \frac{x \text{ inches}}{7 \text{ hours}}$

$$4x = 12 \times 7$$
$$x = 21$$

36. Average Rate

Average rate is *not* simply the average of the rates.

$$\text{Average } A \text{ per } B = \frac{\text{Total } A}{\text{Total } B}$$

$$\text{Average Speed} = \frac{\text{Total distance}}{\text{Total time}}$$

To find the average speed for 120 miles at 40 mph and 120 miles at 60 mph, **don't just average the two speeds**. First, figure out the total distance and the total time. The total distance is $120 + 120 = 240$ miles. The times are 3 hours for the first leg and 2 hours for the second leg, or 5 hours total. The average speed, then, is $\frac{240}{5} = 48$ miles per hour.

AVERAGES

37. Average Formula

To find the average of a set of numbers, **add them up and divide by the number of terms**.

$$\text{Average} = \frac{\text{Sum of the terms}}{\text{Number of terms}}$$

To find the average of the 5 numbers 12, 15, 23, 40, and 40, first add them: $12 + 15 + 23 + 40 + 40 = 130$. Then, divide the sum by 5: $130 \div 5 = 26$.

38. Average of Evenly Spaced Numbers

To find the average of evenly spaced numbers, just **average the smallest and the largest**. The average of all the integers from 13 through 77 is the same as the average of 13 and 77:

$$\frac{13 + 77}{2} = \frac{90}{2} = 45$$

39. Using the Average to Find the Sum

$$\text{Sum} = (\text{Average}) \times (\text{Number of terms})$$

If the average of 10 numbers is 50, then they add up to 10×50, or 500.

40. Finding the Missing Number

To find a missing number when you're given the average, **use the sum**. If the average of 4 numbers is 7, then the sum of those 4 numbers is 4×7, or 28. Suppose that 3 of the numbers are 3, 5, and 8. These 3 numbers add up to 16 of that 28, which leaves 12 for the fourth number.

41. Median and Mode

The median of a set of numbers is the **value that falls in the middle of the set**. If you have 5 test scores, and they are 88, 86, 57, 94, and 73, you must first list the scores in increasing or decreasing order: 57, 73, 86, 88, 94.

The median is the middle number, or 86. If there is an even number of values in a set (6 test scores, for instance), simply take the average of the two middle numbers.

The mode of a set of numbers is the **value that appears most often**. If your test scores were 88, 57, 68, 85, 99, 93, 93, 84, and 81, the mode of the scores would be 93 because it appears more often than any other score. If there is a tie for the most common value in a set, the set has more than one mode.

POSSIBILITIES AND PROBABILITY

42. Counting the Possibilities

The fundamental counting principle: If there are **m ways** one event can happen and **n ways** a second event can happen, then there are **m × n ways** for the two events to happen. For example, with 5 shirts and 7 pairs of pants to choose from, you can have $5 \times 7 = 35$ different outfits.

43. Probability

$$\text{Probability} = \frac{\text{Favorable Outcomes}}{\text{Total Possible outcomes}}$$

For example, if you have 12 shirts in a drawer and 9 of them are white, the probability of picking a white shirt at random is $\frac{9}{12} = \frac{3}{4}$. This probability can also be expressed as 0.75 or 75%.

POWERS AND ROOTS

44. Multiplying and Dividing Powers

To multiply powers with the same base, **add the exponents and keep the same base:**

$$x^3 \times x^4 = x^{3+4} = x^7$$

To divide powers with the same base, **subtract the exponents and keep the same base:**

$$y^{13} \div y^8 = y^{13-8} = y^5$$

45. Raising Powers to Powers

To raise a term that already has exponents to another power, **multiply the exponents:**

$$(x^3)^4 = x^{3 \times 4} = x^{12}$$

46. Simplifying Square Roots

To simplify a square root, **factor out the perfect squares** under the radical, unsquare them, and put the result in front:

$$\sqrt{12} = \sqrt{4 \times 3} = \sqrt{4} \times \sqrt{3} = 2\sqrt{3}$$

47. Adding and Subtracting Roots

You can add or subtract radical expressions **when the part under the radicals is the same:**

$$2\sqrt{3} + 3\sqrt{3} = 5\sqrt{3}$$

Don't try to add or subtract when the radical parts are different. There's not much you can do with an expression like this one:

$$3\sqrt{5} + 4\sqrt{7}$$

48. Multiplying and Dividing Roots

The product of square roots is equal to the **square root of the product:**

$$\sqrt{3} \times \sqrt{5} = \sqrt{3 \times 5} = \sqrt{15}$$

The quotient of square roots is equal to the **square root of the quotient:**

$$\frac{\sqrt{6}}{\sqrt{3}} = \sqrt{\frac{6}{3}} = \sqrt{2}$$

49. Negative Exponent and Rational Exponent

To find the value of a number raised to a negative exponent, simply rewrite the number, without the negative sign, as the bottom of a fraction with 1 as the numerator of the fraction: $3^{-2} = \frac{1}{3^2} = \frac{1}{9}$.

If x is a positive number and a is a nonzero number, then $x^{\frac{1}{a}} = \sqrt[a]{x}$. Therefore, $4^{\frac{1}{2}} = \sqrt[2]{4} = \sqrt{4} = 2$. Finally, if p and q are integers, then $x^{\frac{p}{q}} = \sqrt[q]{x^p}$. So $8^{\frac{2}{3}} = \sqrt[3]{8^2} = \sqrt[3]{64} = 4$.

ABSOLUTE VALUE

50. Determining Absolute Value

The absolute value of a number is the distance of the number from zero on the number line. Because absolute value is a distance, it is always positive. The absolute value of 7 is 7; this is expressed $|7| = 7$. Similarly, the absolute value of −7 is 7: $|-7| = 7$. Every positive number is the absolute value of two numbers: itself and its negative.

ALGEBRAIC EXPRESSIONS

51. Evaluating an Expression

To evaluate an algebraic expression, **plug in** the given values for the unknowns and calculate according to **PEMDAS**. To find the value of $x^2 + 5x - 6$ when $x = -2$, plug in −2 for x: $(-2)^2 + 5(-2) - 6 = -12$.

52. Adding and Subtracting Monomials

To combine like terms, **keep the variable part unchanged while adding or subtracting the coefficients**:

$$2a + 3a = (2 + 3)a = 5a$$

53. Adding and Subtracting Polynomials

To add or subtract polynomials, **combine like terms**:

$$(3x^2 + 5x - 7) - (x^2 + 12) =$$
$$(3x^2 - x^2) + 5x + (-7 - 12) =$$
$$2x^2 + 5x - 19$$

54. Multiplying Monomials

To multiply monomials, **multiply the coefficients and the variables separately**:

$$2a \times 3a = (2 \times 3)(a \times a) = 6a^2$$

55. Multiplying Binomials—FOIL

To multiply binomials, use **FOIL**. To multiply $(x + 3)$ by $(x + 4)$, first multiply the **F**irst terms: $x \times x = x^2$. Next the **O**uter terms: $x \times 4 = 4x$. Then the **I**nner terms: $3 \times x = 3x$. And finally the **L**ast terms: $3 \times 4 = 12$. Then add and combine like terms:

$$x^2 + 4x + 3x + 12 = x^2 + 7x + 12$$

56. Multiplying Other Polynomials

FOIL works only when you want to multiply two binomials. If you want to multiply polynomials with more than two terms, make sure you **multiply each term in the first polynomial by each term in the second**.

$$(x^2 + 3x + 4)(x + 5) =$$
$$x^2(x + 5) + 3x(x + 5) + 4(x + 5) =$$
$$x^3 + 5x^2 + 3x^2 + 15x + 4x + 20 =$$
$$x^3 + 8x^2 + 19x + 20$$

After multiplying two polynomials together, the number of terms in your expression before simplifying should equal the number of terms in one polynomial multiplied by the number of terms in the second. In the example, you should have $3 \times 2 = 6$ terms in the product before you simplify like terms.

FACTORING ALGEBRAIC EXPRESSIONS

57. Factoring out a Common Divisor

A factor common to all terms of a polynomial can be **factored out**. All three terms in the polynomial $3x^3 + 12x^2 - 6x$ contain a factor of $3x$. Pulling out the common factor yields $3x(x^2 + 4x - 2)$.

58. Factoring the Difference of Squares

One of the test maker's favorite factorables is the **difference of squares**:

$$a^2 - b^2 = (a - b)(a + b)$$

$x^2 - 9$, for example, factors to $(x - 3)(x + 3)$.

59. Factoring the Square of a Binomial

Recognize polynomials that are squares of binomials:

$$a^2 + 2ab + b^2 = (a + b)^2$$
$$a^2 - 2ab + b^2 = (a - b)^2$$

For example, $4x^2 + 12x + 9$ factors to $(2x + 3)^2$, and $n^2 - 10n + 25$ factors to $(n - 5)^2$.

60. Factoring Other Polynomials—FOIL in Reverse

To factor a quadratic expression, **think about what binomials you could use FOIL on to get that quadratic expression**. To factor $x^2 - 5x + 6$, think about what First terms will produce x^2, what Last terms will produce +6, and what Outer and Inner terms will produce $-5x$. Some common sense—and a little trial and error—lead you to $(x - 2)(x - 3)$.

61. Simplifying an Algebraic Fraction

Simplifying an algebraic fraction is a lot like simplifying a numerical fraction. The general idea is to **find factors common to the numerator and denominator and cancel them**. Thus, simplifying an algebraic fraction begins with factoring.

For example, to simplify $\dfrac{x^2 - x - 12}{x^2 - 9}$, first factor the numerator and denominator:

$$\frac{x^2 - x - 12}{x^2 - 9} = \frac{(x-4)(x+3)}{(x-3)(x+3)}$$

Canceling $x + 3$ from the numerator and denominator leaves you with $= \dfrac{(x-4)}{(x-3)}$.

SOLVING EQUATIONS

62. Solving a Linear Equation

To solve an equation, do whatever is necessary to both sides to **isolate the variable**. To solve the equation $5x - 12 = -2x + 9$, first get all the x's on one side by adding $2x$ to both sides: $7x - 12 = 9$. Then add 12 to both sides: $7x = 21$. Then divide both sides by 7: $x = 3$.

63. Solving "In Terms Of"

To solve an equation for one variable **in terms of** another means to **isolate the one variable on one side of the equation**, leaving an expression containing the other variable on the other side of the equation. To solve the equation $3x - 10y = -5x + 6y$ for x in terms of y, isolate x:

$$3x - 10y = -5x + 6y$$
$$3x + 5x = 6y + 10y$$
$$8x = 16y$$
$$x = 2y$$

64. Translating from English into Algebra

To translate from English into algebra, look for the keywords and systematically turn phrases into algebraic expressions and sentences into equations. Be careful about order, especially when subtraction is called for.

Example: Celine and Remi play tennis. Last year, Celine won 3 more than twice the number of matches that Remi won. If Celine won 11 more matches than Remi, how many matches did Celine win?

Setup: You are given two sets of information. One way to solve this is to write a system of equations—one equation for each set of information. Use variables that relate well to what they represent. For example, use r to represent Remi's winning matches, and use c to represent Celine's winning matches. The phrase "Celine won 3 more than twice Remi," can be written as $c = 2r + 3$. The phrase "Celine won 11 more matches than Remi," can be written as $c = r + 11$.

65. Solving a Quadratic Equation

To solve a quadratic equation, put it in the "$ax^2 + bx + c = 0$" form, **factor** the left side (if you can) and set each factor equal to 0 separately to get the two solutions. To solve $x^2 + 12 = 7x$, first rewrite it as $x^2 - 7x + 12 = 0$. Then factor the left side:

$$(x - 3)(x - 4) = 0$$
$$x - 3 = 0 \text{ or } x - 4 = 0$$
$$x = 3 \text{ or } 4$$

66. Solving a System of Equations

You can solve for two variables only if you have two distinct equations. Two forms of the same equation will not be adequate. **Combine the equations** in such a way that **one of the variables adds or subtracts out**. To solve the two equations $4x + 3y = 8$ and $x + y = 3$, multiply both sides of the second equation by -3 to get $-3x - 3y = -9$. Now add the two equations; the $3y$ and the $-3y$ cancel out, leaving $x = -1$. Plug that back into either one of the original equations, and you'll find that $y = 4$.

67. Solving an Inequality

To solve an inequality, do whatever is necessary to both sides to **isolate the variable**. Just remember that when you **multiply or divide both sides by a negative number**, you must **reverse the sign**. To solve $-5x + 7 < -3$, subtract 7 from both sides to get $-5x < -10$. Now divide both sides by -5, remembering to reverse the sign: $x > 2$.

68. Radical Equations

A radical equation contains at least one radical expression. Solve radical equations by using standard rules of algebra. If $5\sqrt{x} - 2 = 13$, then $5\sqrt{x} = 15$ and $\sqrt{x} = 3$, so $x = 9$.

FUNCTIONS

69. Function Notation and Evaluation

Standard function notation is written $f(x)$ and read "f of 4." To evaluate the function $f(x) = 2x + 3$ for $f(4)$, replace x with 4 and simplify: $f(4) = 2(4) + 3 = 11$.

70. Direct and Inverse Variation

In direct variation, $y = kx$, where k is a nonzero constant. In direct variation, the variable y changes directly as x does. If a unit of Currency A is worth 2 units of Currency B, then $A = 2B$. If the number of units of B were to double, the number of units of A would double, and so on for halving, tripling, etc. In inverse variation, $xy = k$, where x and y are variables and k is a constant. A famous inverse relationship is $rate \times time = distance$, where distance is constant. Imagine having to cover a distance of 24 miles. If you were to travel at 12 miles per hour, you'd need 2 hours. But if you were to halve your rate, you would have to double your time. This is just another way of saying that rate and time vary inversely.

71. Domain and Range of a Function

The domain of a function is the set of values for which the function is defined. For example, the domain of $f(x) = \dfrac{1}{1-x^2}$ is all values of x except 1 and −1, because for those values the denominator has a value of 0 and is therefore undefined. The range of a function is the set of outputs or results of the function. For example, the range of $f(x) = x^2$ is all numbers greater than or equal to zero, because x^2 cannot be negative.

COORDINATE GEOMETRY

72. Finding the Distance Between Two Points

To find the distance between points, **use the Pythagorean theorem** or **special right triangles**. The difference between the x's is one leg and the difference between the y's is the other.

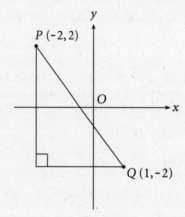

In the figure above, PQ is the hypotenuse of a 3-4-5 triangle, so $PQ = 5$.

You can also use the **distance formula**:

$$d = \sqrt{(x_1 - x_2)^2 + (y_1 - y_2)^2}$$

To find the distance between $R(3,6)$ and $S(5,-2)$:

$$d = \sqrt{(3-5)^2 + [6-(-2)]^2}$$

$$d = \sqrt{(-2)^2 + (8)^2}$$

$$d = \sqrt{68} = 2\sqrt{17}$$

73. Using Two Points to Find the Slope

$$\text{Slope} = \frac{\text{Change in } y}{\text{Change in } x} = \frac{\text{Rise}}{\text{Run}}$$

The slope of the line that contains the points $(2, 3)$ and $(0, -1)$ is

$$\frac{y_2 - y_1}{x_2 - x_1} = \frac{3 - (-1)}{2 - 0} = \frac{4}{2} = 2$$

74. Using an Equation to Find the Slope

To find the slope of a line from an equation, put the equation into the **slope-intercept** form:

$$y = mx + b$$

The **slope is m**. To find the slope of the equation $3x + 2y = 4$, rearrange it:

$$3x + 2y = 4$$
$$2y = -3x + 4$$
$$y = -\frac{3}{2}x + 2$$

The slope is $-\frac{3}{2}$.

75. Using an Equation to Find an Intercept

To find the y-intercept, you can either put the equation into $y = mx + b$ (slope-intercept) form—in which case b is the y-intercept—or you can just **plug $x = 0$** into the equation and **solve for y**. To find the x-intercept, plug $y = 0$ into the equation and **solve for x**.

76. Finding the Midpoint

The midpoint of two points on a line segment is the average of the x-coordinates of the end points and the average of the y-coordinates of the end points. If the end points are (x_1, y_1) and (x_2, y_2), the midpoint is $\left(\frac{x_1 + x_2}{2}, \frac{y_1 + y_2}{2}\right)$. The midpoint of $(3, 5)$ and $(9, 1)$ is $\left(\frac{3 + 9}{2}, \frac{5 + 1}{2}\right)$, or $(6, 3)$.

LINES AND ANGLES

77. Intersecting Lines

When two lines intersect, **adjacent angles are supplementary, and vertical angles are equal**.

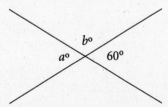

In the figure above, the angles marked $a°$ and $b°$ are adjacent and supplementary, so $a + b = 180$. Furthermore, the angles marked $a°$ and $60°$ are vertical and equal, so $a = 60$.

78. Parallel Lines and Transversals

A transversal across parallel lines forms **four equal acute angles and four equal obtuse angles**. If the transversal meets the lines at a right angle, then all eight angles are right angles.

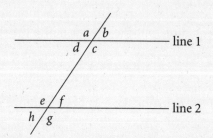

In the figure above, line 1 is parallel to line 2. Angles *a, c, e,* and *g* are obtuse, so they are all equal. Angles *b, d, f,* and *h* are acute, so they are all equal.

Furthermore, **any of the acute angles is supplementary to any of the obtuse angles**. Angles *a* and *h* are supplementary, as are *b* and *e, c* and *f,* and so on.

TRIANGLES—GENERAL

79. Interior and Exterior Angles of a Triangle

The three angles of any triangle **add up to 180 degrees**.

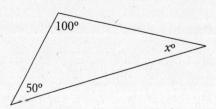

In the figure above, $x + 50 + 100 = 180$, so $x = 30$.

An exterior angle of a triangle is equal to the **sum of the remote interior angles**.

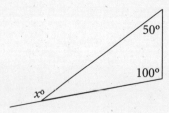

In the figure above, the exterior angle labeled $x°$ is equal to the sum of the remote angles: $x = 50 + 100 = 150$.

The three exterior angles of a triangle **add up to 360 degrees.**

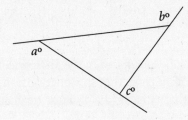

In the figure above, $a + b + c = 360$.

80. Similar Triangles

Similar triangles have the same shape: **Corresponding angles are equal, and corresponding sides are proportional.**

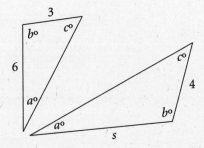

The triangles above are similar because they have the same angles. The side of length 3 corresponds to the side of length 4, and the side of length 6 corresponds to the side of length s.

$$\frac{3}{4} = \frac{6}{s}$$
$$3s = 24$$
$$s = 8$$

81. Area of a Triangle

$$\text{Area of Triangle} = \frac{1}{2} \text{(base)(height)}$$

The height is the perpendicular distance between the side that's chosen as the base and the opposite vertex.

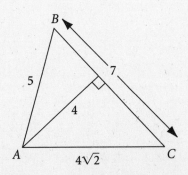

In the triangle above, 4 is the height when 7 is chosen as the base.

$$\text{Area} = \frac{1}{2}\,bh = \frac{1}{2}\,(7)(4) = 14$$

82 Triangle Inequality Theorem

The length of one side of a triangle must be **greater than the difference and less than the sum** of the lengths of the other two sides. For example, if it is given that the length of one side is 3 and the length of another side is 7, then you know that the length of the third side must be greater than $7 - 3 = 4$ and less than $7 + 3 = 10$.

83. Isosceles and Equilateral Triangles

An isosceles triangle is a triangle that has **two equal sides**. Not only are two sides equal, but the angles opposite the equal sides, called **base angles**, are also equal.

Equilateral triangles are triangles in which **all three sides are equal**. Since all the sides are equal, all the angles are also equal. All three angles in an equilateral triangle measure 60 degrees, regardless of the lengths of sides.

RIGHT TRIANGLES

84. Pythagorean Theorem

For all right triangles:

$$(\text{leg}_1)^2 + (\text{leg}_2)^2 = (\text{hypotenuse})^2$$

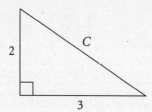

If one leg is 2 and the other leg is 3, then

$$2^2 + 3^2 = c^2$$
$$c^2 = 4 + 9$$
$$c = \sqrt{13}$$

85. The 3-4-5 Triangle

If a right triangle's leg-to-leg ratio is 3:4, or if the leg-to-hypotenuse ratio is 3:5 or 4:5, it's a 3-4-5 triangle and you don't need to use the Pythagorean theorem to find the third side. Just figure out what multiple of 3-4-5 it is.

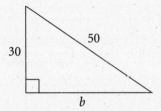

In the right triangle shown, one leg is 30 and the hypotenuse is 50. This is 10 times 3-4-5. The other leg is 40.

86. The 5-12-13 Triangle

If a right triangle's leg-to-leg ratio is 5:12, or if the leg-to-hypotenuse ratio is 5:13 or 12:13, then it's a 5-12-13 triangle and you don't need to use the Pythagorean theorem to find the third side. Just figure out what multiple of 5-12-13 it is.

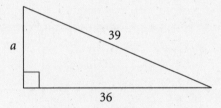

Here one leg is 36 and the hypotenuse is 39. This is 3 times 5-12-13. The other leg is 15.

87. The 30-60-90 Triangle

The sides of a 30-60-90 triangle are in a ratio of $x : x\sqrt{3} : 2x$. You don't need the Pythagorean theorem if you know the length of one side.

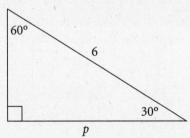

If the hypotenuse is 6, then the shorter leg is half that, or 3; and then the longer leg is equal to the short leg times $\sqrt{3}$, or $p = 3\sqrt{3}$.

88. The 45-45-90 Triangle

The sides of a 45-45-90 triangle are in a ratio of $x : x : x\sqrt{2}$.

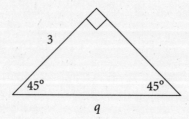

If one leg has a length of 3, then the other leg also has a length of 3, and the hypotenuse is equal to a leg times $\sqrt{2}$, or $q = 3\sqrt{2}$.

OTHER POLYGONS

89. Characteristics of a Rectangle

A rectangle is a **four-sided figure with four right angles**. Opposite sides are equal. Diagonals are equal.

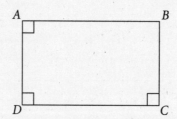

Quadrilateral *ABCD* above is shown to have three right angles. The fourth angle therefore also measures 90 degrees, and *ABCD* is a rectangle. The **perimeter** of a rectangle is equal to the sum of the lengths of the four sides, which is equivalent to **2(length + width)**.

Area of Rectangle = length × width

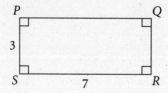

The area of a 7-by-3 rectangle is $7 \times 3 = 21$.

90. Characteristics of a Parallelogram

A parallelogram has **two pairs of parallel sides**. Opposite sides are equal. Opposite angles are equal. Consecutive angles add up to 180 degrees.

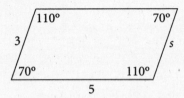

In the figure above, s is the length of the side opposite the 3, so $s = 3$.

Area of Parallelogram = base × height

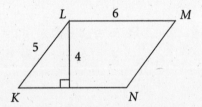

In parallelogram *KLMN* above, 4 is the height when *LM* or *KN* is used as the base. Base × height = $6 \times 4 = 24$.

91. Characteristics of a Square

A square is a **rectangle with four equal sides**.

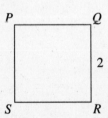

If *PQRS* is a square, all sides are the same length as *QR*. The **perimeter** of a square is equal to four times the length of one side.

Area of Square = (side)^2

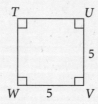

The square above, with sides of length 5, has an area of $5^2 = 25$.

92. Interior Angles of a Polygon

The **sum of the measures of the interior angles of a polygon** $= (n-2) \times 180$, where n is the number of sides.

Sum of the angles $= (n-2) \times 180$

The eight angles of an octagon, for example, add up to $(8-2) \times 180 = 1{,}080$.

CIRCLES

93. Circumference of a Circle

Circumference = 2πr

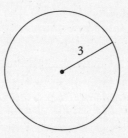

In the circle above, the radius has a length of 3, so the circumference is $2\pi(3) = 6\pi$.

94. Length of an Arc

An **arc** is a piece of the circumference. If n is the degree measure of the arc's central angle, then the formula is this:

$$\text{Length of an arc} = \left(\frac{n}{360}\right)(2\pi r)$$

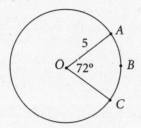

In the figure above, the radius has a length of 5, and the measure of the central angle is 72 degrees. The arc length is $\frac{72}{360}$ or $\frac{1}{5}$ of the circumference:

$$\left(\frac{72}{360}\right)(2\pi)(5) = \left(\frac{1}{5}\right)(10\pi) = 2\pi$$

95. Area of a Circle

$$\text{Area of a Circle} = \pi r^2$$

The area of the circle is $\pi(4)^2 = 16\pi$.

96. Area of a Sector

A **sector** is a piece of the area of a circle. If n is the degree measure of the sector's central angle, then the formula is this:

$$\text{Area of a sector} = \left(\frac{n}{360}\right)(\pi r^2)$$

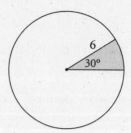

In the figure above, the radius has a length of 6, and the measure of the sector's central angle is 30 degrees. The sector has $\frac{30}{360}$ or $\frac{1}{12}$ of the area of the circle:

$$\left(\frac{30}{360}\right)(\pi)(6^2) = \left(\frac{1}{12}\right)(36\pi) = 3\pi$$

97. Tangency

When a line is tangent to a circle, the radius of the circle is perpendicular to the line at the point of contact.

SOLIDS

98. Surface Area of a Rectangular Solid

The surface of a rectangular solid consists of three pairs of identical faces. To find the surface area, find the area of each face and add them up. If the length is l, the width is w, and the height is h, the formula is this:

Surface area = $2lw + 2wh + 2lh$

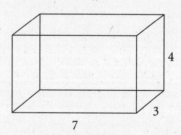

The surface area of the box above is $(2 \times 7 \times 3) + (2 \times 3 \times 4) + (2 \times 7 \times 4) = 42 + 24 + 56 = 122$

99. Volume of a Rectangular Solid

Volume of a rectangular solid = lwh

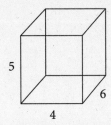

The volume of a 4-by-5-by-6 box is $4 \times 5 \times 6 = 120$.

A cube is a rectangular solid with length, width, and height all equal. If s is the length of an edge of a cube, the volume formula is this:

Volume of a cube = s^3

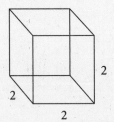

The volume of this cube is $2^3 = 8$.

100. Volume of a Cylinder

Volume of a cylinder = $\pi r^2 h$

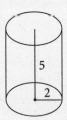

In the cylinder above, $r = 2$ and $h = 5$. Therefore, Volume $= \pi(2^2)(5) = 20\pi$.